the AMAZING SPIDER-MAN

PRESENTS:
AMERICAN SON

THE OSBORN IDENTITY
Writer: **BRIAN REED**
Artist: **PHILIPPE BRIONES** WITH
**PATRICK OLLIFFE, CHAD
HARDIN, WAYNE FAUCHER
& STEPHEN SEGOVIA**
Colorists: **JEROMY COX** WITH
CHRIS SOTOMAYOR
Letterer: **DAVE LANPHEAR**
Cover Artist: **MARKO DJURDJEVIC**

"BARGAIN DONUTS"
Writer: **JOE CARAMAGNA**
Artist: **TODD NAUCK**
Colorist: **CHRIS CHUCKRY**
Letterer: **VC'S JOE SABINO**

"HEROIC RAGE"
Writer: **BRIAN REED**
Penciler: **CHAD HARDIN**
Inker: **VICTOR OLAZABA**
Colorists: **CHRIS SOTOMAYOR** WITH
JEROMY COX
Letterer: **VC'S JOE SABINO**

Editor: **THOMAS BRENNAN**
Supervising Editor: **STEPHEN WACKER**

Collection Editor: **NICOLE BOOSE** • Editorial Assistants: **JAMES EMMETT** & **JOE HOCHSTEIN**
Assistant Editors: **ALEX STARBUCK** & **NELSON RIBEIRO**
Editors, Special Projects: **JENNIFER GRÜNWALD** & **MARK D. BEAZLEY**
Senior Editor, Special Projects: **JEFF YOUNGQUIST** • Senior Vice President of Sales: **DAVID GABRIEL**
Collection Designer: **JEFF POWELL** • Production: **JERRY KALINOWSKI**

Editor in Chief: **JOE QUESADA** • Publisher: **DAN BUCKLEY** • Executive Producer: **ALAN FINE**

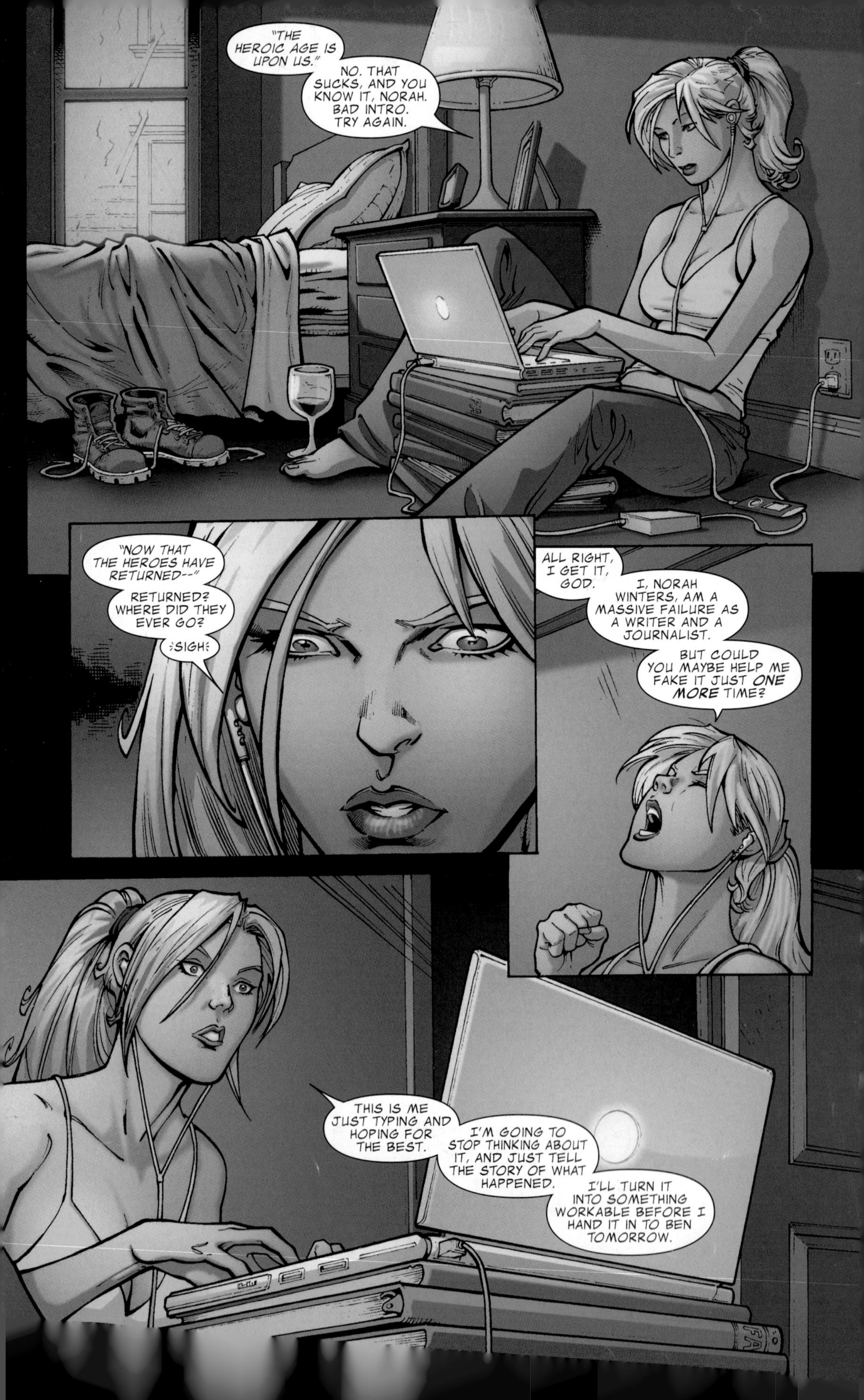
"THE HEROIC AGE IS UPON US."
NO. THAT SUCKS, AND YOU KNOW IT, NORAH. BAD INTRO. TRY AGAIN.
"NOW THAT THE HEROES HAVE RETURNED--"
RETURNED? WHERE DID THEY EVER GO?
SIGH
ALL RIGHT, I GET IT, GOD.
I, NORAH WINTERS, AM A MASSIVE FAILURE AS A WRITER AND A JOURNALIST.
BUT COULD YOU MAYBE HELP ME FAKE IT JUST ONE MORE TIME?
THIS IS ME JUST TYPING AND HOPING FOR THE BEST.
I'M GOING TO STOP THINKING ABOUT IT, AND JUST TELL THE STORY OF WHAT HAPPENED.
I'LL TURN IT INTO SOMETHING WORKABLE BEFORE I HAND IT IN TO BEN TOMORROW.

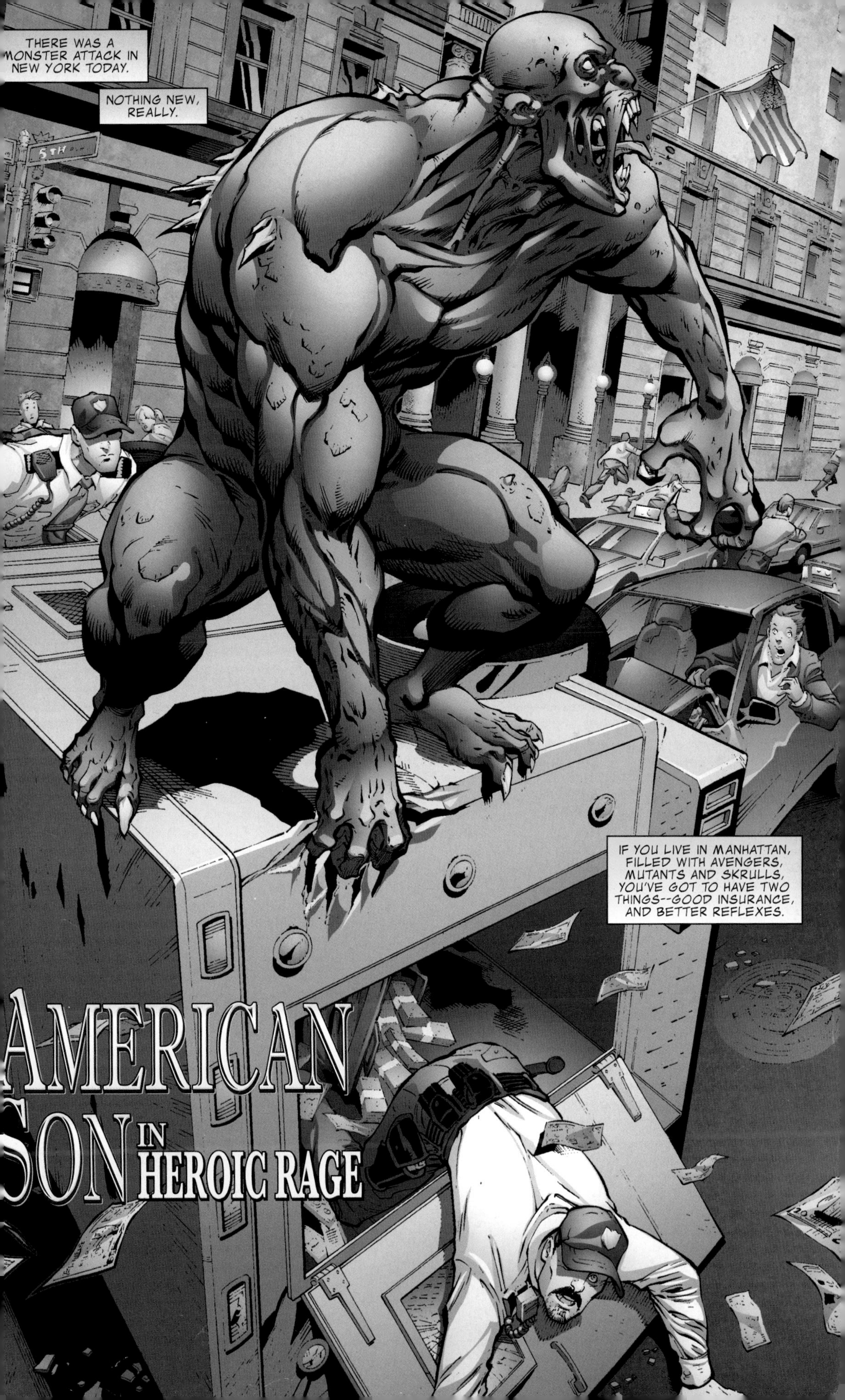
THERE WAS A MONSTER ATTACK IN NEW YORK TODAY.
NOTHING NEW, REALLY.
5TH
IF YOU LIVE IN MANHATTAN, FILLED WITH AVENGERS, MUTANTS AND SKRULLS, YOU'VE GOT TO HAVE TWO THINGS--GOOD INSURANCE, AND BETTER REFLEXES.
AMERICAN SON IN HEROIC RAGE

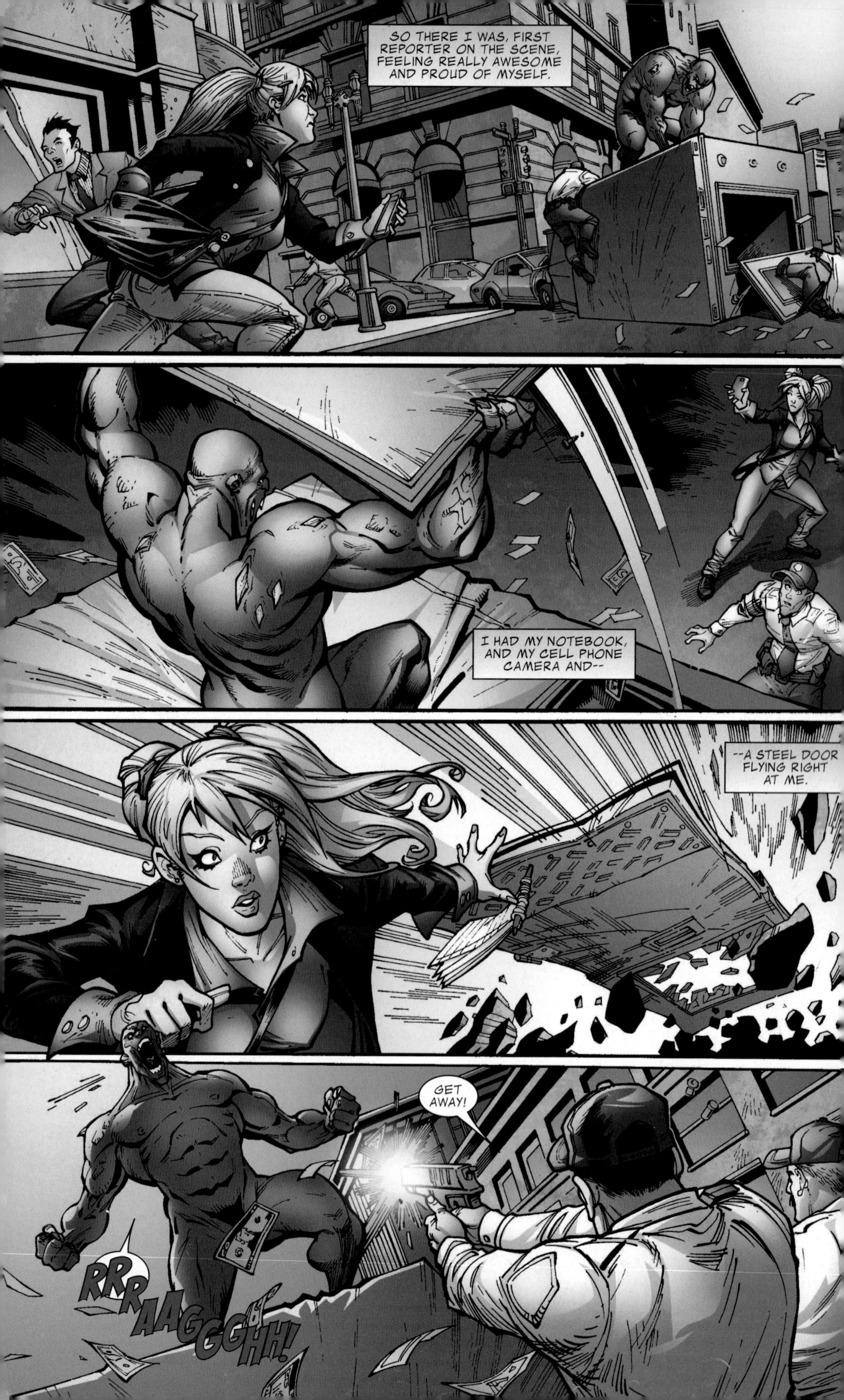
SO THERE I WAS, FIRST REPORTER ON THE SCENE, FEELING REALLY AWESOME AND PROUD OF MYSELF.
I HAD MY NOTEBOOK, AND MY CELL PHONE CAMERA AND--
--A STEEL DOOR FLYING RIGHT AT ME.
GET AWAY!
RRRAAGGGHH!

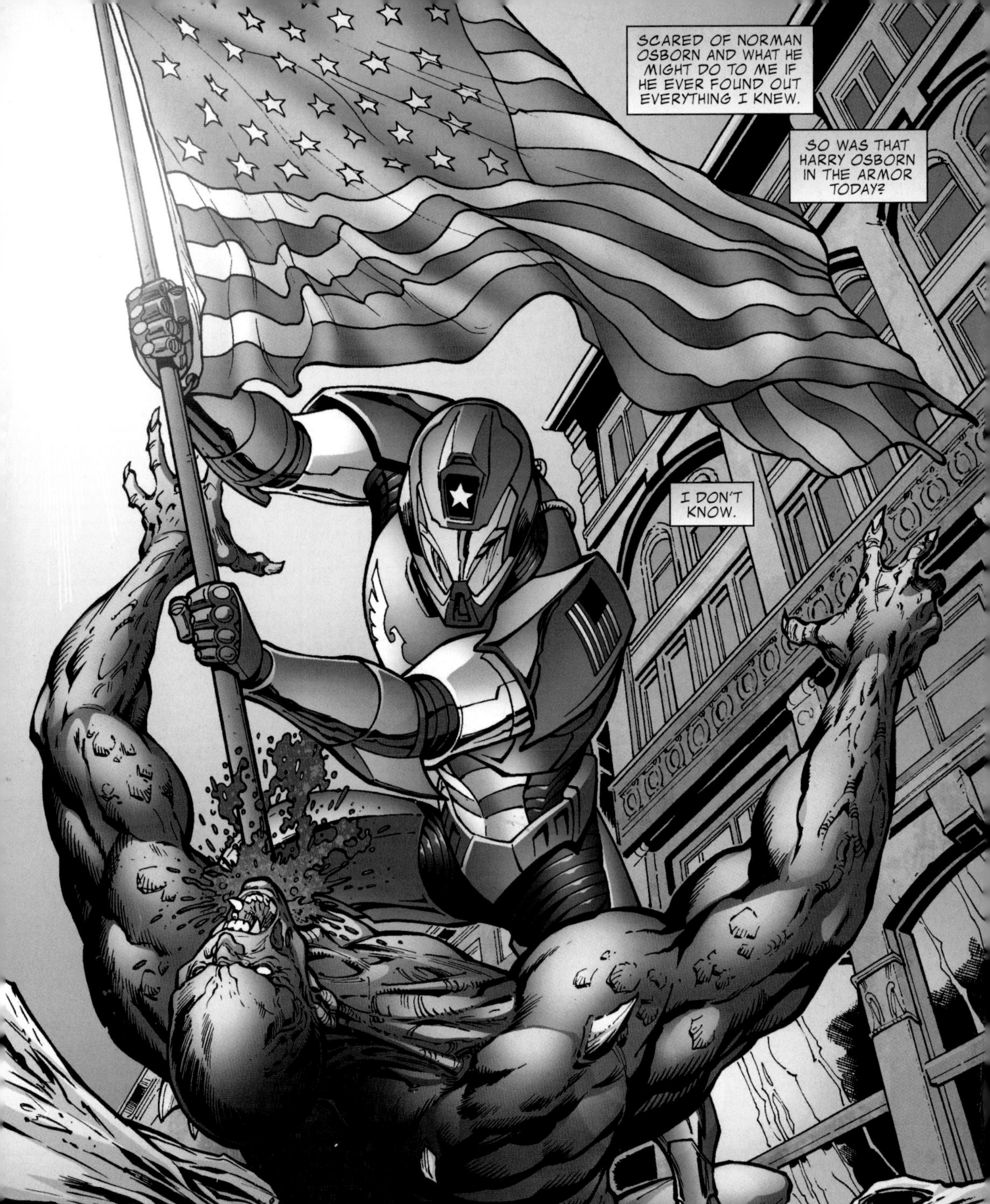
SCARED OF NORMAN OSBORN AND WHAT HE MIGHT DO TO ME IF HE EVER FOUND OUT EVERYTHING I KNEW.
SO WAS THAT HARRY OSBORN IN THE ARMOR TODAY?
I DON'T KNOW.
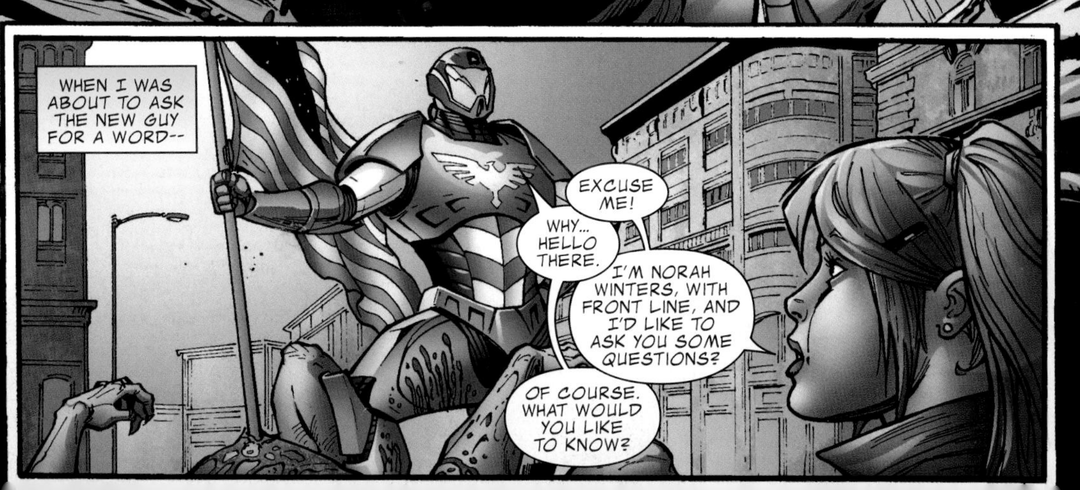
WHEN I WAS ABOUT TO ASK THE NEW GUY FOR A WORD--
EXCUSE ME!
WHY... HELLO THERE.
I'M NORAH WINTERS, WITH FRONT LINE, AND I'D LIKE TO ASK YOU SOME QUESTIONS?
OF COURSE. WHAT WOULD YOU LIKE TO KNOW?

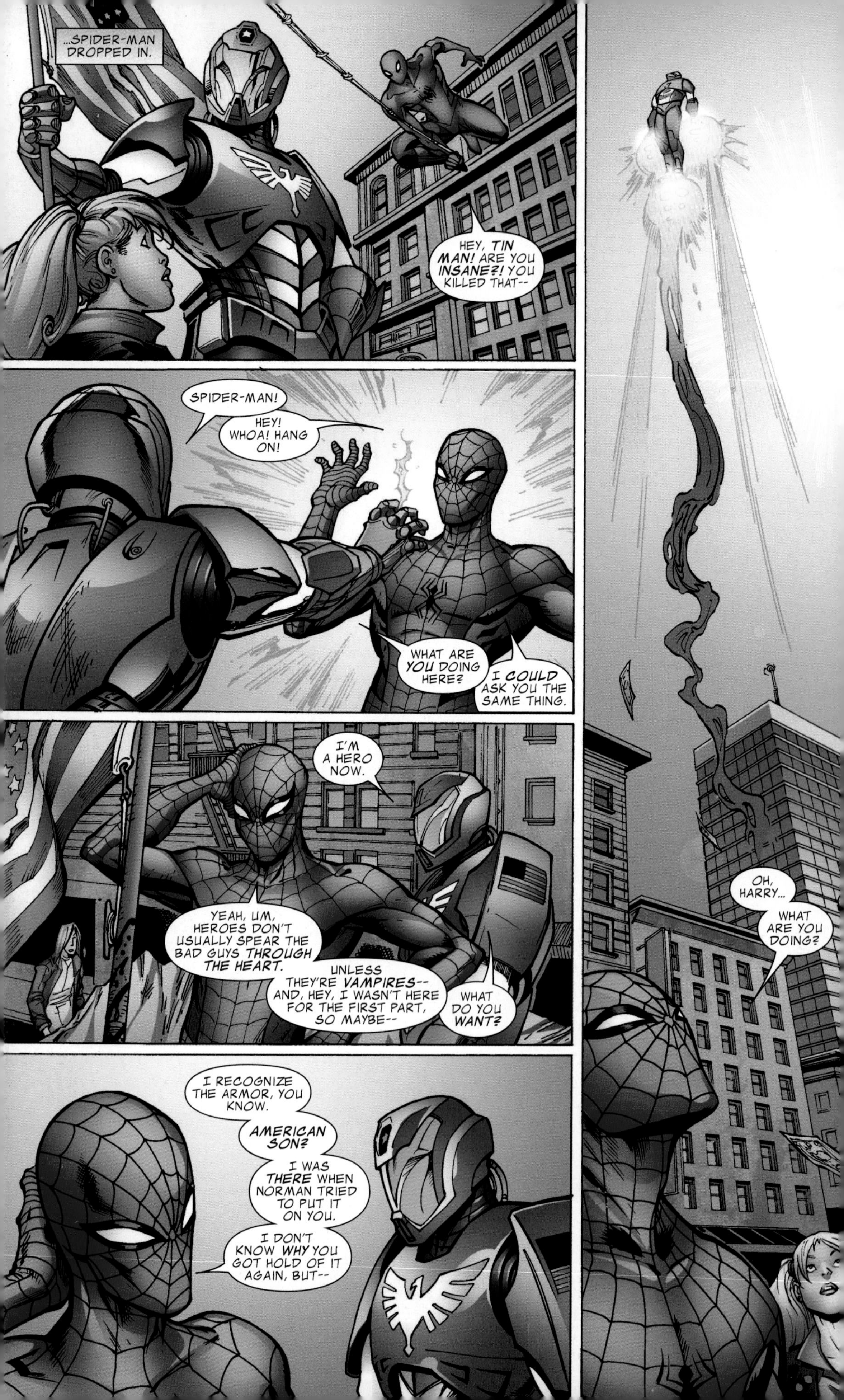
...SPIDER-MAN DROPPED IN.
HEY, TIN MAN! ARE YOU INSANE?! YOU KILLED THAT--
SPIDER-MAN!
HEY! WHOA! HANG ON!
WHAT ARE YOU DOING HERE?
I COULD ASK YOU THE SAME THING.
I'M A HERO NOW.
YEAH, UM, HEROES DON'T USUALLY SPEAR THE BAD GUYS THROUGH THE HEART.
UNLESS THEY'RE VAMPIRES-- AND, HEY, I WASN'T HERE FOR THE FIRST PART, SO MAYBE--
WHAT DO YOU WANT?
I RECOGNIZE THE ARMOR, YOU KNOW.
AMERICAN SON?
I WAS THERE WHEN NORMAN TRIED TO PUT IT ON YOU.
I DON'T KNOW WHY YOU GOT HOLD OF IT AGAIN, BUT--
OH, HARRY...
WHAT ARE YOU DOING?

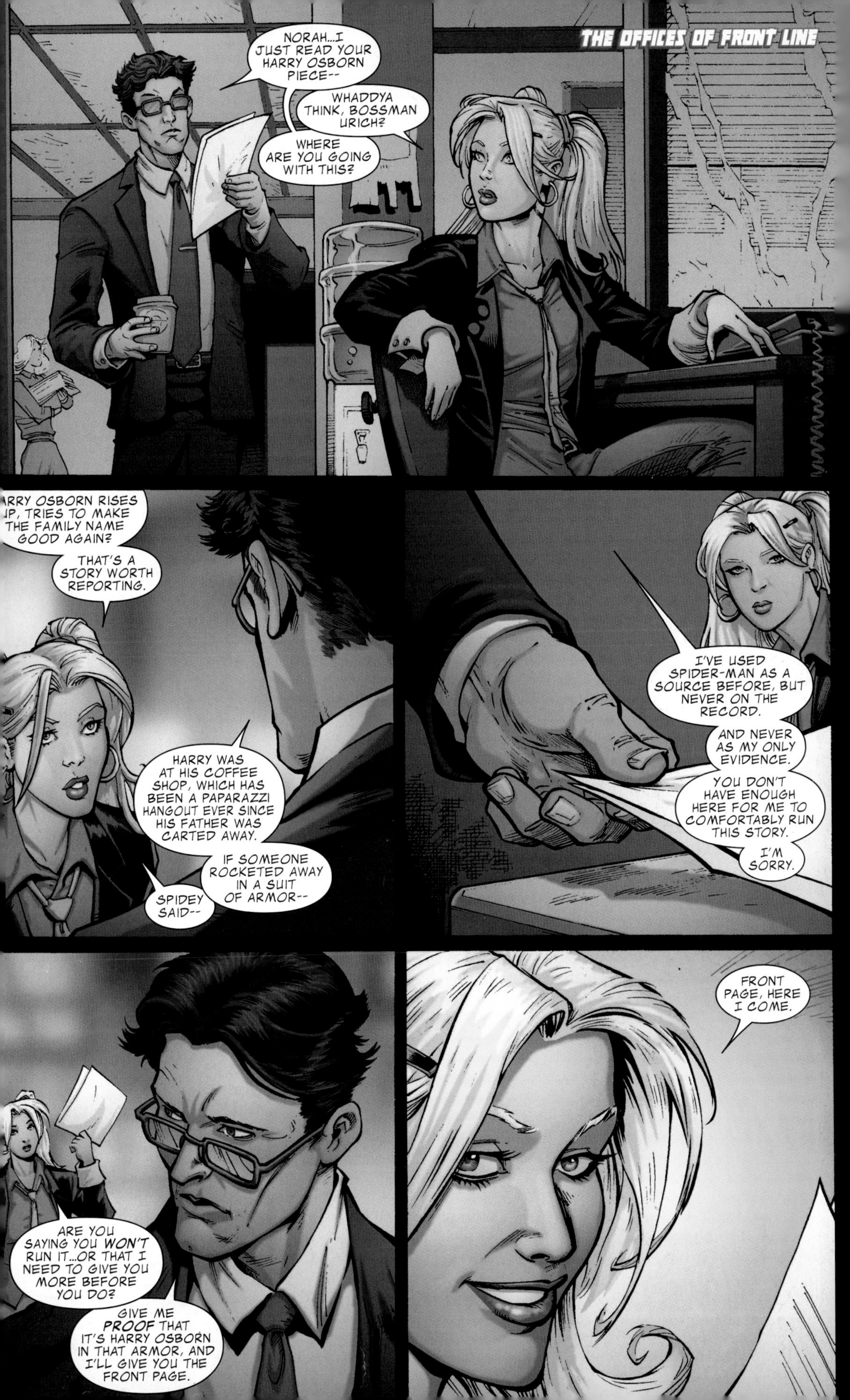
THE OFFICES OF FRONT LINE
NORAH...I JUST READ YOUR HARRY OSBORN PIECE--
WHADDYA THINK, BOSSMAN URICH?
WHERE ARE YOU GOING WITH THIS?
ARRY OSBORN RISES UP, TRIES TO MAKE THE FAMILY NAME GOOD AGAIN?
THAT'S A STORY WORTH REPORTING.
HARRY WAS AT HIS COFFEE SHOP, WHICH HAS BEEN A PAPARAZZI HANGOUT EVER SINCE HIS FATHER WAS CARTED AWAY.
IF SOMEONE ROCKETED AWAY IN A SUIT OF ARMOR--
SPIDEY SAID--
I'VE USED SPIDER-MAN AS A SOURCE BEFORE, BUT NEVER ON THE RECORD.
AND NEVER AS MY ONLY EVIDENCE.
YOU DON'T HAVE ENOUGH HERE FOR ME TO COMFORTABLY RUN THIS STORY.
I'M SORRY.
ARE YOU SAYING YOU WON'T RUN IT...OR THAT I NEED TO GIVE YOU MORE BEFORE YOU DO?
GIVE ME PROOF THAT IT'S HARRY OSBORN IN THAT ARMOR, AND I'LL GIVE YOU THE FRONT PAGE.
FRONT PAGE, HERE I COME.

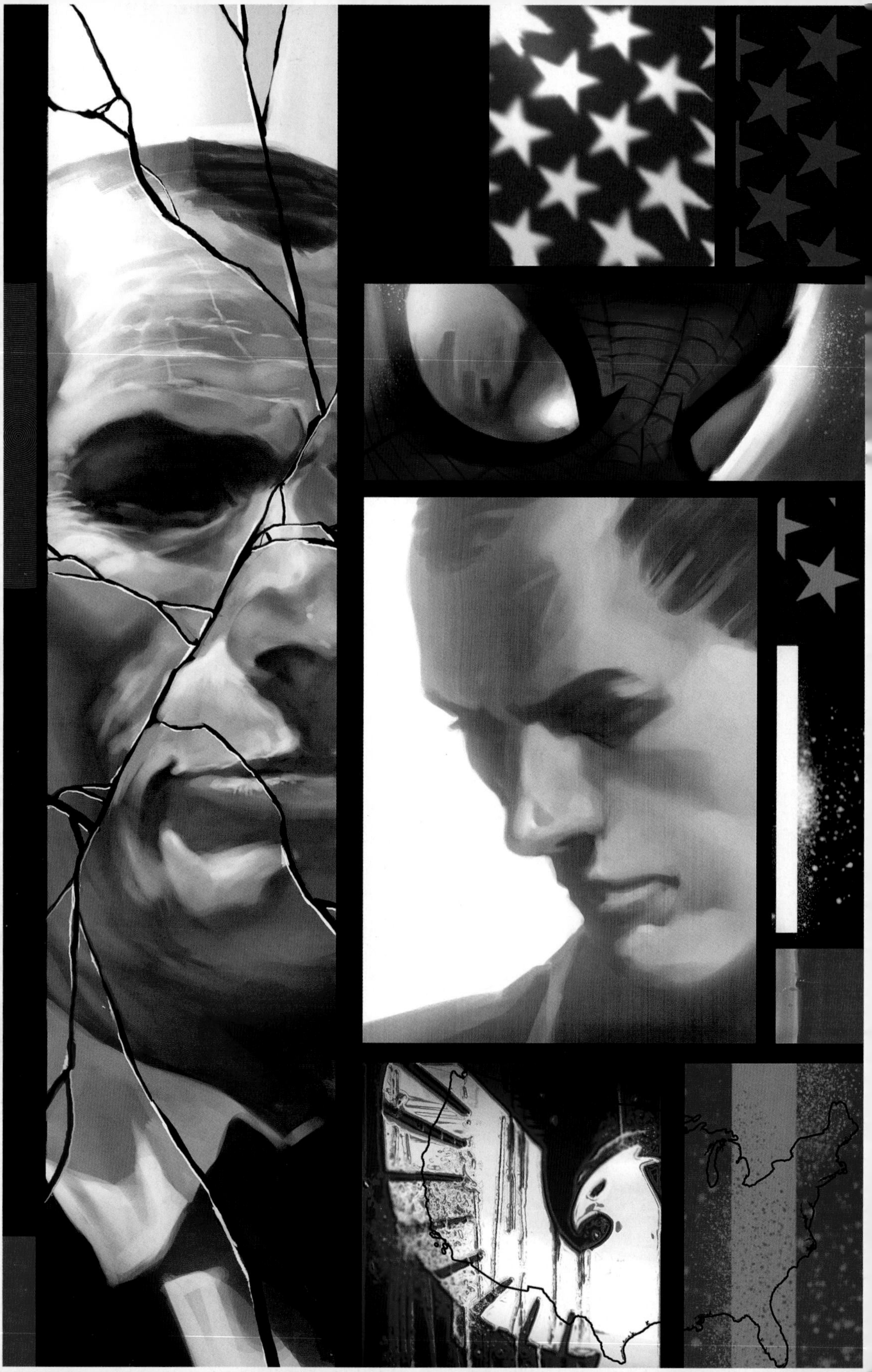

AMAZING SPIDER-MAN PRESENTS: AMERICAN SON #1

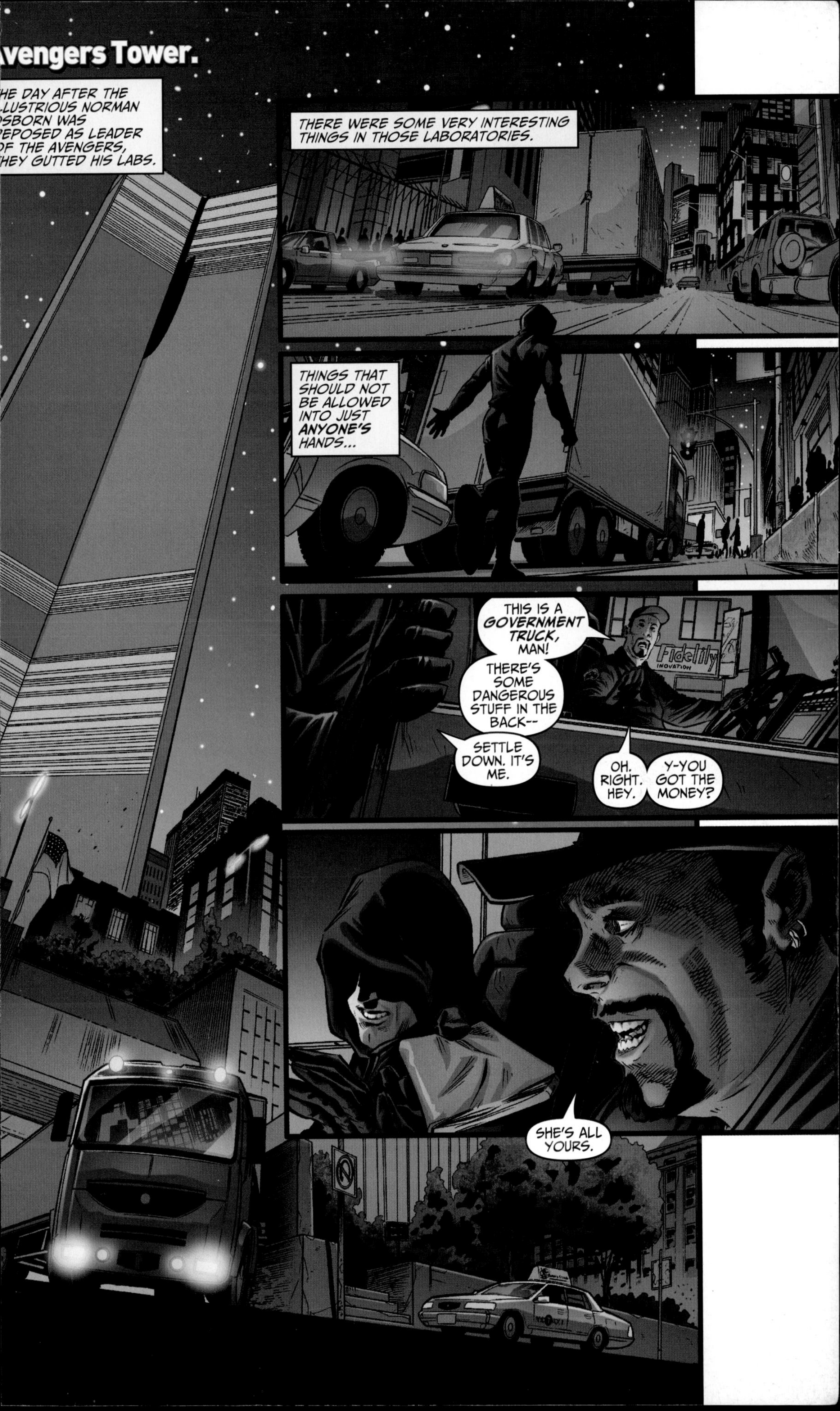
Avengers Tower.
HE DAY AFTER THE
-LUSTRIOUS NORMAN
OSBORN WAS
EPOSED AS LEADER
OF THE AVENGERS,
HEY GUTTED HIS LABS.
THERE WERE SOME VERY INTERESTING THINGS IN THOSE LABORATORIES.
THINGS THAT SHOULD NOT BE ALLOWED INTO JUST ANYONE'S HANDS...
THIS IS A GOVERNMENT TRUCK, MAN!
THERE'S SOME DANGEROUS STUFF IN THE BACK--
SETTLE DOWN. IT'S ME.
OH. RIGHT. HEY.
Y-YOU GOT THE MONEY?
SHE'S ALL YOURS.

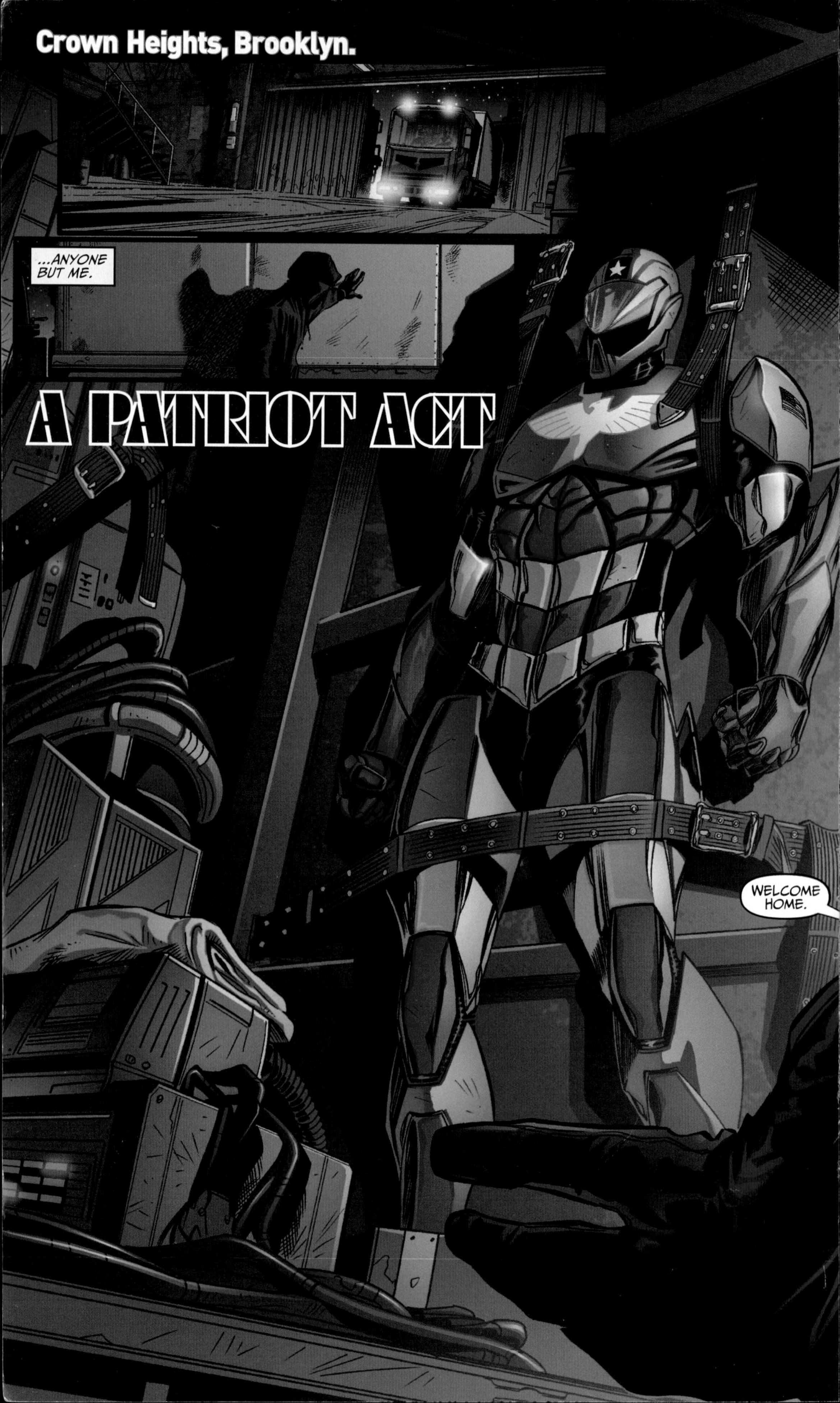

Crown Heights, Brooklyn.
...ANYONE BUT ME.
A PATRIOT ACT
WELCOME HOME.

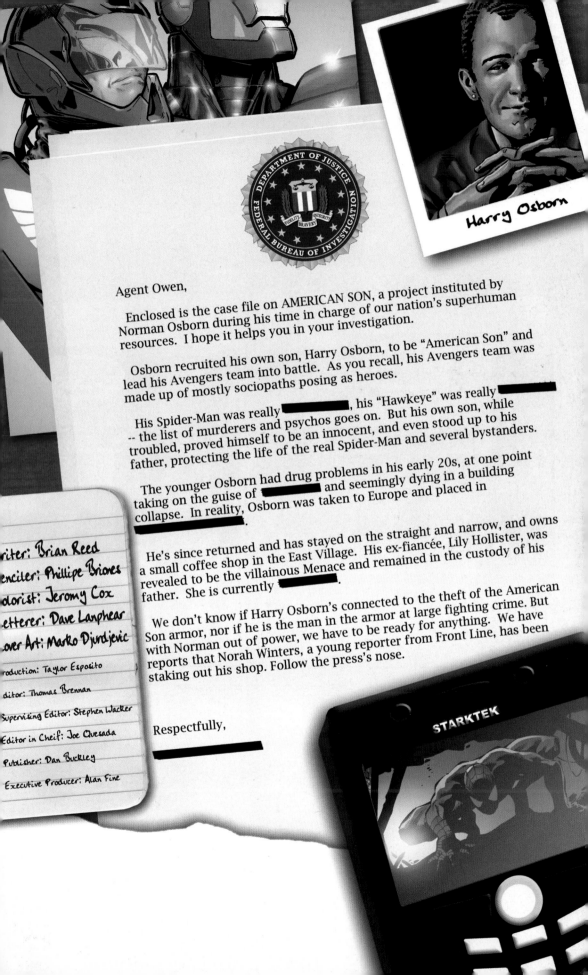

Harry Osborn

Agent Owen,

Enclosed is the case file on AMERICAN SON, a project instituted by Norman Osborn during his time in charge of our nation's superhuman resources. I hope it helps you in your investigation.

Osborn recruited his own son, Harry Osborn, to be "American Son" and lead his Avengers team into battle. As you recall, his Avengers team was made up of mostly sociopaths posing as heroes.

His Spider-Man was really [redacted], his "Hawkeye" was really [redacted] -- the list of murderers and psychos goes on. But his own son, while troubled, proved himself to be an innocent, and even stood up to his father, protecting the life of the real Spider-Man and several bystanders.

The younger Osborn had drug problems in his early 20s, at one point taking on the guise of [redacted] and seemingly dying in a building collapse. In reality, Osborn was taken to Europe and placed in [redacted].

He's since returned and has stayed on the straight and narrow, and owns a small coffee shop in the East Village. His ex-fiancée, Lily Hollister, was revealed to be the villainous Menace and remained in the custody of his father. She is currently [redacted].

We don't know if Harry Osborn's connected to the theft of the American Son armor, nor if he is the man in the armor at large fighting crime. But with Norman out of power, we have to be ready for anything. We have reports that Norah Winters, a young reporter from Front Line, has been staking out his shop. Follow the press's nose.

Respectfully,

[redacted]

riter: Brian Reed
enciler: Phillipe Briones
olorist: Jeromy Cox
etterer: Dave Lanphear
over Art: Marko Djurdjevic
roduction: Taylor Esposito
ditor: Thomas Brennan
Supervising Editor: Stephen Wacker
Editor in Cheif: Joe Quesada
Publisher: Dan Buckley
Executive Producer: Alan Fine

STARKTEK

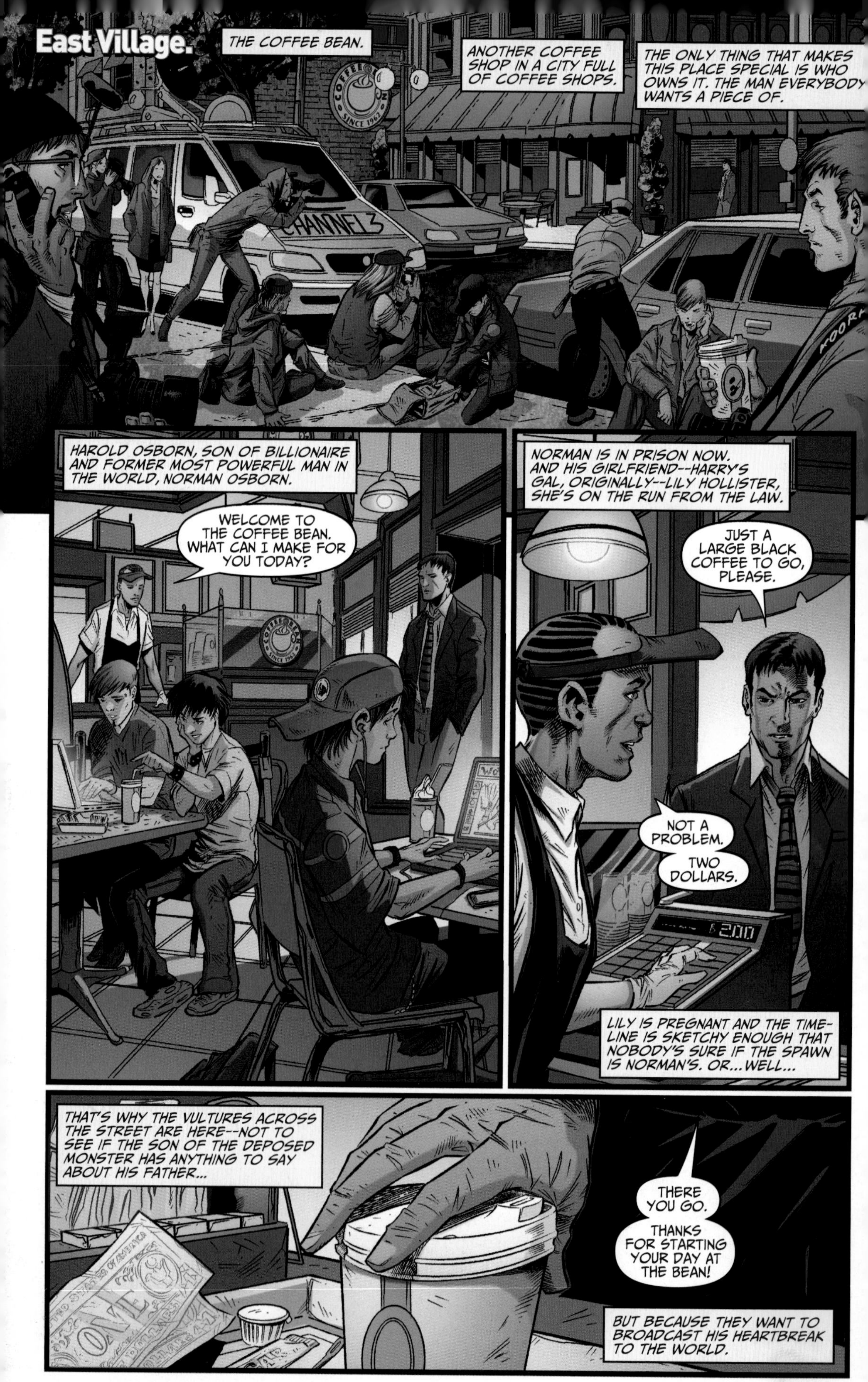
East Village.
THE COFFEE BEAN.
ANOTHER COFFEE SHOP IN A CITY FULL OF COFFEE SHOPS.
THE ONLY THING THAT MAKES THIS PLACE SPECIAL IS WHO OWNS IT. THE MAN EVERYBODY WANTS A PIECE OF.
CHANNEL 3
HAROLD OSBORN, SON OF BILLIONAIRE AND FORMER MOST POWERFUL MAN IN THE WORLD, NORMAN OSBORN.
WELCOME TO THE COFFEE BEAN. WHAT CAN I MAKE FOR YOU TODAY?
NORMAN IS IN PRISON NOW. AND HIS GIRLFRIEND--HARRY'S GAL, ORIGINALLY--LILY HOLLISTER, SHE'S ON THE RUN FROM THE LAW.
JUST A LARGE BLACK COFFEE TO GO, PLEASE.
NOT A PROBLEM.
TWO DOLLARS.
LILY IS PREGNANT AND THE TIME-LINE IS SKETCHY ENOUGH THAT NOBODY'S SURE IF THE SPAWN IS NORMAN'S. OR...WELL...
THAT'S WHY THE VULTURES ACROSS THE STREET ARE HERE--NOT TO SEE IF THE SON OF THE DEPOSED MONSTER HAS ANYTHING TO SAY ABOUT HIS FATHER...
THERE YOU GO.
THANKS FOR STARTING YOUR DAY AT THE BEAN!
BUT BECAUSE THEY WANT TO BROADCAST HIS HEARTBREAK TO THE WORLD.

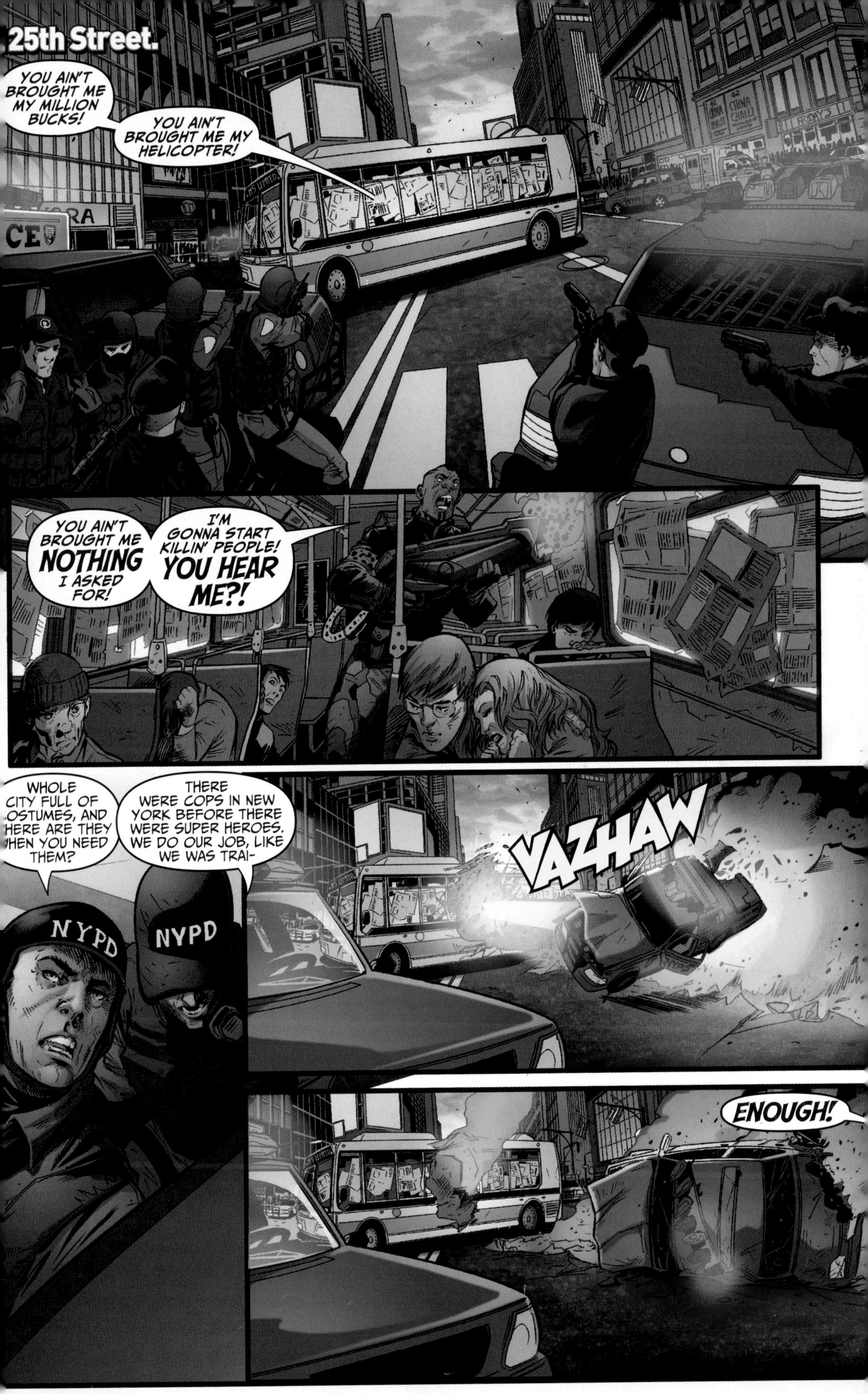
25th Street.
YOU AIN'T BROUGHT ME MY MILLION BUCKS!
YOU AIN'T BROUGHT ME MY HELICOPTER!
YOU AIN'T BROUGHT ME NOTHING I ASKED FOR!
I'M GONNA START KILLIN' PEOPLE! YOU HEAR ME?!
WHOLE CITY FULL OF COSTUMES, AND WHERE ARE THEY WHEN YOU NEED THEM?
THERE WERE COPS IN NEW YORK BEFORE THERE WERE SUPER HEROES. WE DO OUR JOB, LIKE WE WAS TRAI-
NYPD
NYPD
VAZHAW
ENOUGH!

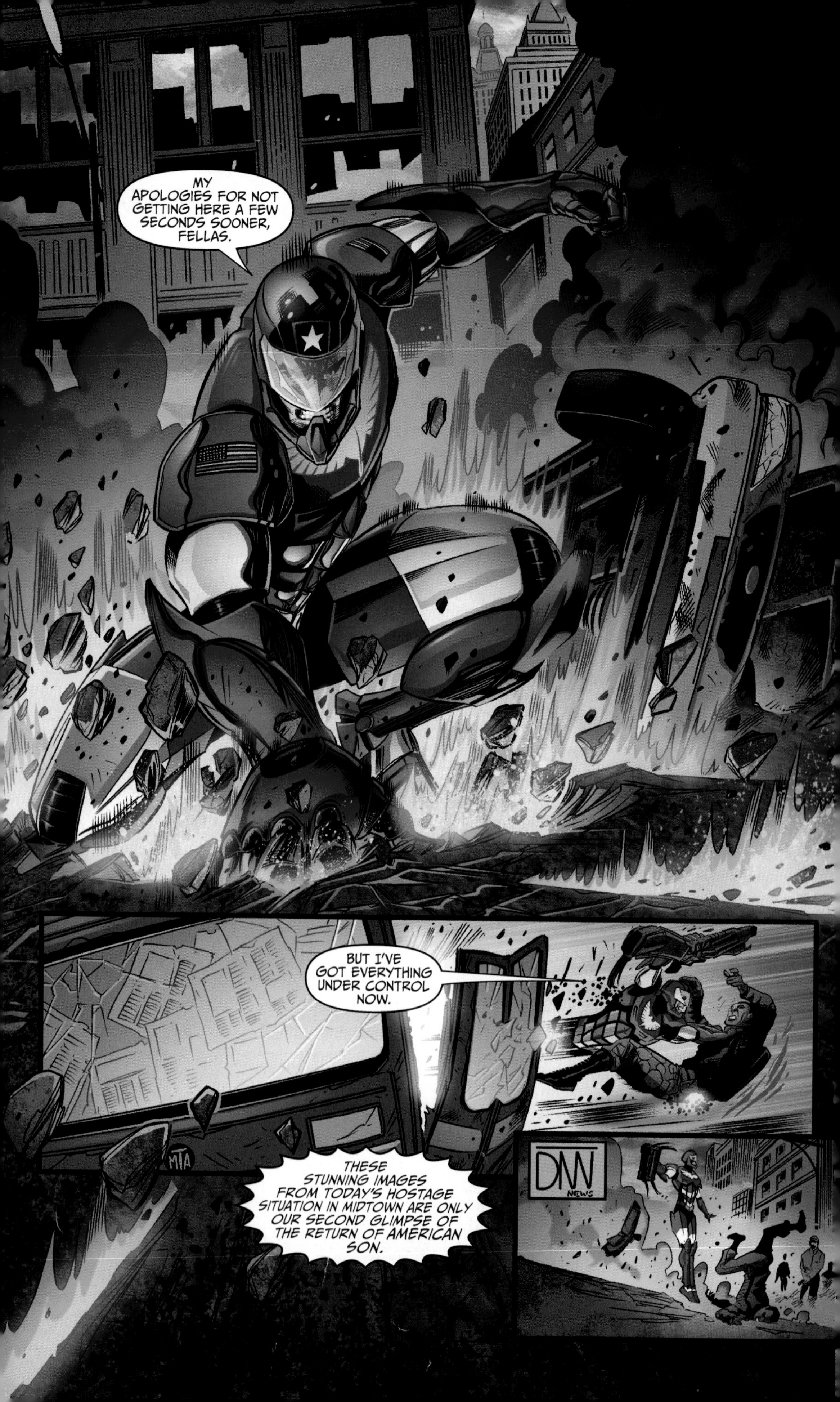

MY APOLOGIES FOR NOT GETTING HERE A FEW SECONDS SOONER, FELLAS.
BUT I'VE GOT EVERYTHING UNDER CONTROL NOW.
THESE STUNNING IMAGES FROM TODAY'S HOSTAGE SITUATION IN MIDTOWN ARE ONLY OUR SECOND GLIMPSE OF THE RETURN OF AMERICAN SON.
DNN NEWS

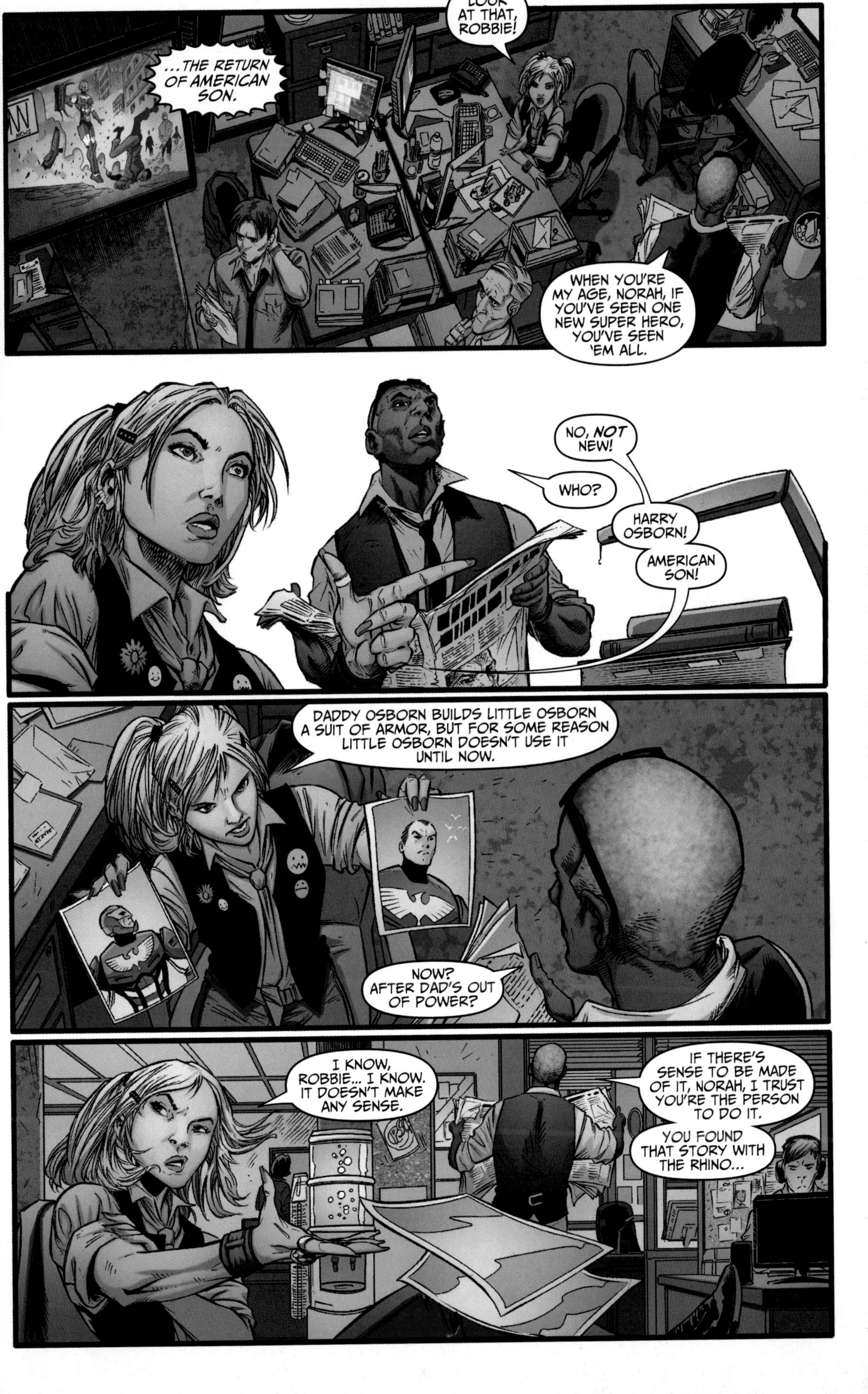
...THE RETURN OF AMERICAN SON.
LOOK AT THAT, ROBBIE!
WHEN YOU'RE MY AGE, NORAH, IF YOU'VE SEEN ONE NEW SUPER HERO, YOU'VE SEEN 'EM ALL.
NO, NOT NEW!
WHO?
HARRY OSBORN!
AMERICAN SON!
DADDY OSBORN BUILDS LITTLE OSBORN A SUIT OF ARMOR, BUT FOR SOME REASON LITTLE OSBORN DOESN'T USE IT UNTIL NOW.
NOW? AFTER DAD'S OUT OF POWER?
I KNOW, ROBBIE... I KNOW. IT DOESN'T MAKE ANY SENSE.
IF THERE'S SENSE TO BE MADE OF IT, NORAH, I TRUST YOU'RE THE PERSON TO DO IT.
YOU FOUND THAT STORY WITH THE RHINO...

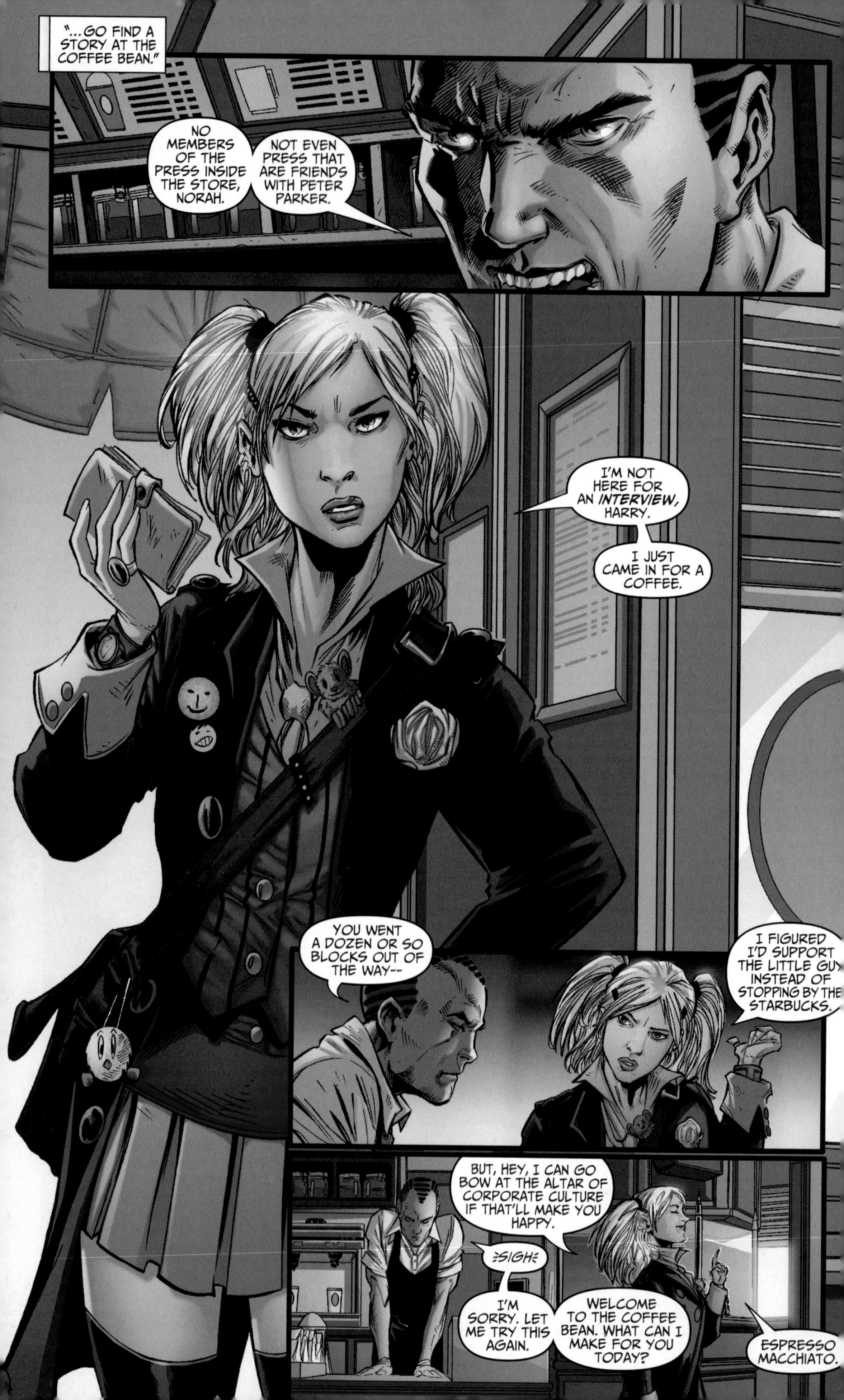
"...GO FIND A STORY AT THE COFFEE BEAN."
NO MEMBERS OF THE PRESS INSIDE THE STORE, NORAH.
NOT EVEN PRESS THAT ARE FRIENDS WITH PETER PARKER.
I'M NOT HERE FOR AN *INTERVIEW,* HARRY.
I JUST CAME IN FOR A COFFEE.
YOU WENT A DOZEN OR SO BLOCKS OUT OF THE WAY--
I FIGURED I'D SUPPORT THE LITTLE GUY INSTEAD OF STOPPING BY THE STARBUCKS.
BUT, HEY, I CAN GO BOW AT THE ALTAR OF CORPORATE CULTURE IF THAT'LL MAKE YOU HAPPY.
SIGH
I'M SORRY. LET ME TRY THIS AGAIN.
WELCOME TO THE COFFEE BEAN. WHAT CAN I MAKE FOR YOU TODAY?
ESPRESSO MACCHIATO.

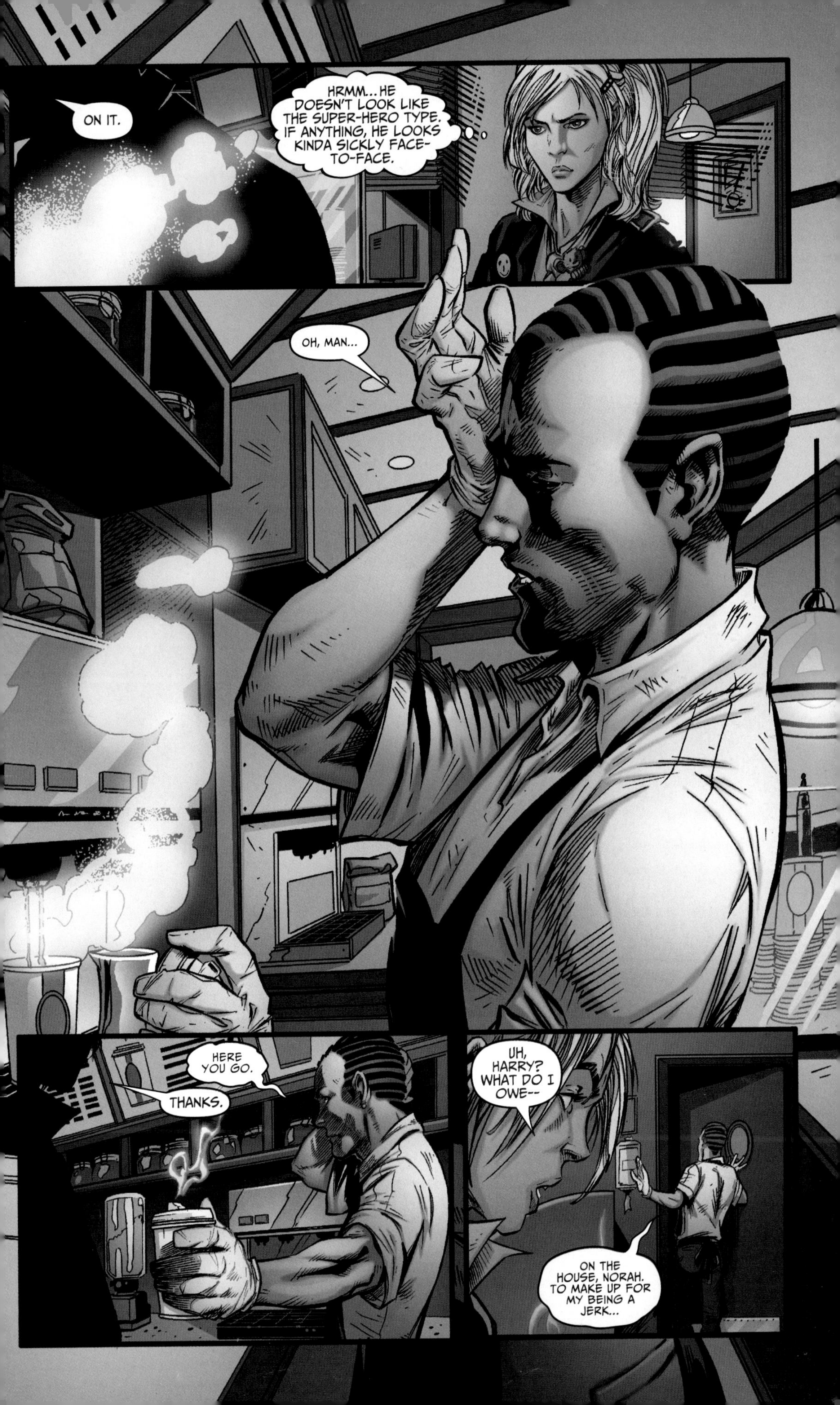

ON IT.
HRMM...HE DOESN'T LOOK LIKE THE SUPER-HERO TYPE. IF ANYTHING, HE LOOKS KINDA SICKLY FACE-TO-FACE.
OH, MAN...
HERE YOU GO.
THANKS.
UH, HARRY? WHAT DO I OWE--
ON THE HOUSE, NORAH. TO MAKE UP FOR MY BEING A JERK...

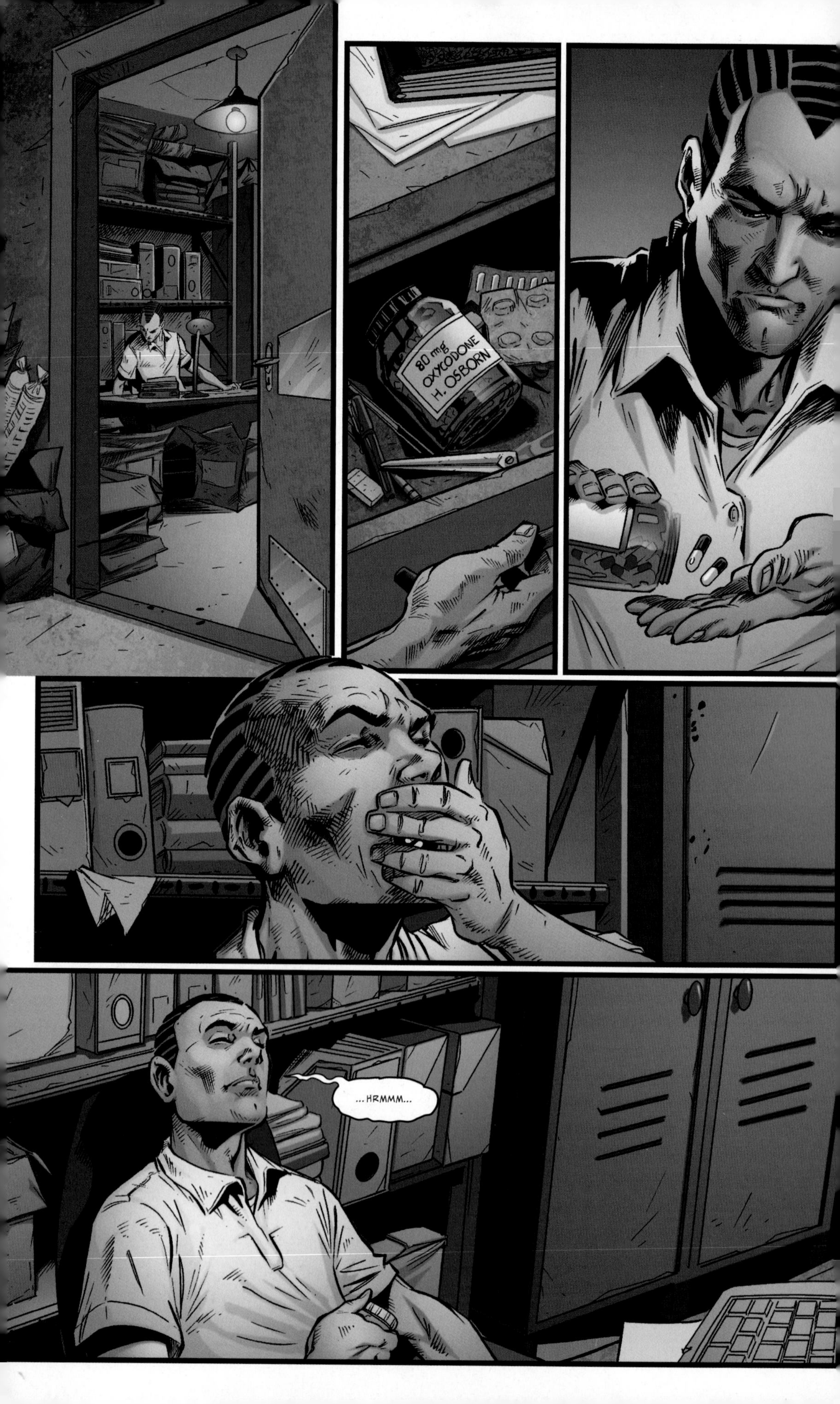
80 mg
OXYCODONE
H. OSBORN
...HRMMM...

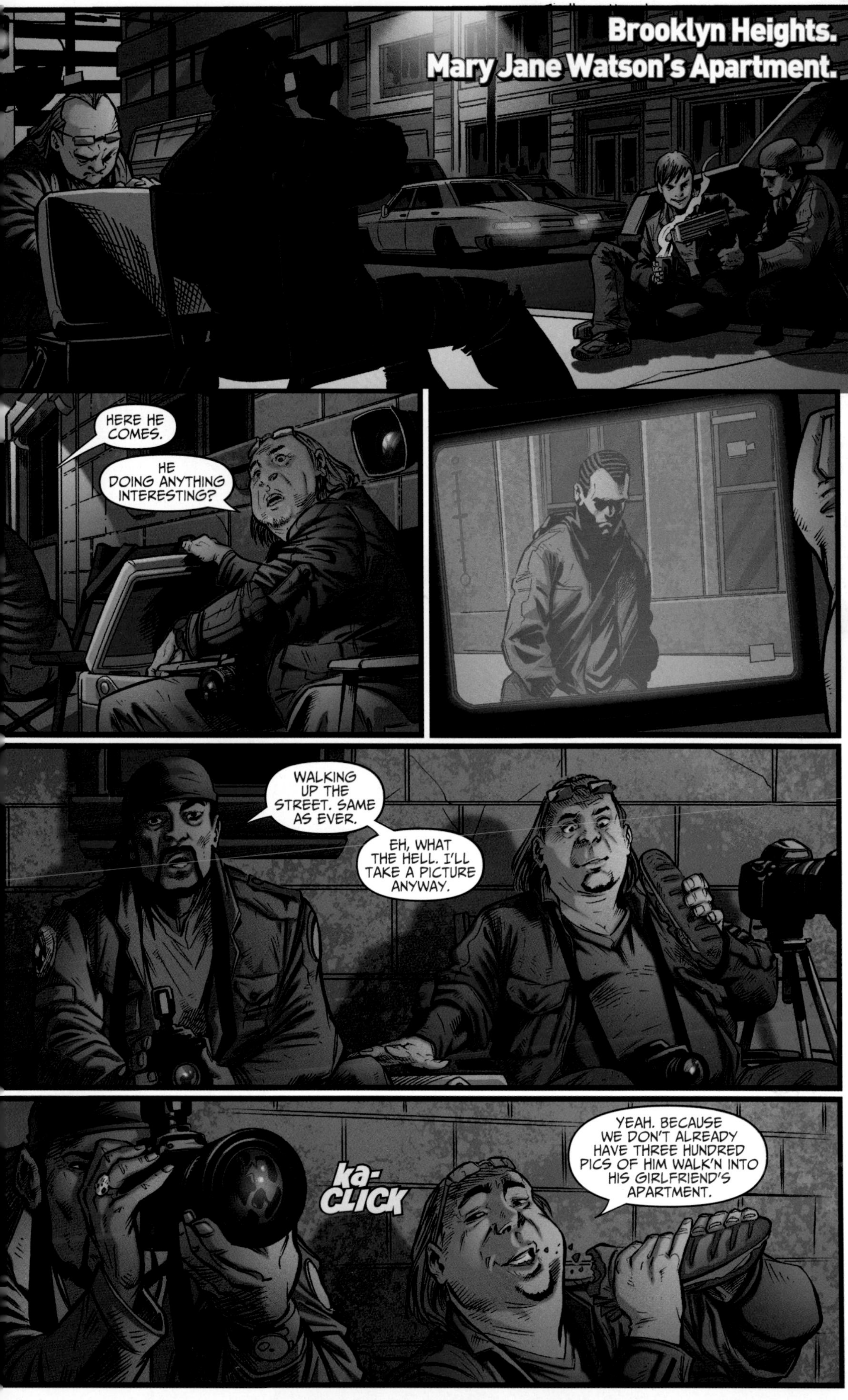
Brooklyn Heights.
Mary Jane Watson's Apartment.
HERE HE COMES.
HE DOING ANYTHING INTERESTING?
WALKING UP THE STREET. SAME AS EVER.
EH, WHAT THE HELL. I'LL TAKE A PICTURE ANYWAY.
KA-CLICK
YEAH. BECAUSE WE DON'T ALREADY HAVE THREE HUNDRED PICS OF HIM WALK'N INTO HIS GIRLFRIEND'S APARTMENT.

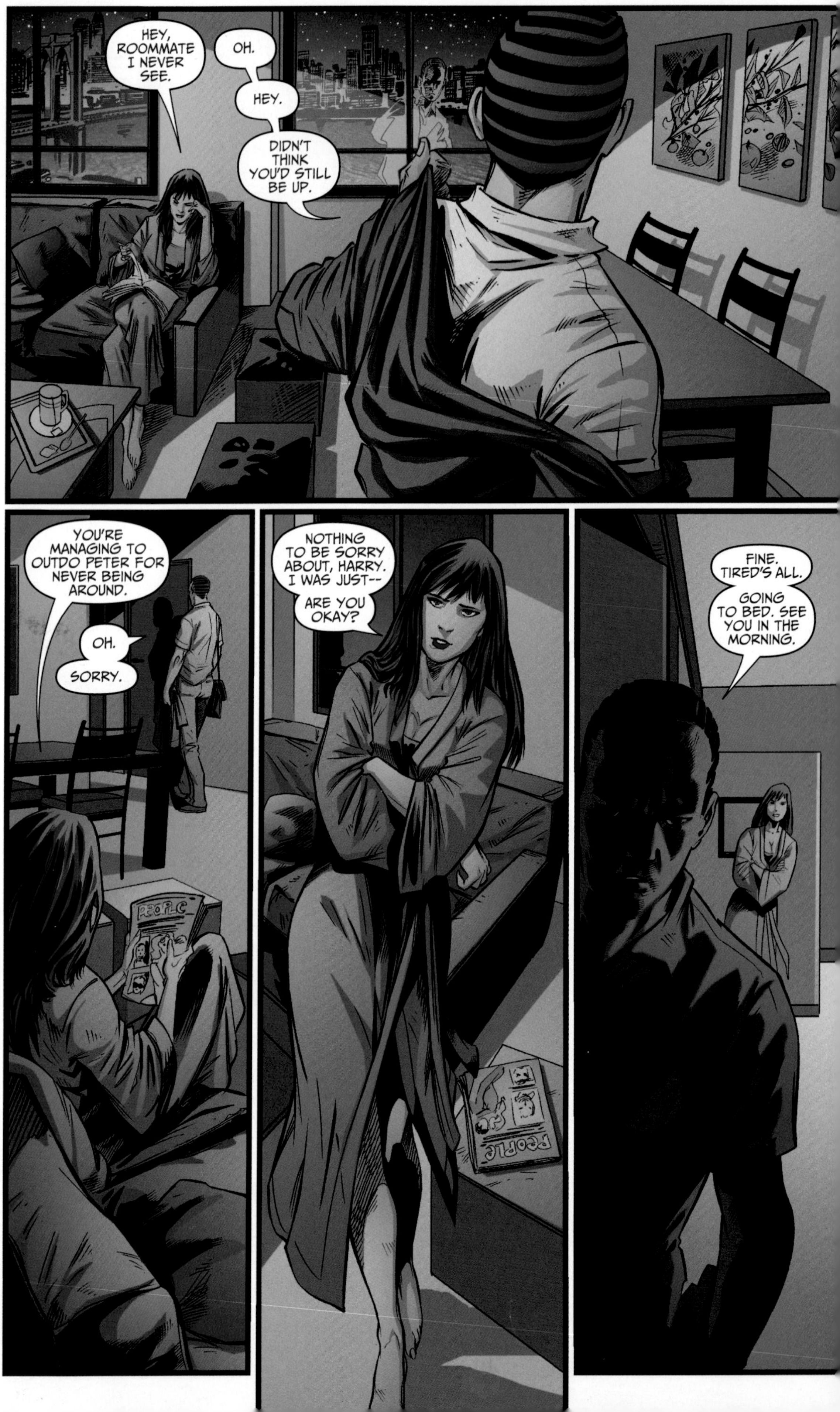
HEY, ROOMMATE I NEVER SEE.
OH.
HEY.
DIDN'T THINK YOU'D STILL BE UP.
YOU'RE MANAGING TO OUTDO PETER FOR NEVER BEING AROUND.
OH.
SORRY.
PEOPLE
NOTHING TO BE SORRY ABOUT, HARRY. I WAS JUST--
ARE YOU OKAY?
PEOPLE
FINE. TIRED'S ALL.
GOING TO BED. SEE YOU IN THE MORNING.

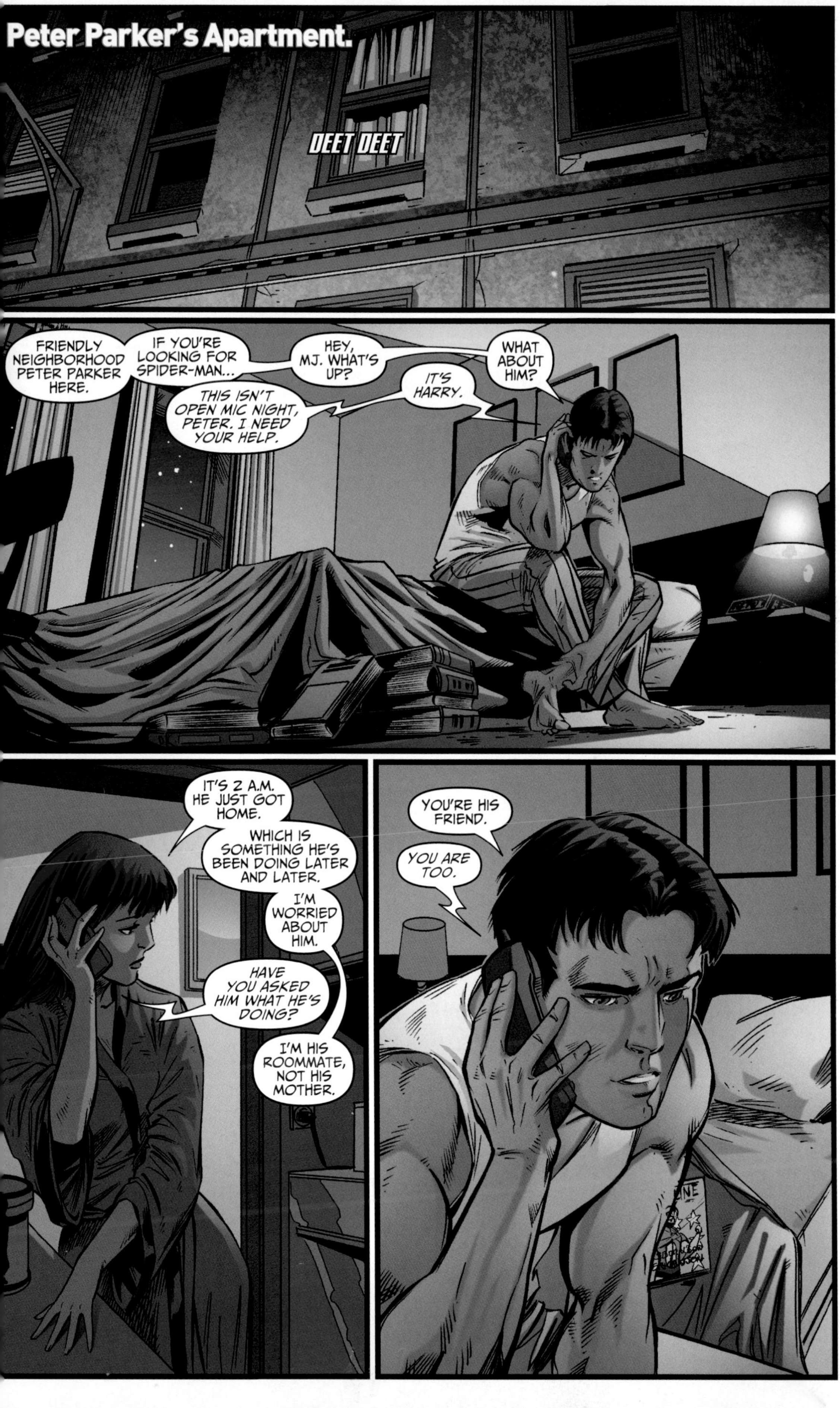
Peter Parker's Apartment.
DEET DEET
FRIENDLY NEIGHBORHOOD PETER PARKER HERE.
IF YOU'RE LOOKING FOR SPIDER-MAN...
THIS ISN'T OPEN MIC NIGHT, PETER. I NEED YOUR HELP.
HEY, MJ. WHAT'S UP?
IT'S HARRY.
WHAT ABOUT HIM?
IT'S 2 A.M. HE JUST GOT HOME.
WHICH IS SOMETHING HE'S BEEN DOING LATER AND LATER.
I'M WORRIED ABOUT HIM.
HAVE YOU ASKED HIM WHAT HE'S DOING?
I'M HIS ROOMMATE, NOT HIS MOTHER.
YOU'RE HIS FRIEND.
YOU ARE TOO.

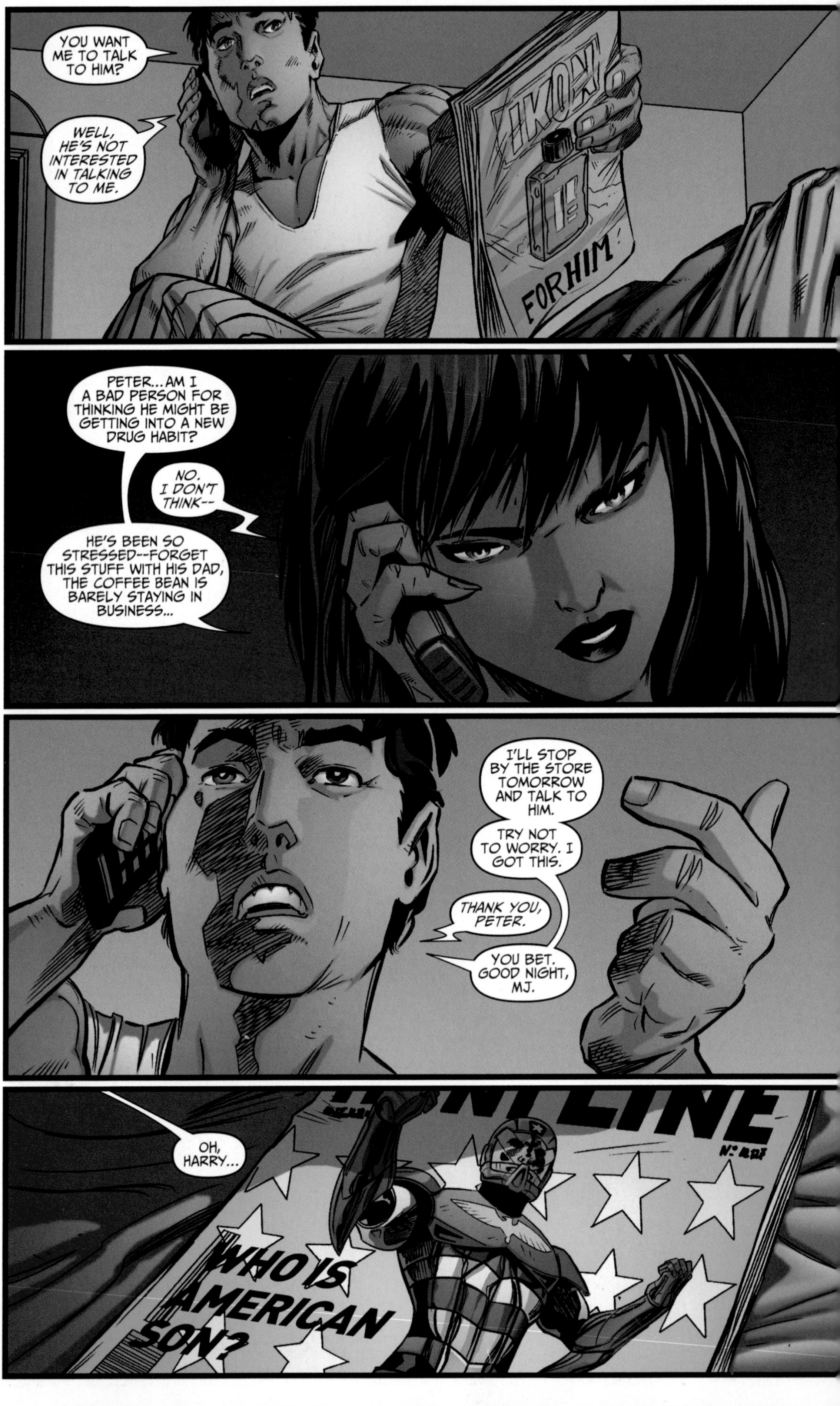
YOU WANT ME TO TALK TO HIM?
WELL, HE'S NOT INTERESTED IN TALKING TO ME.
FOR HIM
PETER...AM I A BAD PERSON FOR THINKING HE MIGHT BE GETTING INTO A NEW DRUG HABIT?
NO. I DON'T THINK--
HE'S BEEN SO STRESSED--FORGET THIS STUFF WITH HIS DAD, THE COFFEE BEAN IS BARELY STAYING IN BUSINESS...
I'LL STOP BY THE STORE TOMORROW AND TALK TO HIM.
TRY NOT TO WORRY. I GOT THIS.
THANK YOU, PETER.
YOU BET. GOOD NIGHT, MJ.
OH, HARRY...
WHO IS AMERICAN SON?

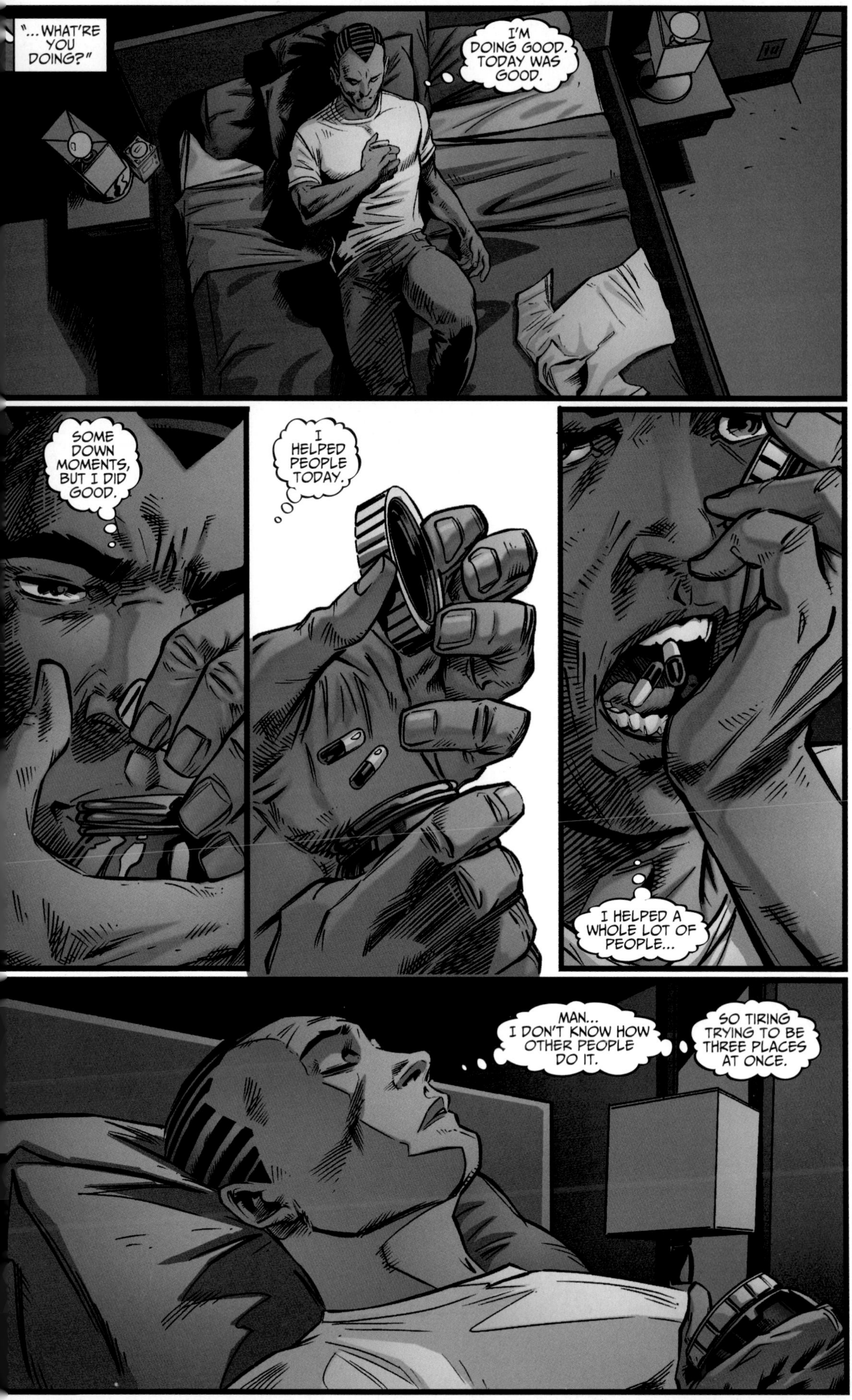
"...WHAT'RE YOU DOING?"
I'M DOING GOOD. TODAY WAS GOOD.
SOME DOWN MOMENTS, BUT I DID GOOD.
I HELPED PEOPLE TODAY.
I HELPED A WHOLE LOT OF PEOPLE...
MAN... I DON'T KNOW HOW OTHER PEOPLE DO IT.
SO TIRING TRYING TO BE THREE PLACES AT ONCE.

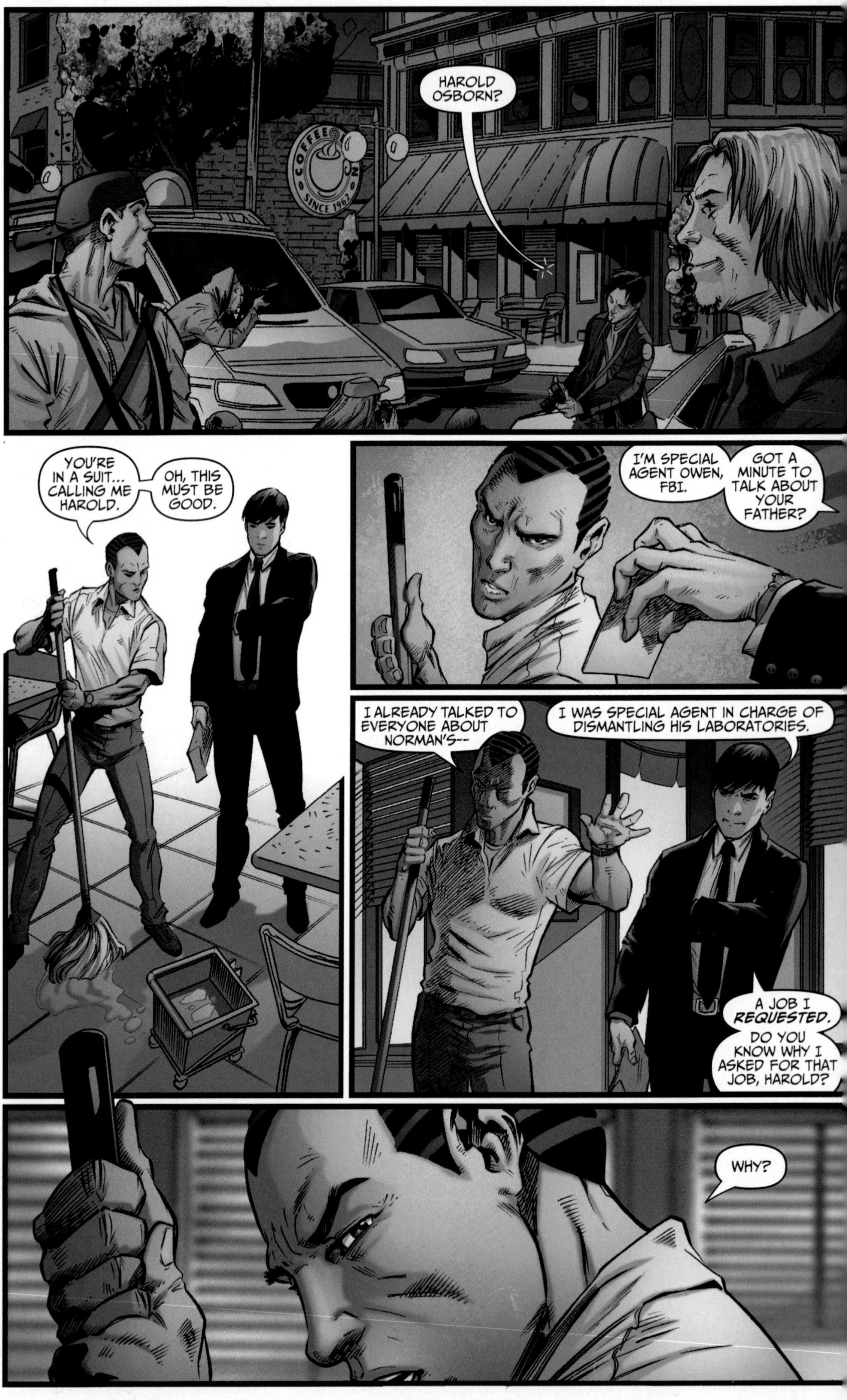
HAROLD OSBORN?
YOU'RE IN A SUIT... CALLING ME HAROLD.
OH, THIS MUST BE GOOD.
I'M SPECIAL AGENT OWEN, FBI.
GOT A MINUTE TO TALK ABOUT YOUR FATHER?
I ALREADY TALKED TO EVERYONE ABOUT NORMAN'S--
I WAS SPECIAL AGENT IN CHARGE OF DISMANTLING HIS LABORATORIES.
A JOB I *REQUESTED.* DO YOU KNOW WHY I ASKED FOR THAT JOB, HAROLD?
WHY?

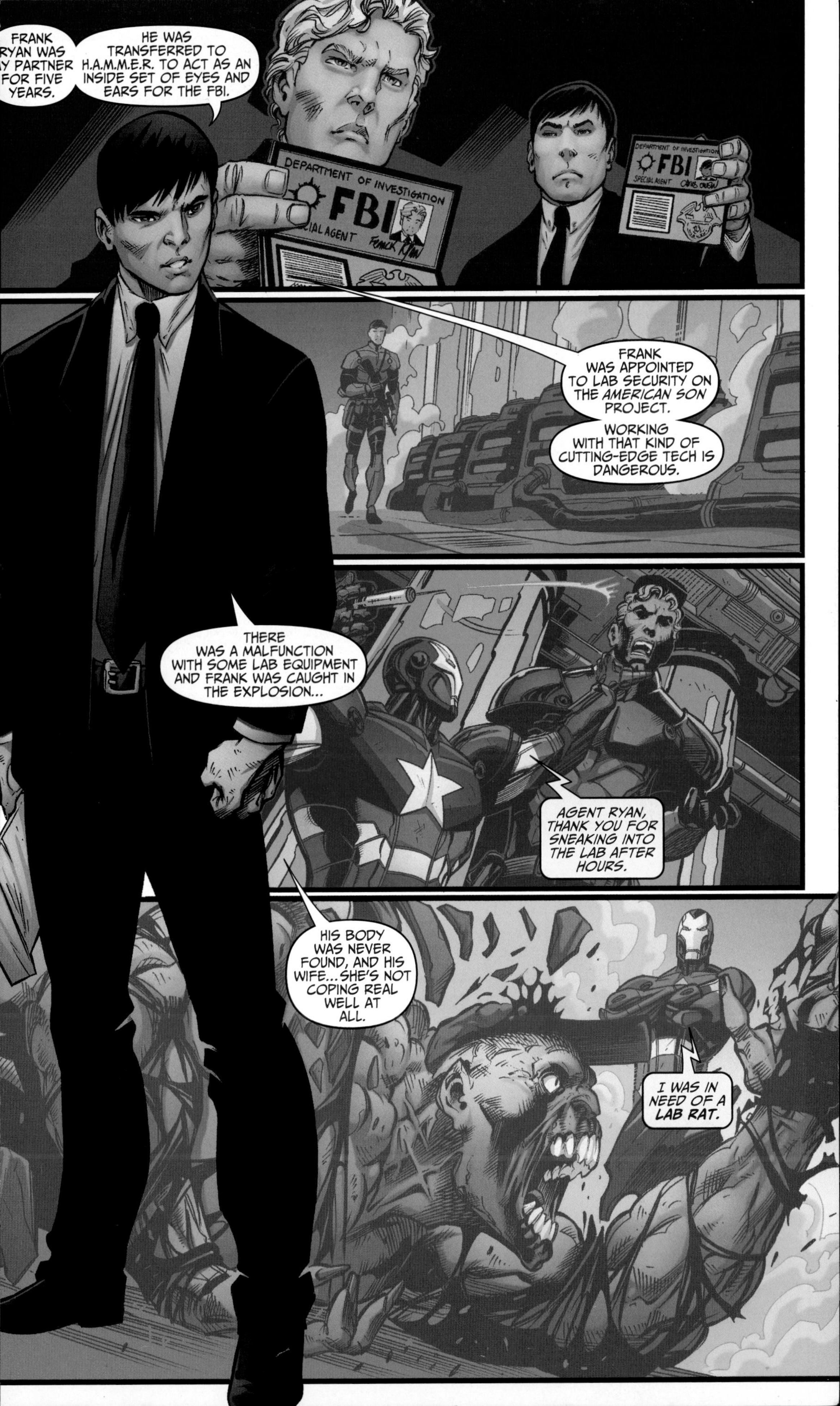

FRANK RYAN WAS MY PARTNER FOR FIVE YEARS.
HE WAS TRANSFERRED TO H.A.M.M.E.R. TO ACT AS AN INSIDE SET OF EYES AND EARS FOR THE FBI.
DEPARTMENT OF INVESTIGATION FBI SPECIAL AGENT
DEPARTMENT OF INVESTIGATION FBI SPECIAL AGENT
FRANK WAS APPOINTED TO LAB SECURITY ON THE AMERICAN SON PROJECT.
WORKING WITH THAT KIND OF CUTTING-EDGE TECH IS DANGEROUS.
THERE WAS A MALFUNCTION WITH SOME LAB EQUIPMENT AND FRANK WAS CAUGHT IN THE EXPLOSION...
AGENT RYAN, THANK YOU FOR SNEAKING INTO THE LAB AFTER HOURS.
HIS BODY WAS NEVER FOUND, AND HIS WIFE... SHE'S NOT COPING REAL WELL AT ALL.
I WAS IN NEED OF A LAB RAT.

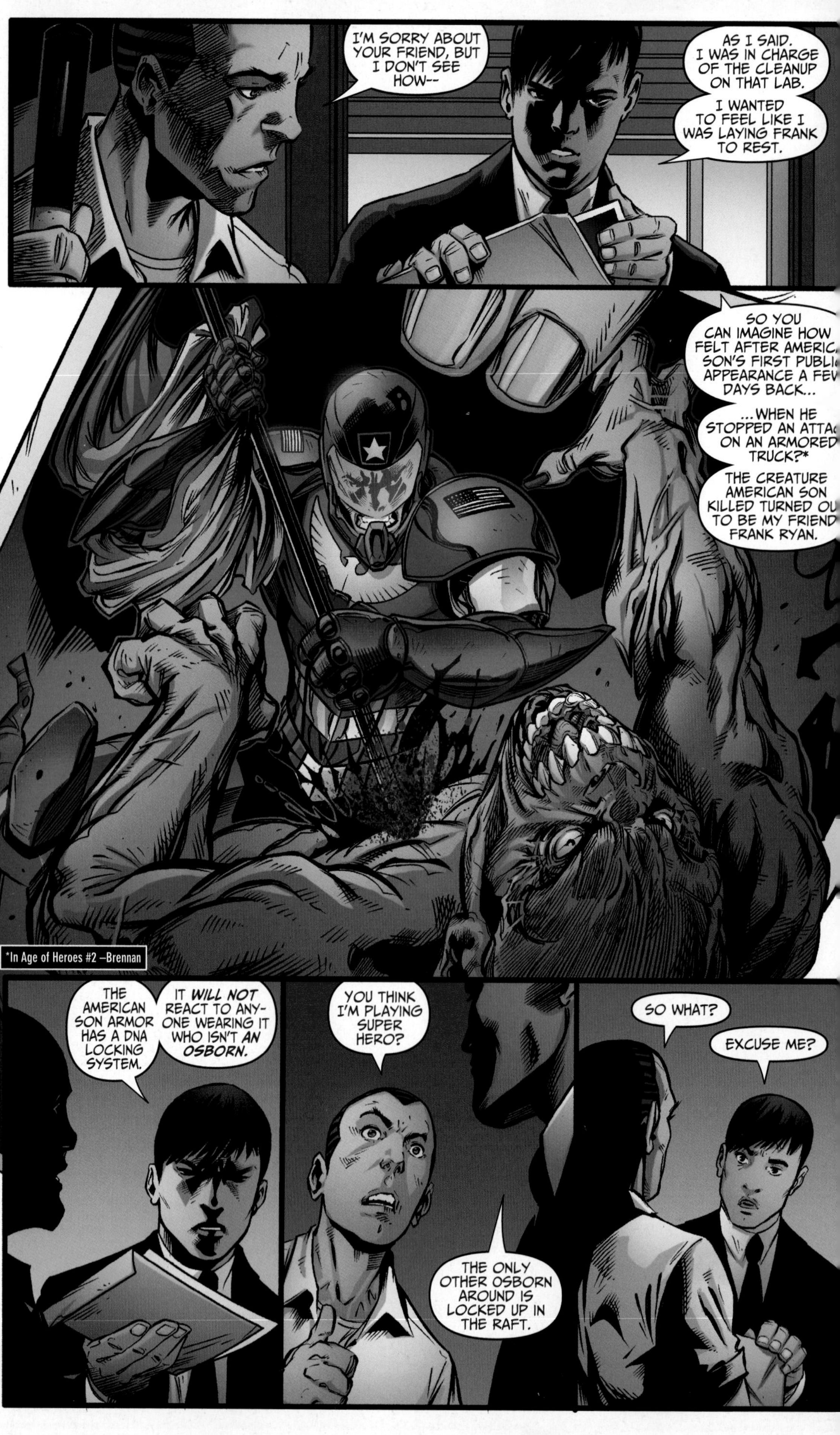
I'M SORRY ABOUT YOUR FRIEND, BUT I DON'T SEE HOW--
AS I SAID. I WAS IN CHARGE OF THE CLEANUP ON THAT LAB.
I WANTED TO FEEL LIKE I WAS LAYING FRANK TO REST.
SO YOU CAN IMAGINE HOW I FELT AFTER AMERICAN SON'S FIRST PUBLIC APPEARANCE A FEW DAYS BACK...
...WHEN HE STOPPED AN ATTACK ON AN ARMORED TRUCK?*
THE CREATURE AMERICAN SON KILLED TURNED OUT TO BE MY FRIEND FRANK RYAN.
*In Age of Heroes #2 –Brennan
THE AMERICAN SON ARMOR HAS A DNA LOCKING SYSTEM.
IT WILL NOT REACT TO ANYONE WEARING IT WHO ISN'T AN OSBORN.
YOU THINK I'M PLAYING SUPER HERO?
THE ONLY OTHER OSBORN AROUND IS LOCKED UP IN THE RAFT.
SO WHAT?
EXCUSE ME?

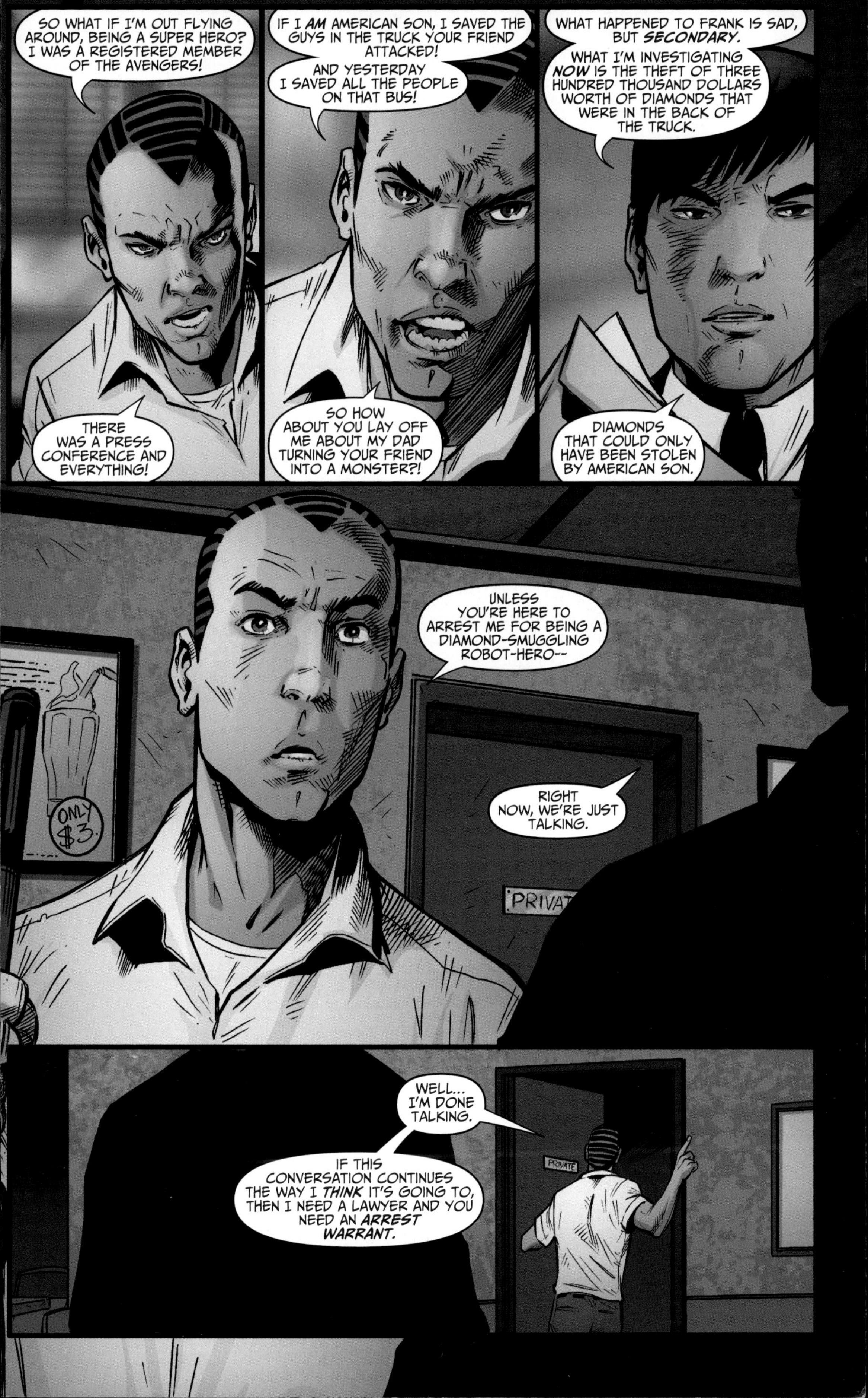
SO WHAT IF I'M OUT FLYING AROUND, BEING A SUPER HERO? I WAS A REGISTERED MEMBER OF THE AVENGERS!
THERE WAS A PRESS CONFERENCE AND EVERYTHING!
IF I *AM* AMERICAN SON, I SAVED THE GUYS IN THE TRUCK YOUR FRIEND ATTACKED!
AND YESTERDAY I SAVED ALL THE PEOPLE ON THAT BUS!
SO HOW ABOUT YOU LAY OFF ME ABOUT MY DAD TURNING YOUR FRIEND INTO A MONSTER?!
WHAT HAPPENED TO FRANK IS SAD, BUT ***SECONDARY.***
WHAT I'M INVESTIGATING ***NOW*** IS THE THEFT OF THREE HUNDRED THOUSAND DOLLARS WORTH OF DIAMONDS THAT WERE IN THE BACK OF THE TRUCK.
DIAMONDS THAT COULD ONLY HAVE BEEN STOLEN BY AMERICAN SON.
ONLY $3.
UNLESS YOU'RE HERE TO ARREST ME FOR BEING A DIAMOND-SMUGGLING ROBOT-HERO--
RIGHT NOW, WE'RE JUST TALKING.
PRIVAT
WELL... I'M DONE TALKING.
IF THIS CONVERSATION CONTINUES THE WAY I *THINK* IT'S GOING TO, THEN I NEED A LAWYER AND YOU NEED AN ***ARREST WARRANT.***
PRIVATE

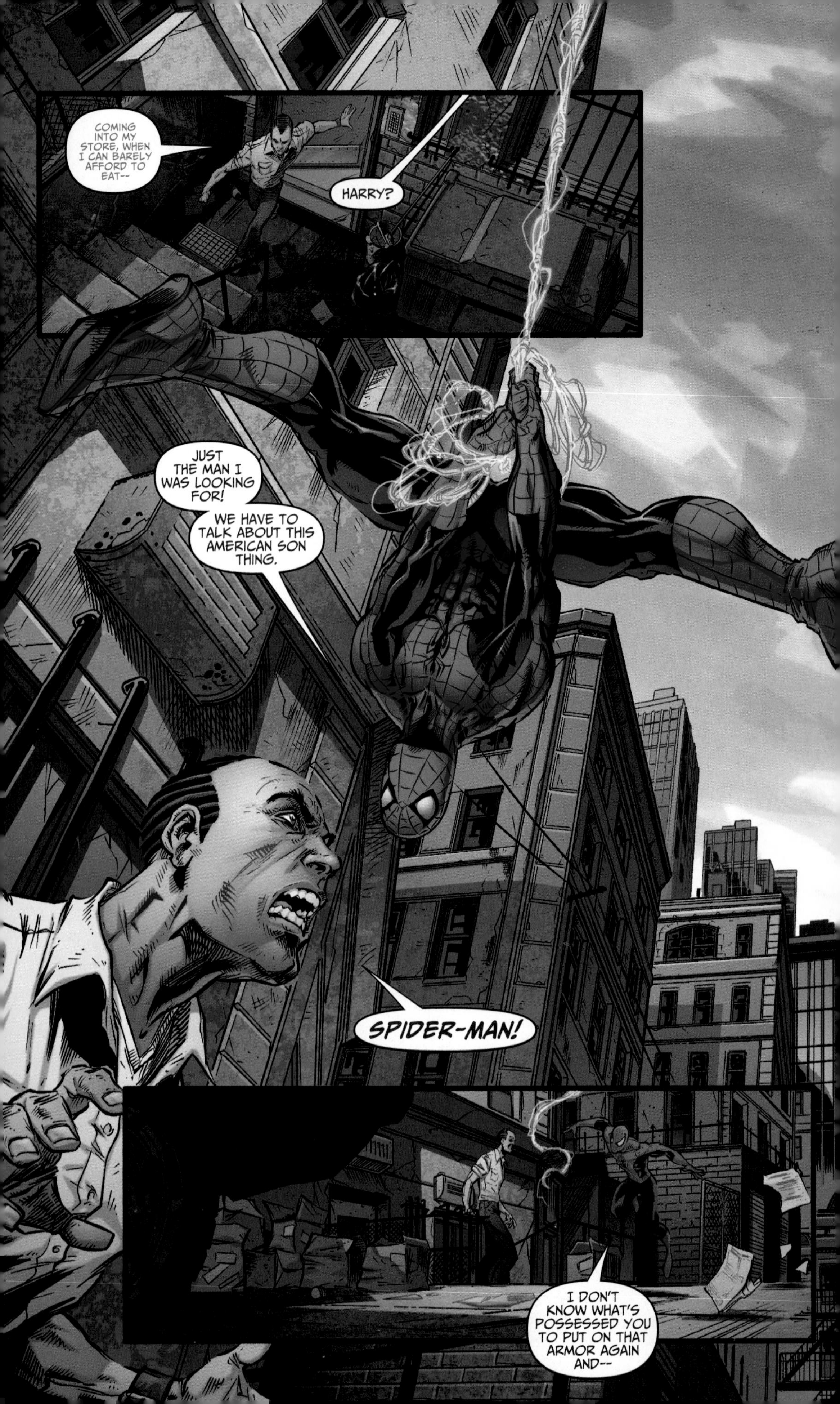

COMING INTO MY STORE, WHEN I CAN BARELY AFFORD TO EAT--
HARRY?
JUST THE MAN I WAS LOOKING FOR!
WE HAVE TO TALK ABOUT THIS AMERICAN SON THING.
SPIDER-MAN!
I DON'T KNOW WHAT'S POSSESSED YOU TO PUT ON THAT ARMOR AGAIN AND--

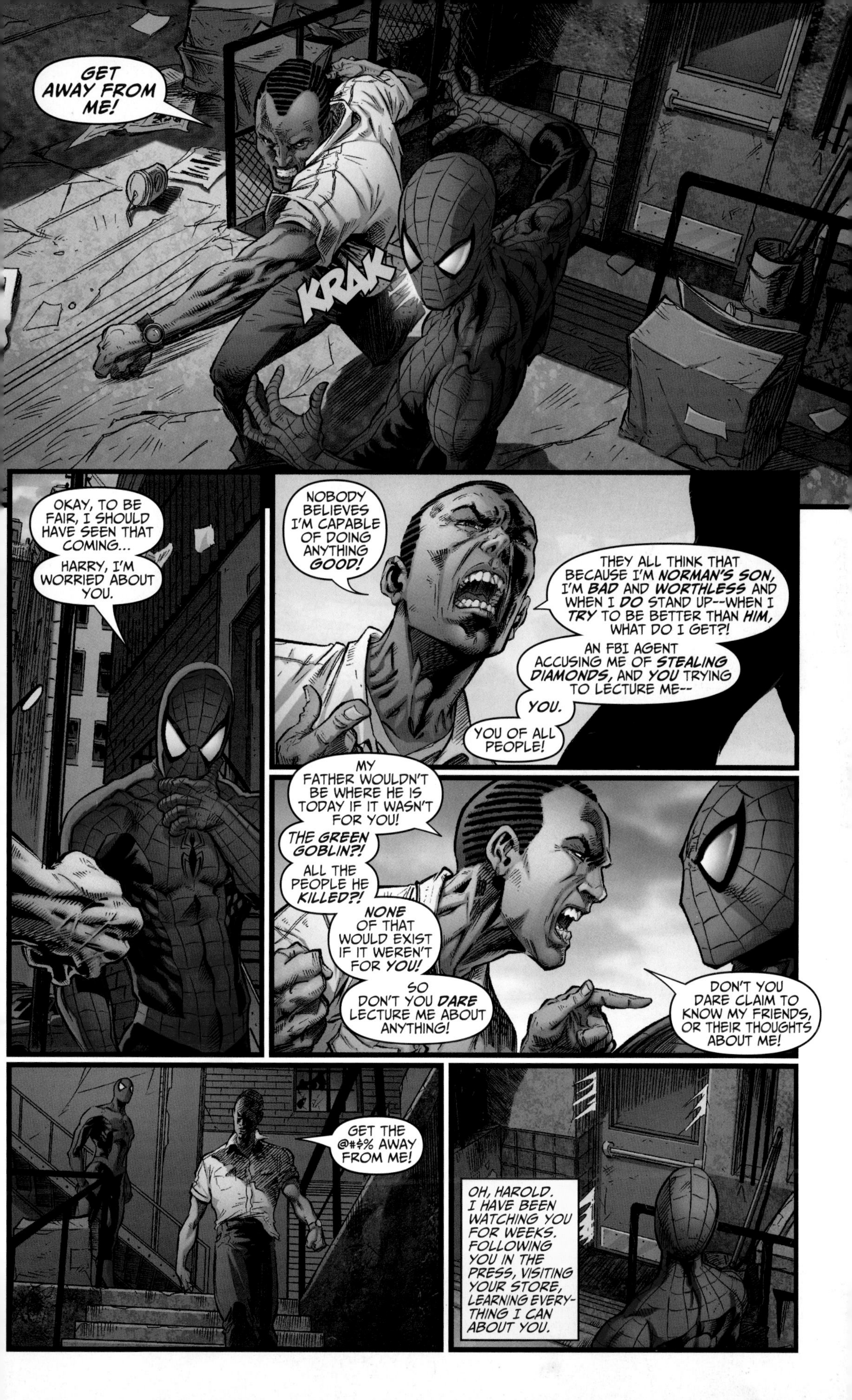
GET AWAY FROM ME!
KRAK
OKAY, TO BE FAIR, I SHOULD HAVE SEEN THAT COMING...
HARRY, I'M WORRIED ABOUT YOU.
NOBODY BELIEVES I'M CAPABLE OF DOING ANYTHING GOOD!
THEY ALL THINK THAT BECAUSE I'M NORMAN'S SON, I'M BAD AND WORTHLESS AND WHEN I DO STAND UP--WHEN I TRY TO BE BETTER THAN HIM, WHAT DO I GET?!
AN FBI AGENT ACCUSING ME OF STEALING DIAMONDS, AND YOU TRYING TO LECTURE ME--
YOU.
YOU OF ALL PEOPLE!
MY FATHER WOULDN'T BE WHERE HE IS TODAY IF IT WASN'T FOR YOU!
THE GREEN GOBLIN?!
ALL THE PEOPLE HE KILLED?!
NONE OF THAT WOULD EXIST IF IT WEREN'T FOR YOU!
SO DON'T YOU DARE LECTURE ME ABOUT ANYTHING!
DON'T YOU DARE CLAIM TO KNOW MY FRIENDS, OR THEIR THOUGHTS ABOUT ME!
GET THE @#$% AWAY FROM ME!
OH, HAROLD. I HAVE BEEN WATCHING YOU FOR WEEKS. FOLLOWING YOU IN THE PRESS, VISITING YOUR STORE, LEARNING EVERYTHING I CAN ABOUT YOU.

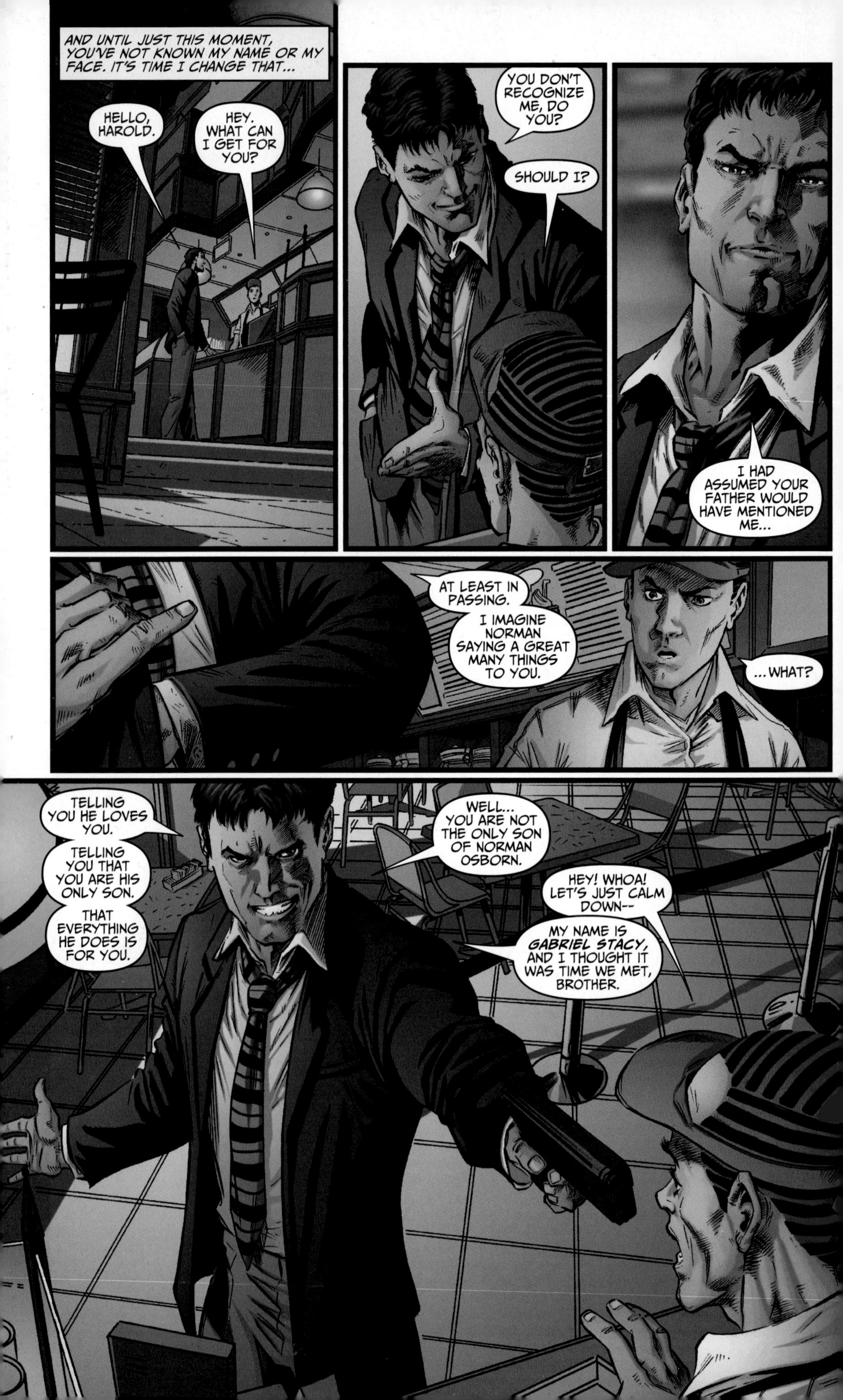
AND UNTIL JUST THIS MOMENT, YOU'VE NOT KNOWN MY NAME OR MY FACE. IT'S TIME I CHANGE THAT...
HELLO, HAROLD.
HEY. WHAT CAN I GET FOR YOU?
YOU DON'T RECOGNIZE ME, DO YOU?
SHOULD I?
I HAD ASSUMED YOUR FATHER WOULD HAVE MENTIONED ME...
AT LEAST IN PASSING.
I IMAGINE NORMAN SAYING A GREAT MANY THINGS TO YOU.
...WHAT?
TELLING YOU HE LOVES YOU.
TELLING YOU THAT YOU ARE HIS ONLY SON.
THAT EVERYTHING HE DOES IS FOR YOU.
WELL... YOU ARE NOT THE ONLY SON OF NORMAN OSBORN.
HEY! WHOA! LET'S JUST CALM DOWN--
MY NAME IS ***GABRIEL STACY***, AND I THOUGHT IT WAS TIME WE MET, BROTHER.

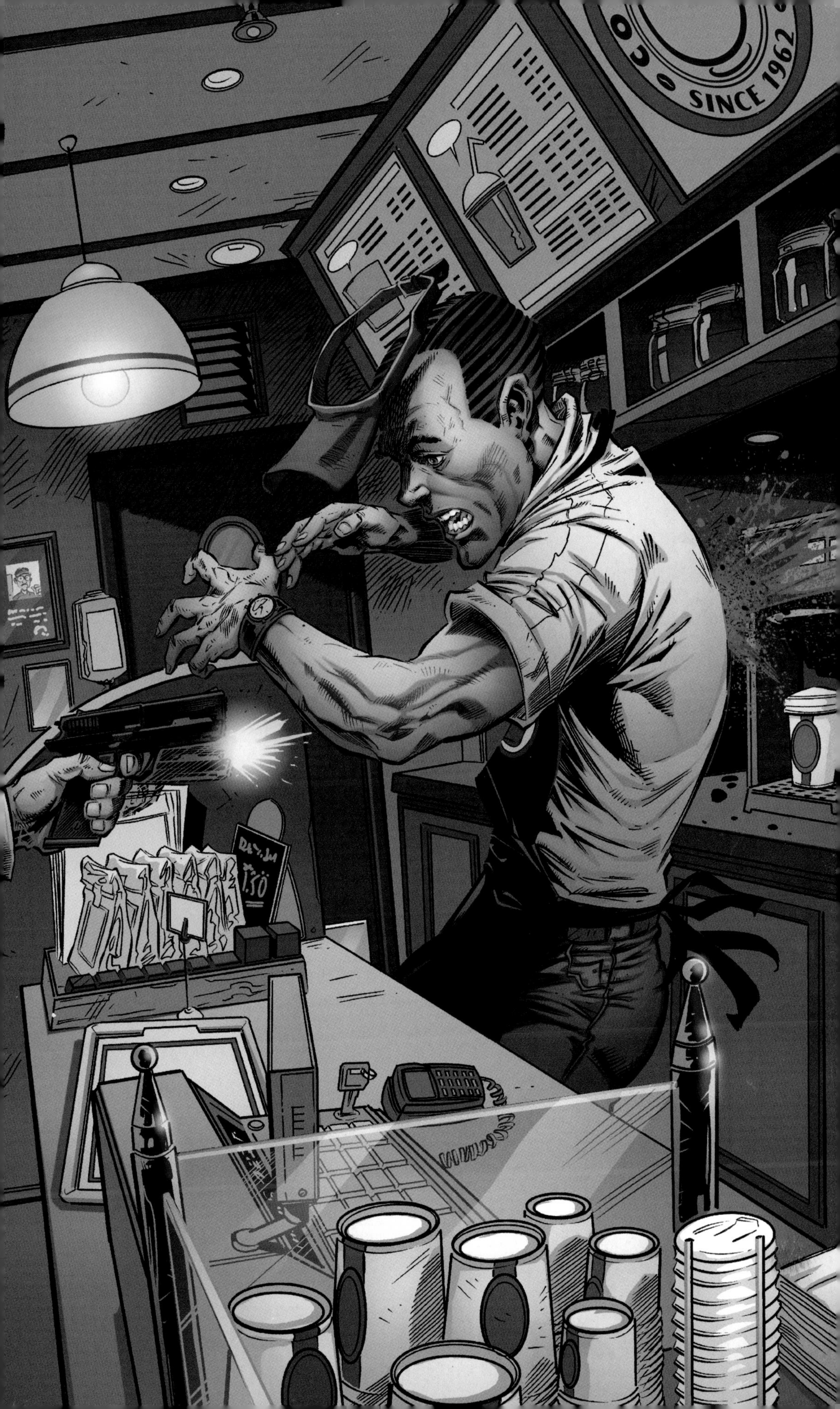
SINCE 1962

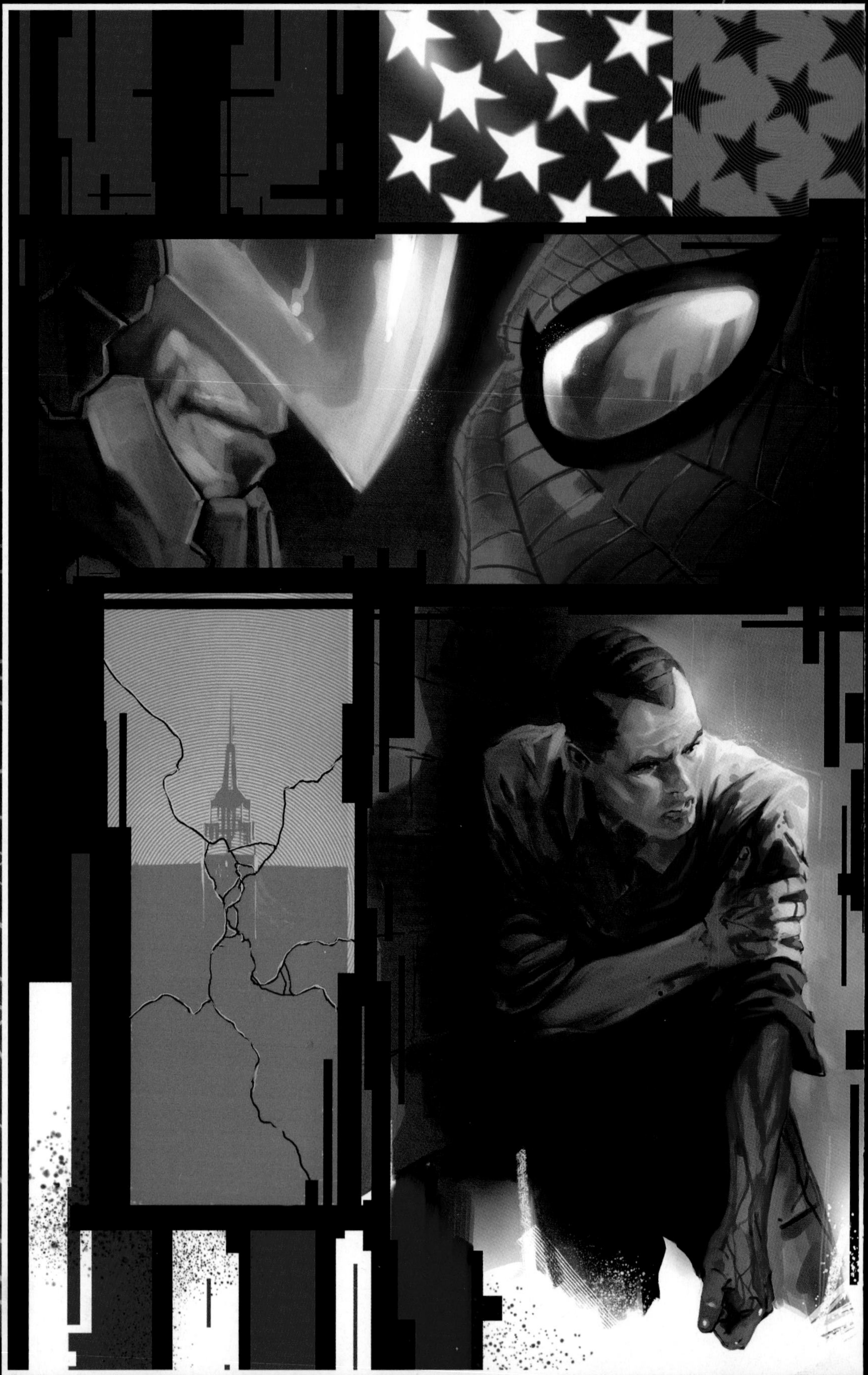

AMAZING SPIDER-MAN PRESENTS: AMERICAN SON #2

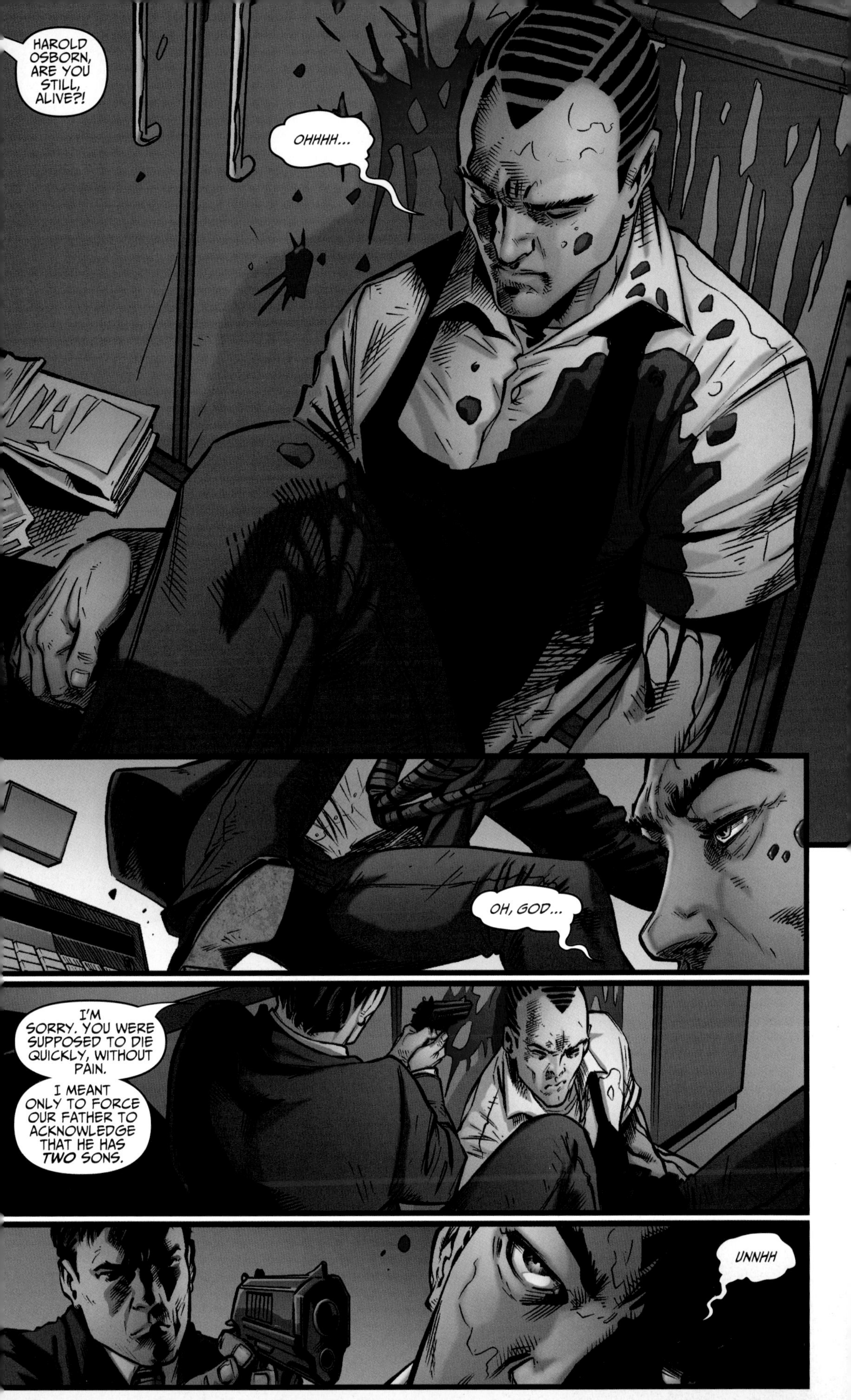
HAROLD OSBORN, ARE YOU STILL, ALIVE?!
OHHHH...
OH, GOD...
I'M SORRY. YOU WERE SUPPOSED TO DIE QUICKLY, WITHOUT PAIN.
I MEANT ONLY TO FORCE OUR FATHER TO ACKNOWLEDGE THAT HE HAS *TWO* SONS.
UNNHH

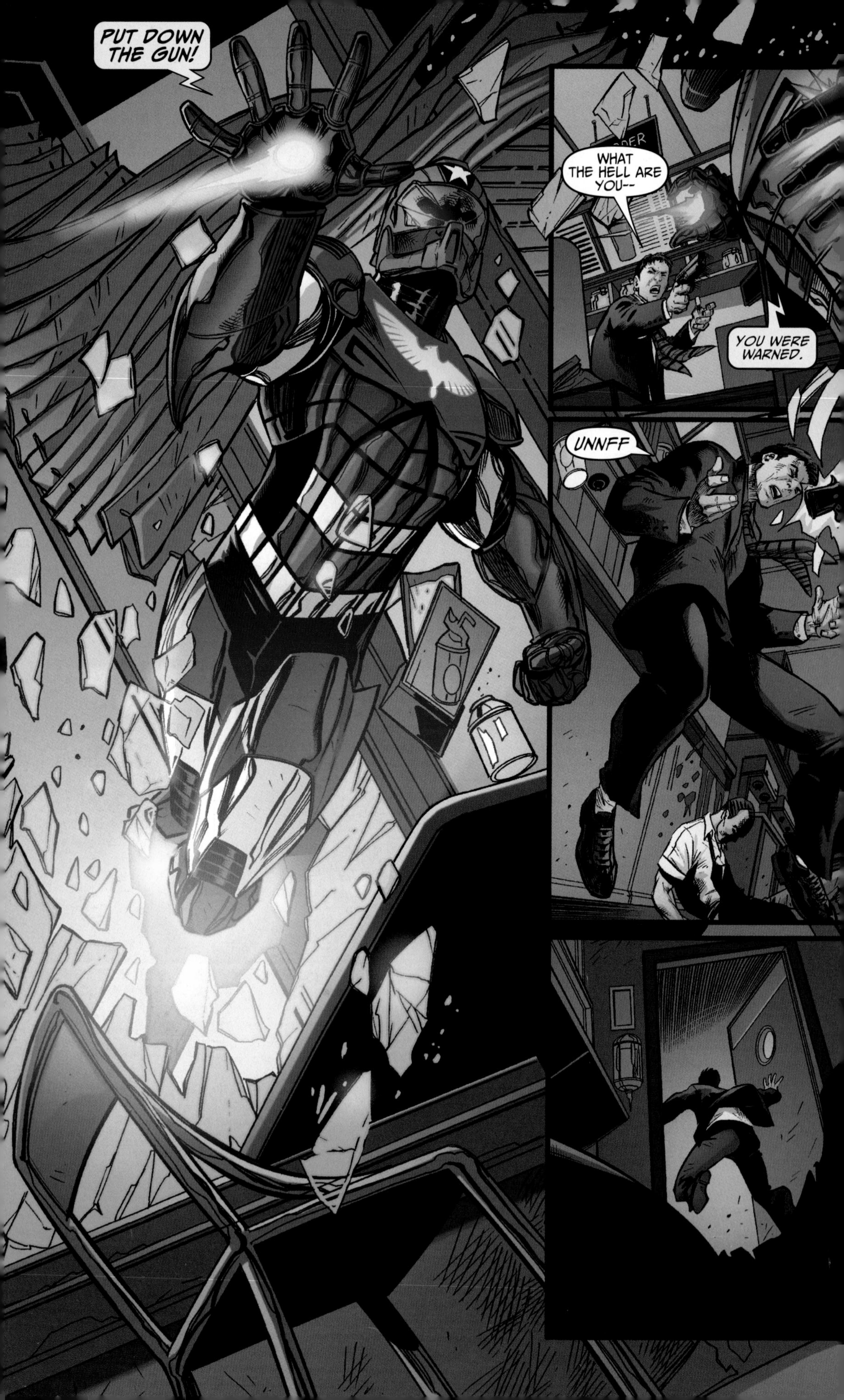
PUT DOWN THE GUN!
WHAT THE HELL ARE YOU--
YOU WERE WARNED.
UNNFF

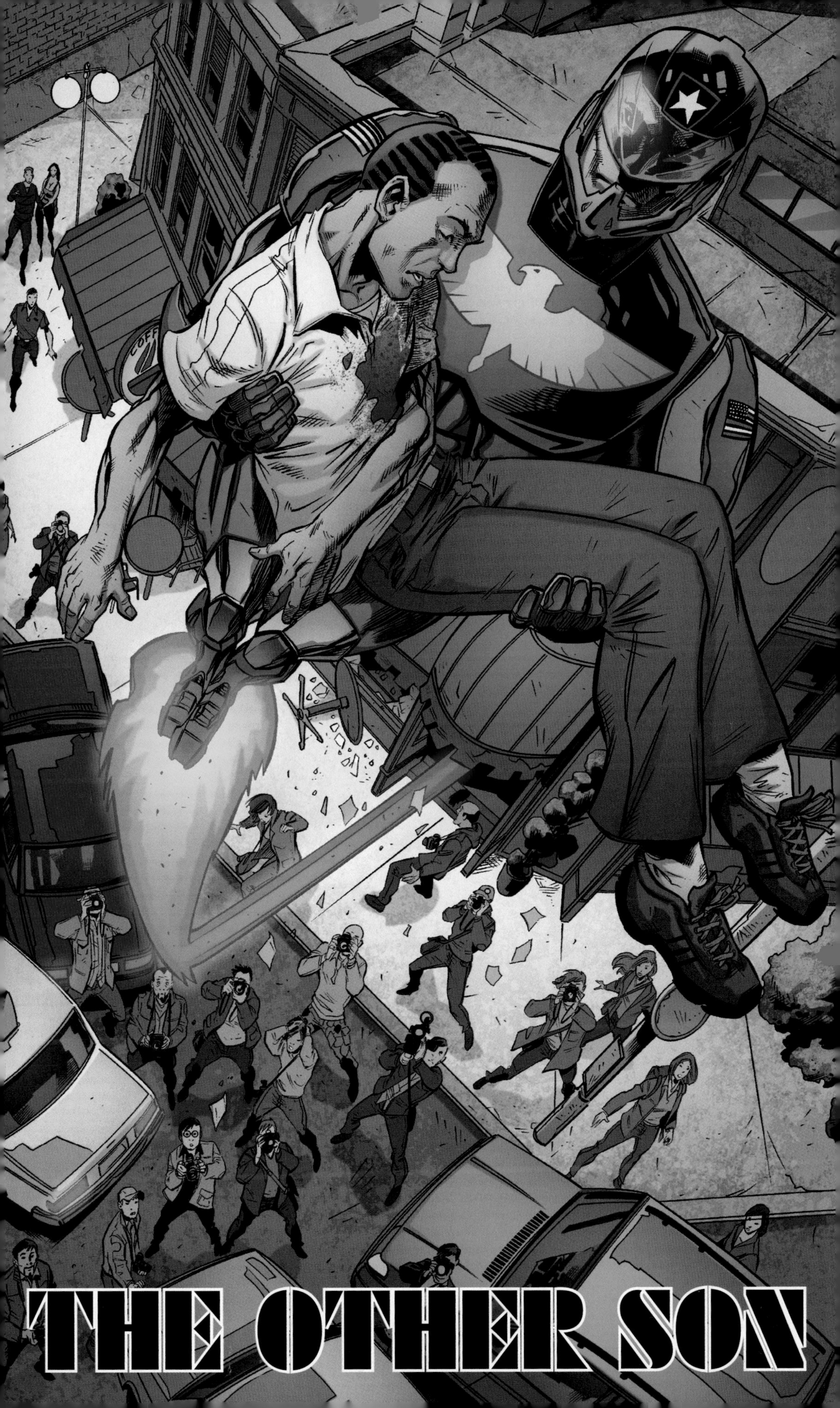
THE OTHER SON

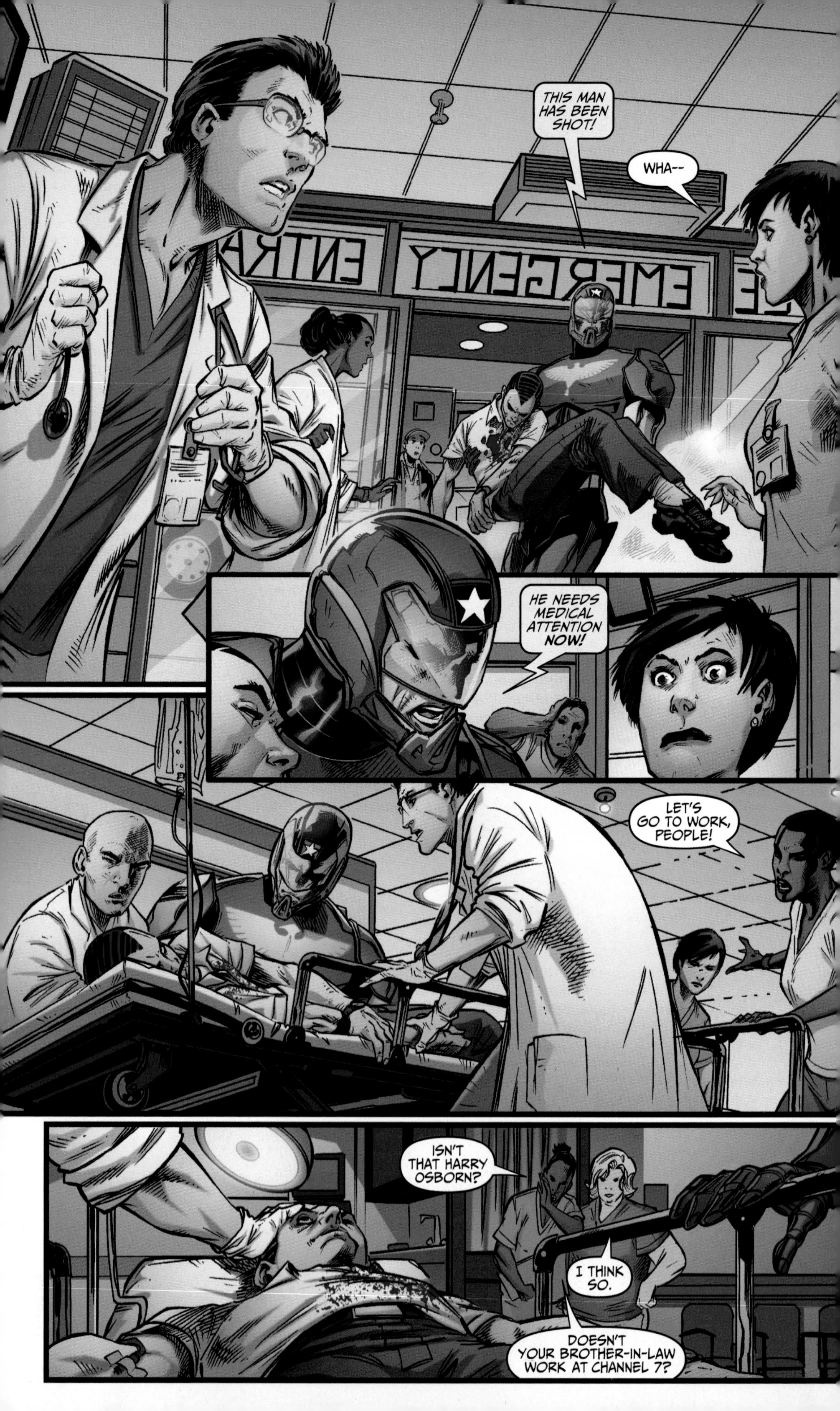
THIS MAN HAS BEEN SHOT!
WHA--
HE NEEDS MEDICAL ATTENTION NOW!
LET'S GO TO WORK, PEOPLE!
ISN'T THAT HARRY OSBORN?
I THINK SO.
DOESN'T YOUR BROTHER-IN-LAW WORK AT CHANNEL 7?

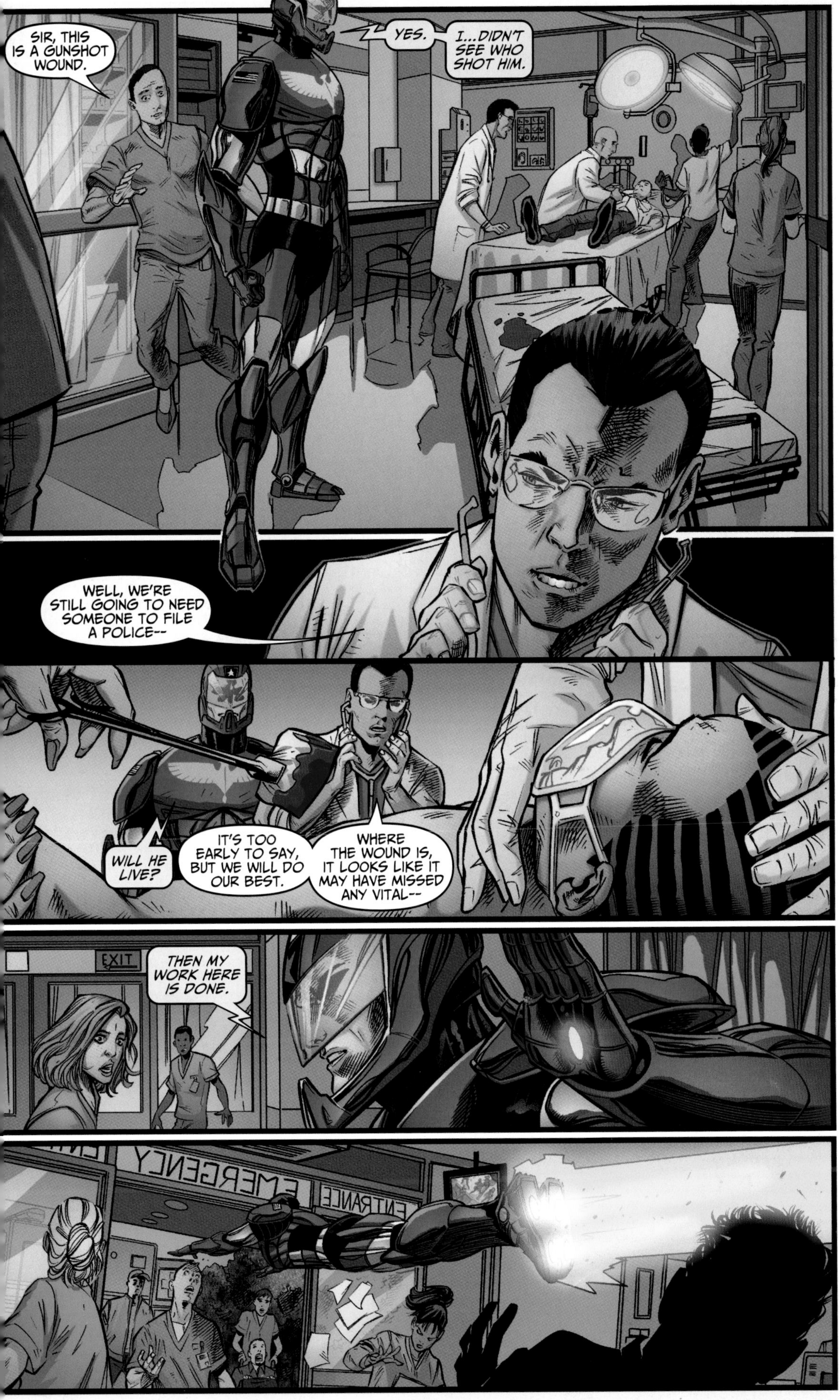
SIR, THIS IS A GUNSHOT WOUND.
YES.
I...DIDN'T SEE WHO SHOT HIM.
WELL, WE'RE STILL GOING TO NEED SOMEONE TO FILE A POLICE--
WILL HE LIVE?
IT'S TOO EARLY TO SAY, BUT WE WILL DO OUR BEST.
WHERE THE WOUND IS, IT LOOKS LIKE IT MAY HAVE MISSED ANY VITAL--
EXIT
THEN MY WORK HERE IS DONE.
EMERGENCY
ENTRANCE

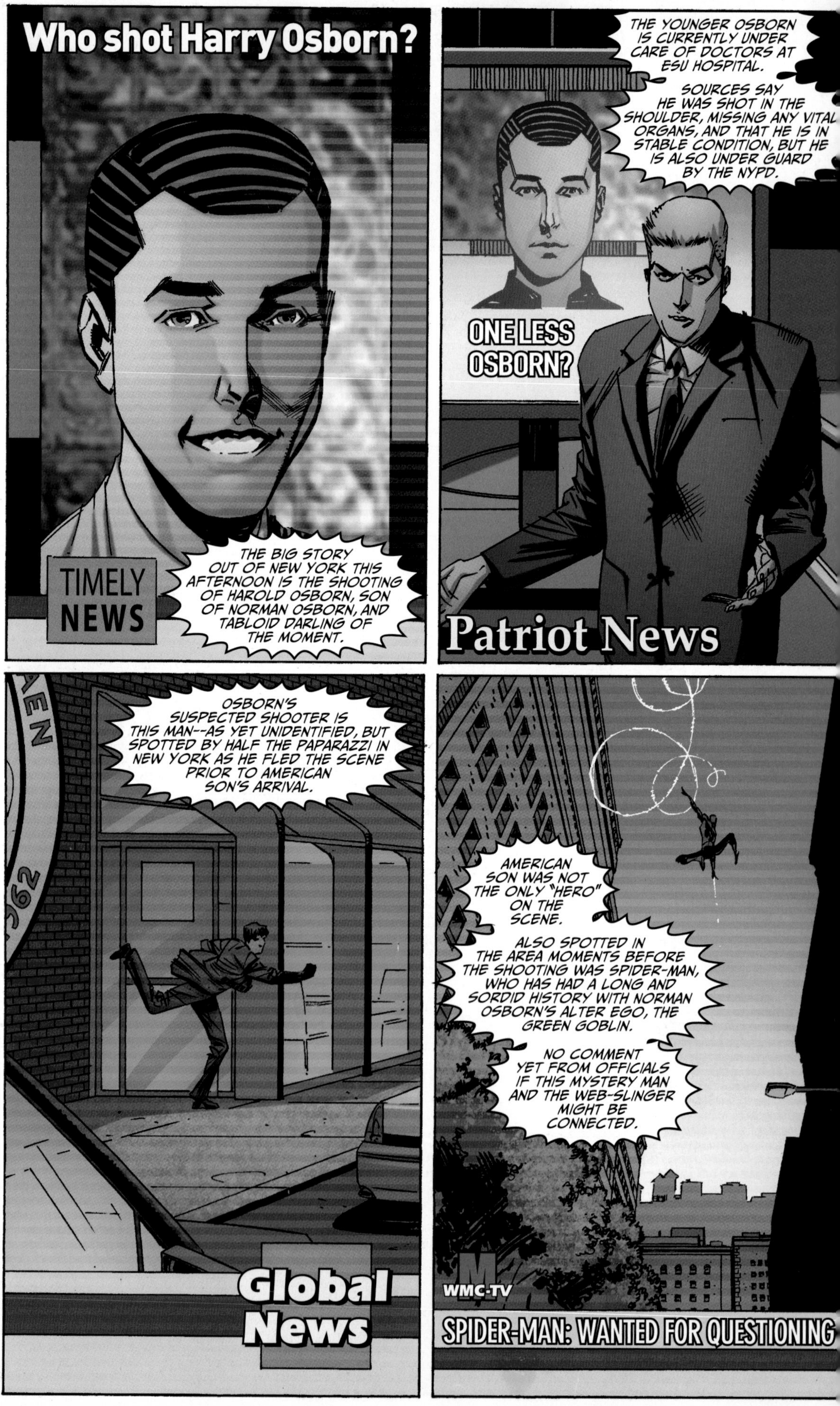

Who shot Harry Osborn?
TIMELY NEWS
THE BIG STORY OUT OF NEW YORK THIS AFTERNOON IS THE SHOOTING OF HAROLD OSBORN, SON OF NORMAN OSBORN, AND TABLOID DARLING OF THE MOMENT.
THE YOUNGER OSBORN IS CURRENTLY UNDER CARE OF DOCTORS AT ESU HOSPITAL.
SOURCES SAY HE WAS SHOT IN THE SHOULDER, MISSING ANY VITAL ORGANS, AND THAT HE IS IN STABLE CONDITION, BUT HE IS ALSO UNDER GUARD BY THE NYPD.
ONE LESS OSBORN?
Patriot News
OSBORN'S SUSPECTED SHOOTER IS THIS MAN--AS YET UNIDENTIFIED, BUT SPOTTED BY HALF THE PAPARAZZI IN NEW YORK AS HE FLED THE SCENE PRIOR TO AMERICAN SON'S ARRIVAL.
Global News
AMERICAN SON WAS NOT THE ONLY "HERO" ON THE SCENE.
ALSO SPOTTED IN THE AREA MOMENTS BEFORE THE SHOOTING WAS SPIDER-MAN, WHO HAS HAD A LONG AND SORDID HISTORY WITH NORMAN OSBORN'S ALTER EGO, THE GREEN GOBLIN.
NO COMMENT YET FROM OFFICIALS IF THIS MYSTERY MAN AND THE WEB-SLINGER MIGHT BE CONNECTED.
WMC-TV
SPIDER-MAN: WANTED FOR QUESTIONING

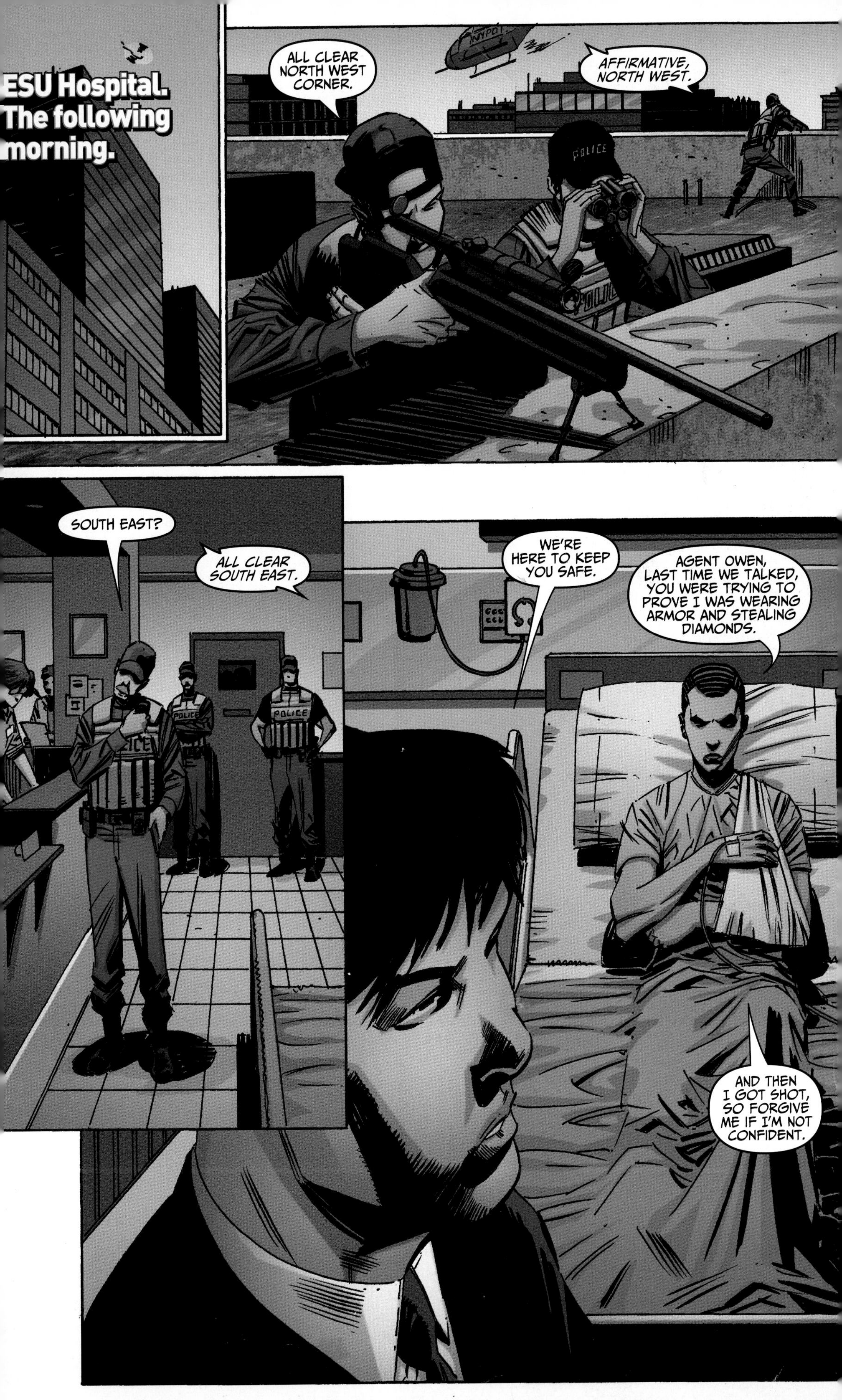
ESU Hospital. The following morning.
ALL CLEAR NORTH WEST CORNER.
AFFIRMATIVE, NORTH WEST.
SOUTH EAST?
ALL CLEAR SOUTH EAST.
WE'RE HERE TO KEEP YOU SAFE.
AGENT OWEN, LAST TIME WE TALKED, YOU WERE TRYING TO PROVE I WAS WEARING ARMOR AND STEALING DIAMONDS.
AND THEN I GOT SHOT, SO FORGIVE ME IF I'M NOT CONFIDENT.

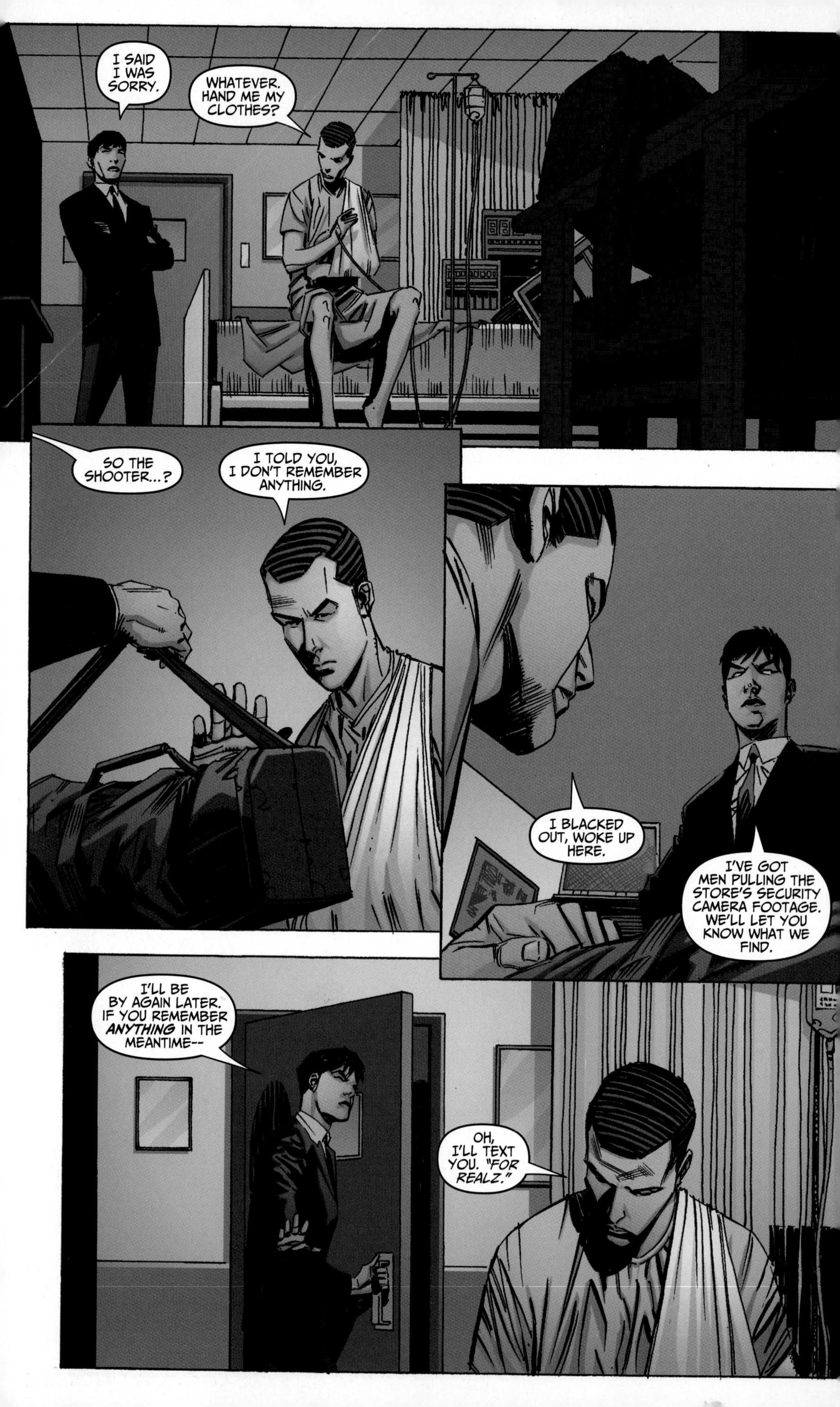
I SAID I WAS SORRY.
WHATEVER. HAND ME MY CLOTHES?
SO THE SHOOTER...?
I TOLD YOU, I DON'T REMEMBER ANYTHING.
I BLACKED OUT, WOKE UP HERE.
I'VE GOT MEN PULLING THE STORE'S SECURITY CAMERA FOOTAGE. WE'LL LET YOU KNOW WHAT WE FIND.
I'LL BE BY AGAIN LATER. IF YOU REMEMBER *ANYTHING* IN THE MEANTIME--
OH, I'LL TEXT YOU. "FOR REALZ."

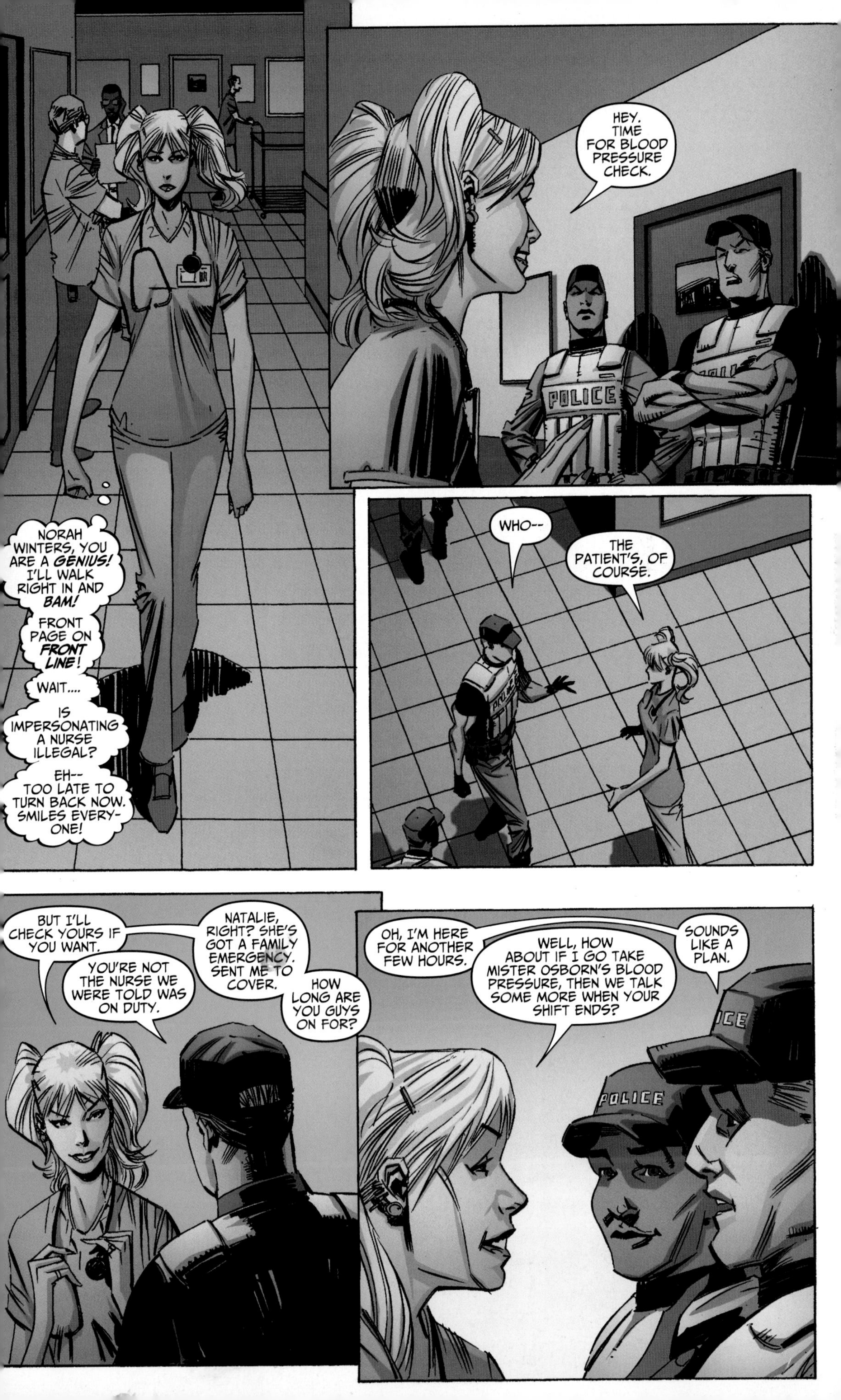
HEY. TIME FOR BLOOD PRESSURE CHECK.
POLICE
NORAH WINTERS, YOU ARE A GENIUS! I'LL WALK RIGHT IN AND BAM!
FRONT PAGE ON FRONT LINE!
WAIT....
IS IMPERSONATING A NURSE ILLEGAL?
EH-- TOO LATE TO TURN BACK NOW. SMILES EVERY-ONE!
WHO--
THE PATIENT'S, OF COURSE.
BUT I'LL CHECK YOURS IF YOU WANT.
YOU'RE NOT THE NURSE WE WERE TOLD WAS ON DUTY.
NATALIE, RIGHT? SHE'S GOT A FAMILY EMERGENCY. SENT ME TO COVER.
HOW LONG ARE YOU GUYS ON FOR?
OH, I'M HERE FOR ANOTHER FEW HOURS.
WELL, HOW ABOUT IF I GO TAKE MISTER OSBORN'S BLOOD PRESSURE, THEN WE TALK SOME MORE WHEN YOUR SHIFT ENDS?
SOUNDS LIKE A PLAN.
POLICE

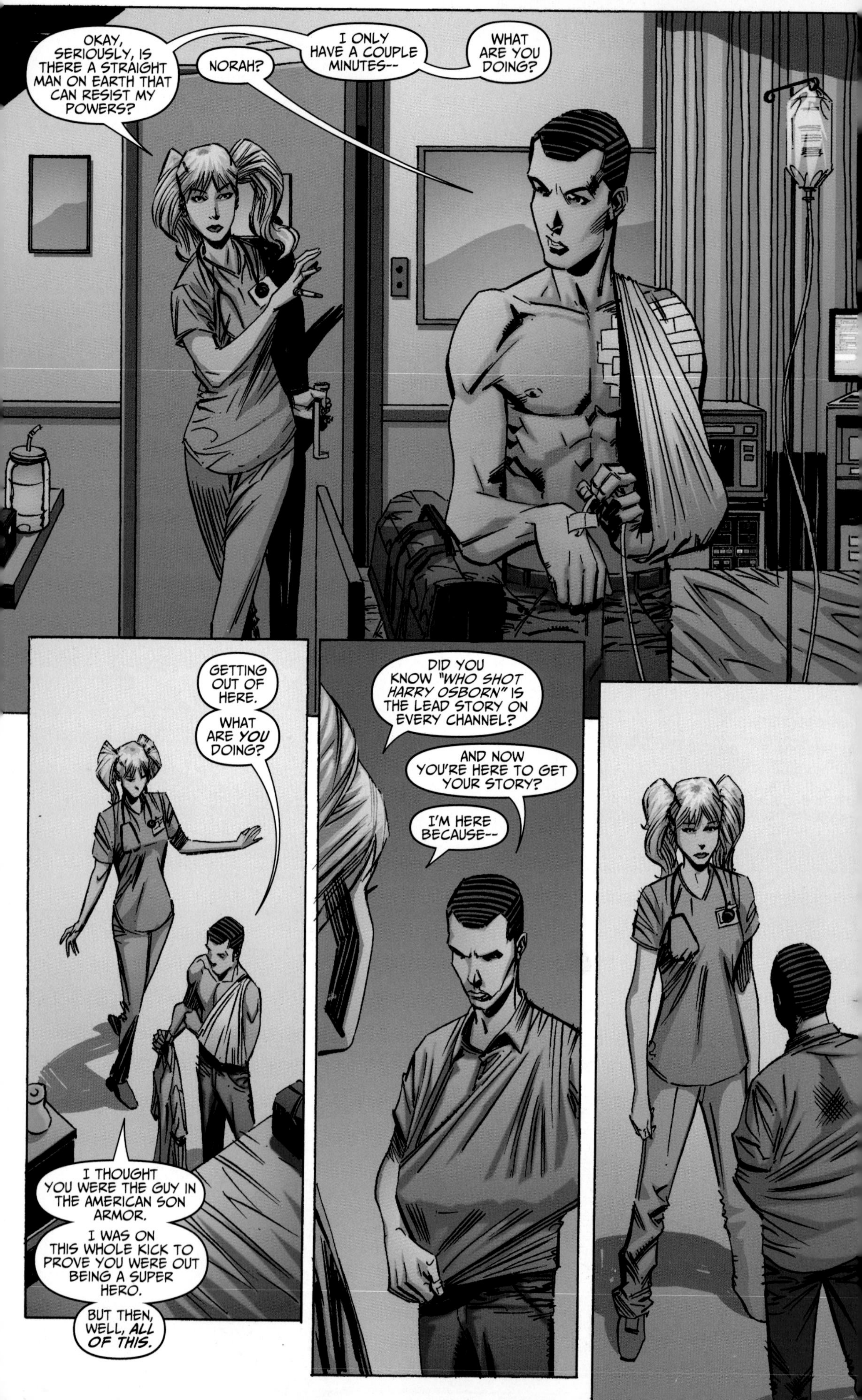

OKAY, SERIOUSLY, IS THERE A STRAIGHT MAN ON EARTH THAT CAN RESIST MY POWERS?
NORAH?
I ONLY HAVE A COUPLE MINUTES--
WHAT ARE YOU DOING?
GETTING OUT OF HERE.
WHAT ARE *YOU* DOING?
I THOUGHT YOU WERE THE GUY IN THE AMERICAN SON ARMOR.
I WAS ON THIS WHOLE KICK TO PROVE YOU WERE OUT BEING A SUPER HERO.
BUT THEN, WELL, ***ALL OF THIS.***
DID YOU KNOW *"WHO SHOT HARRY OSBORN"* IS THE LEAD STORY ON EVERY CHANNEL?
AND NOW YOU'RE HERE TO GET YOUR STORY?
I'M HERE BECAUSE--

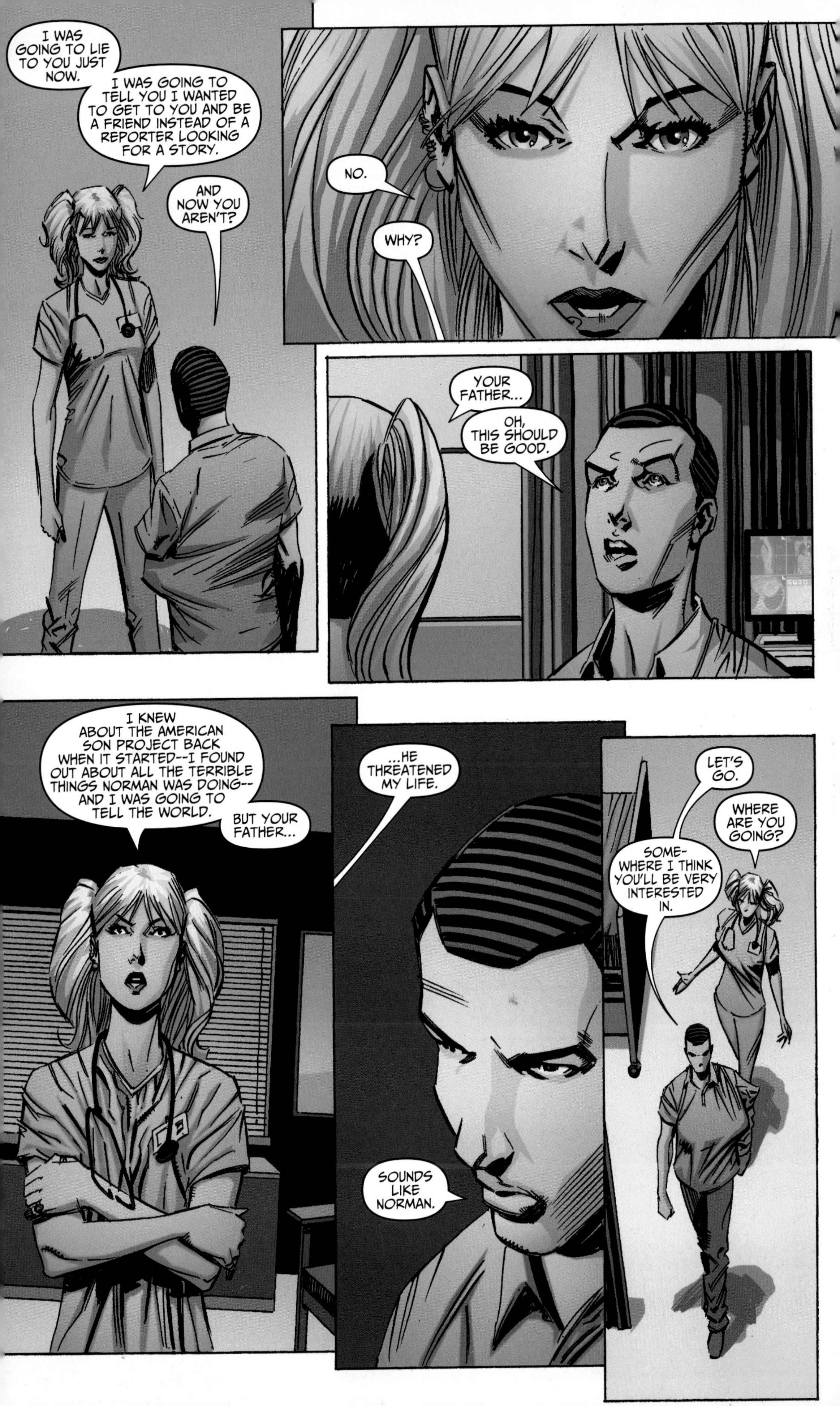
I WAS GOING TO LIE TO YOU JUST NOW.
I WAS GOING TO TELL YOU I WANTED TO GET TO YOU AND BE A FRIEND INSTEAD OF A REPORTER LOOKING FOR A STORY.
AND NOW YOU AREN'T?
NO.
WHY?
YOUR FATHER...
OH, THIS SHOULD BE GOOD.
I KNEW ABOUT THE AMERICAN SON PROJECT BACK WHEN IT STARTED--I FOUND OUT ABOUT ALL THE TERRIBLE THINGS NORMAN WAS DOING--AND I WAS GOING TO TELL THE WORLD.
BUT YOUR FATHER...
...HE THREATENED MY LIFE.
SOUNDS LIKE NORMAN.
LET'S GO.
WHERE ARE YOU GOING?
SOME-WHERE I THINK YOU'LL BE VERY INTERESTED IN.

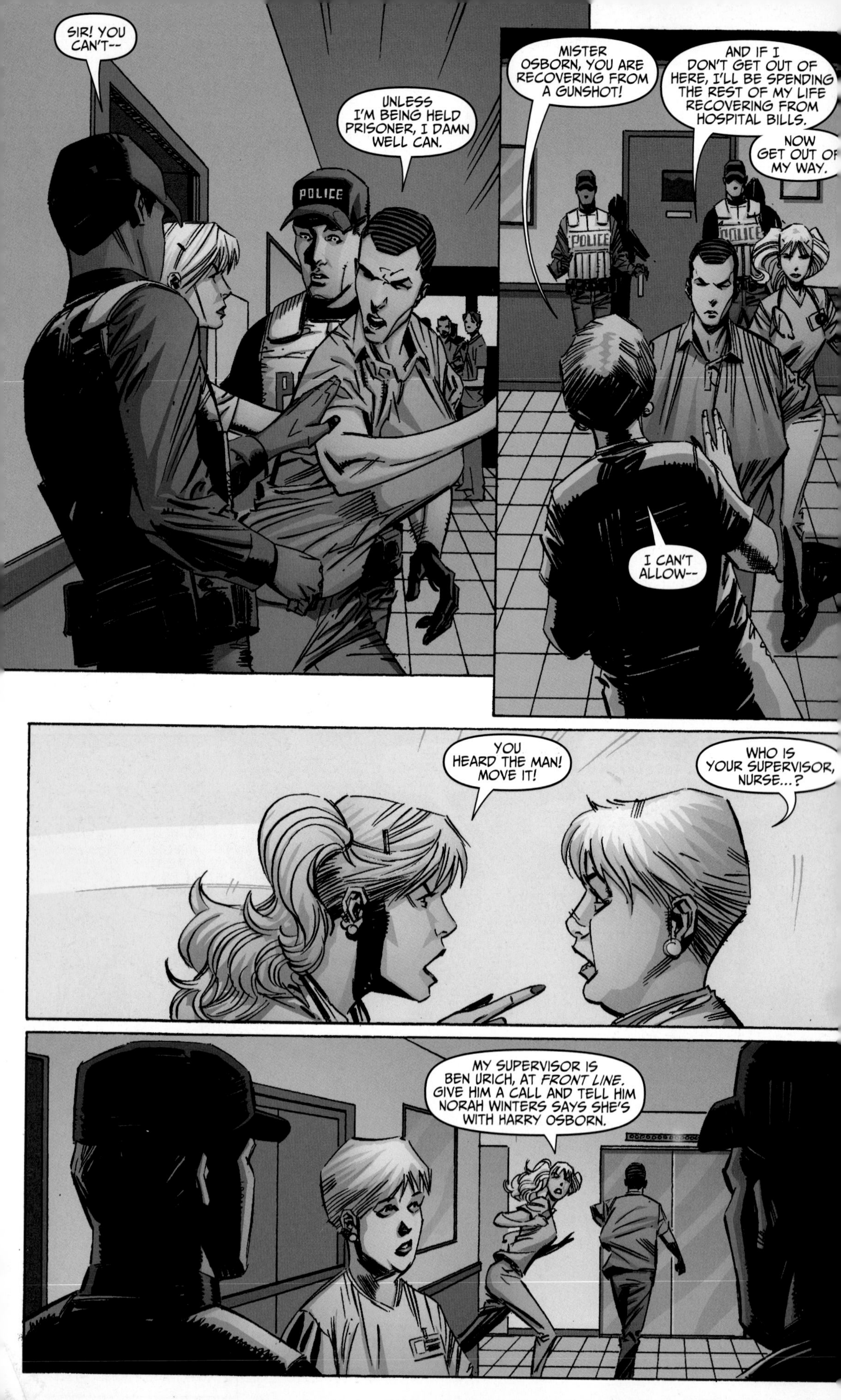

SIR! YOU CAN'T--
UNLESS I'M BEING HELD PRISONER, I DAMN WELL CAN.
POLICE
MISTER OSBORN, YOU ARE RECOVERING FROM A GUNSHOT!
AND IF I DON'T GET OUT OF HERE, I'LL BE SPENDING THE REST OF MY LIFE RECOVERING FROM HOSPITAL BILLS.
NOW GET OUT OF MY WAY.
POLICE
I CAN'T ALLOW--
YOU HEARD THE MAN! MOVE IT!
WHO IS YOUR SUPERVISOR, NURSE...?
MY SUPERVISOR IS BEN URICH, AT *FRONT LINE*. GIVE HIM A CALL AND TELL HIM NORAH WINTERS SAYS SHE'S WITH HARRY OSBORN.

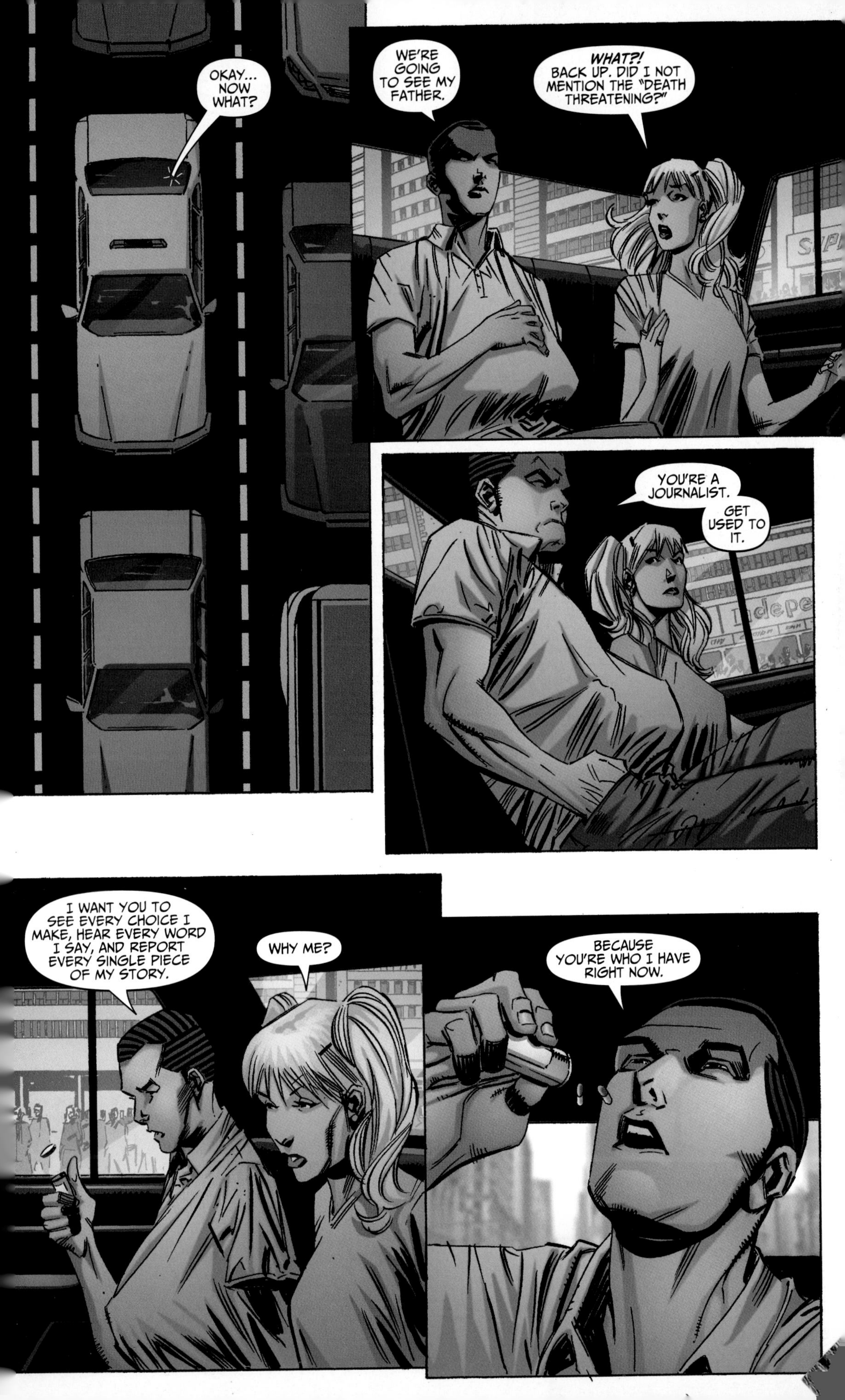
OKAY... NOW WHAT?
WE'RE GOING TO SEE MY FATHER.
WHAT?! BACK UP. DID I NOT MENTION THE "DEATH THREATENING?"
YOU'RE A JOURNALIST.
GET USED TO IT.
I WANT YOU TO SEE EVERY CHOICE I MAKE, HEAR EVERY WORD I SAY, AND REPORT EVERY SINGLE PIECE OF MY STORY.
WHY ME?
BECAUSE YOU'RE WHO I HAVE RIGHT NOW.

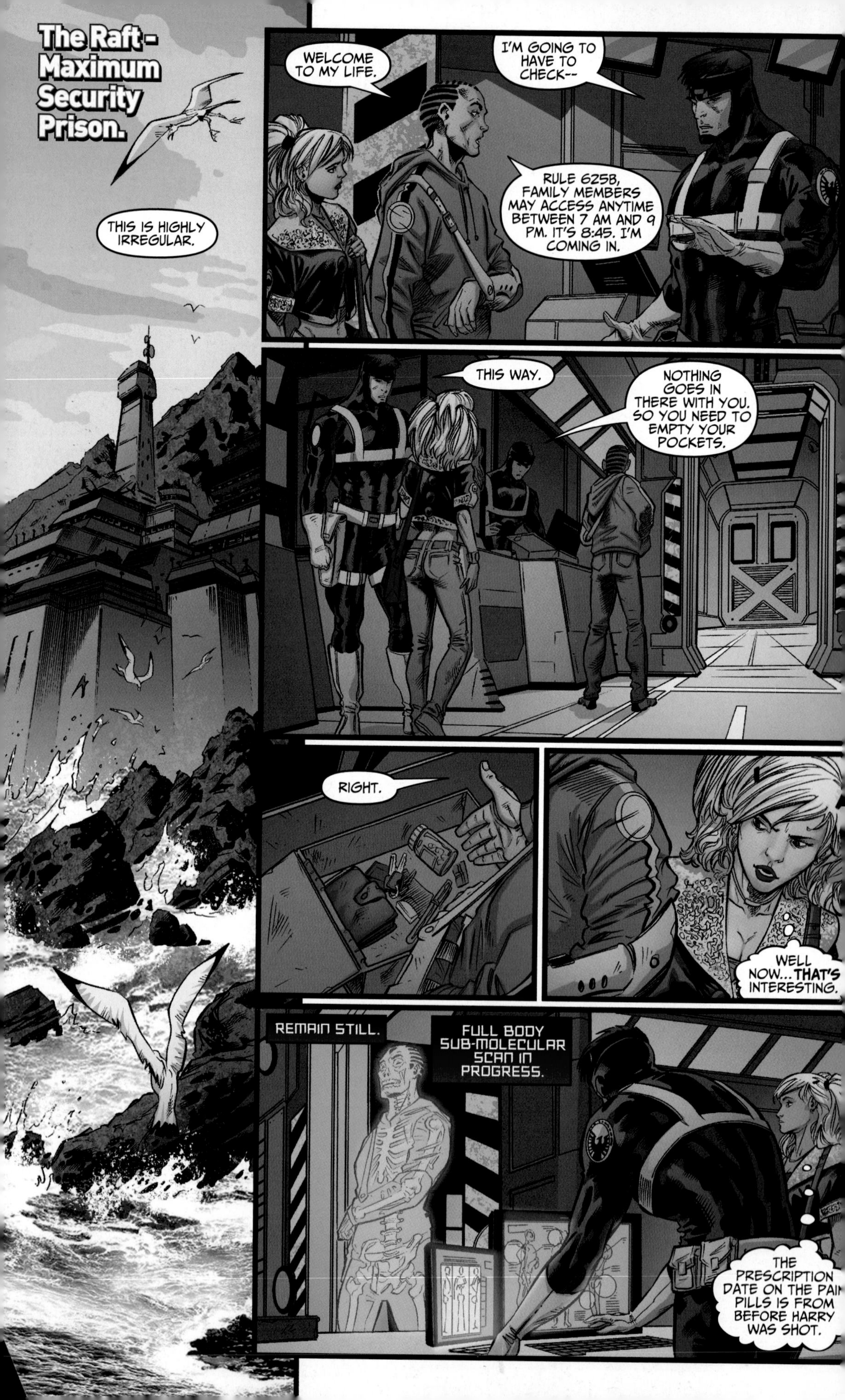
The Raft - Maximum Security Prison.
THIS IS HIGHLY IRREGULAR.
WELCOME TO MY LIFE.
I'M GOING TO HAVE TO CHECK--
RULE 625B, FAMILY MEMBERS MAY ACCESS ANYTIME BETWEEN 7 AM AND 9 PM. IT'S 8:45. I'M COMING IN.
THIS WAY.
NOTHING GOES IN THERE WITH YOU. SO YOU NEED TO EMPTY YOUR POCKETS.
RIGHT.
WELL NOW...THAT'S INTERESTING.
REMAIN STILL.
FULL BODY SUB-MOLECULAR SCAN IN PROGRESS.
THE PRESCRIPTION DATE ON THE PAIN PILLS IS FROM BEFORE HARRY WAS SHOT.

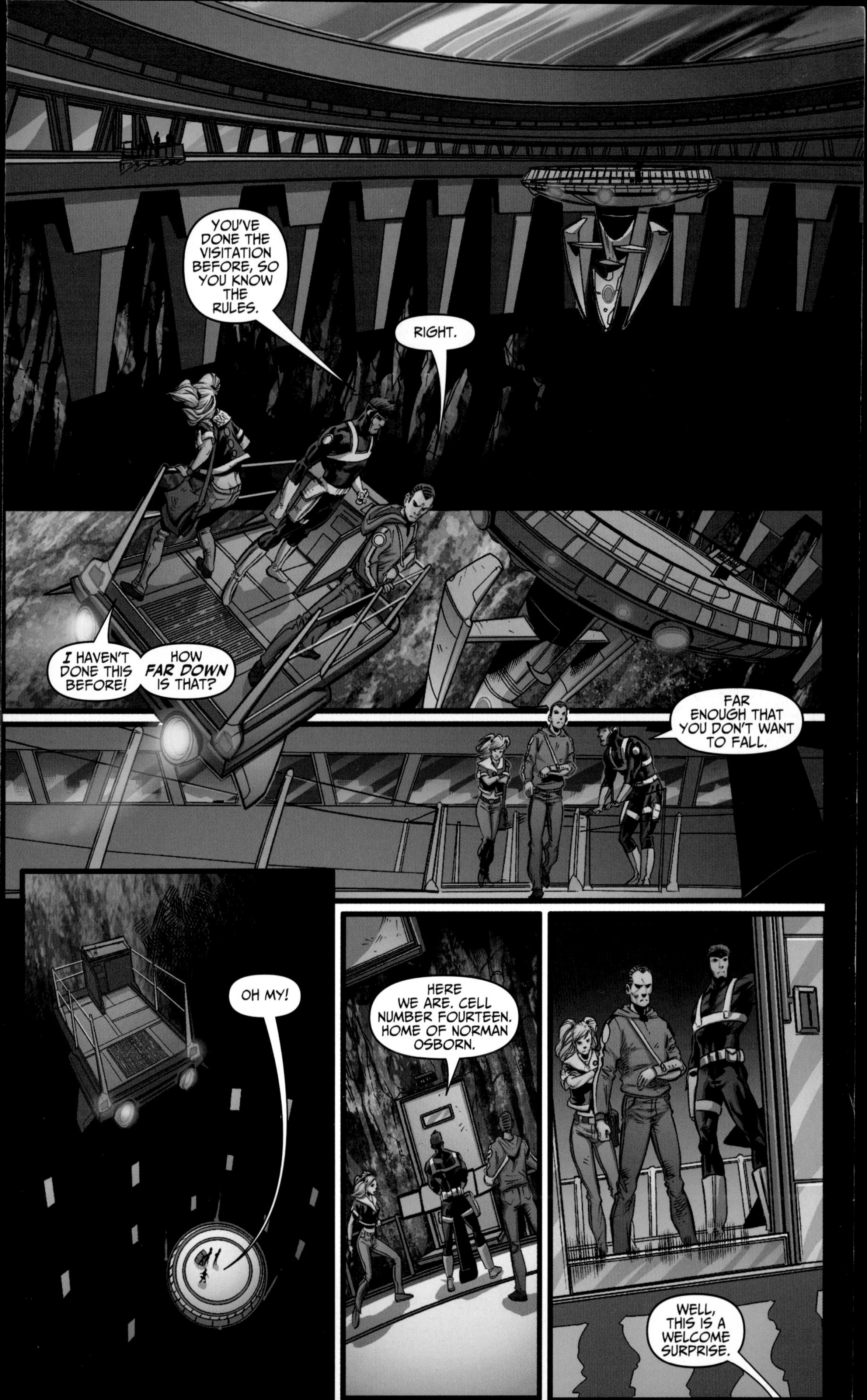

YOU'VE DONE THE VISITATION BEFORE, SO YOU KNOW THE RULES.
RIGHT.
I HAVEN'T DONE THIS BEFORE!
HOW FAR DOWN IS THAT?
FAR ENOUGH THAT YOU DON'T WANT TO FALL.
OH MY!
HERE WE ARE. CELL NUMBER FOURTEEN. HOME OF NORMAN OSBORN.
WELL, THIS IS A WELCOME SURPRISE.

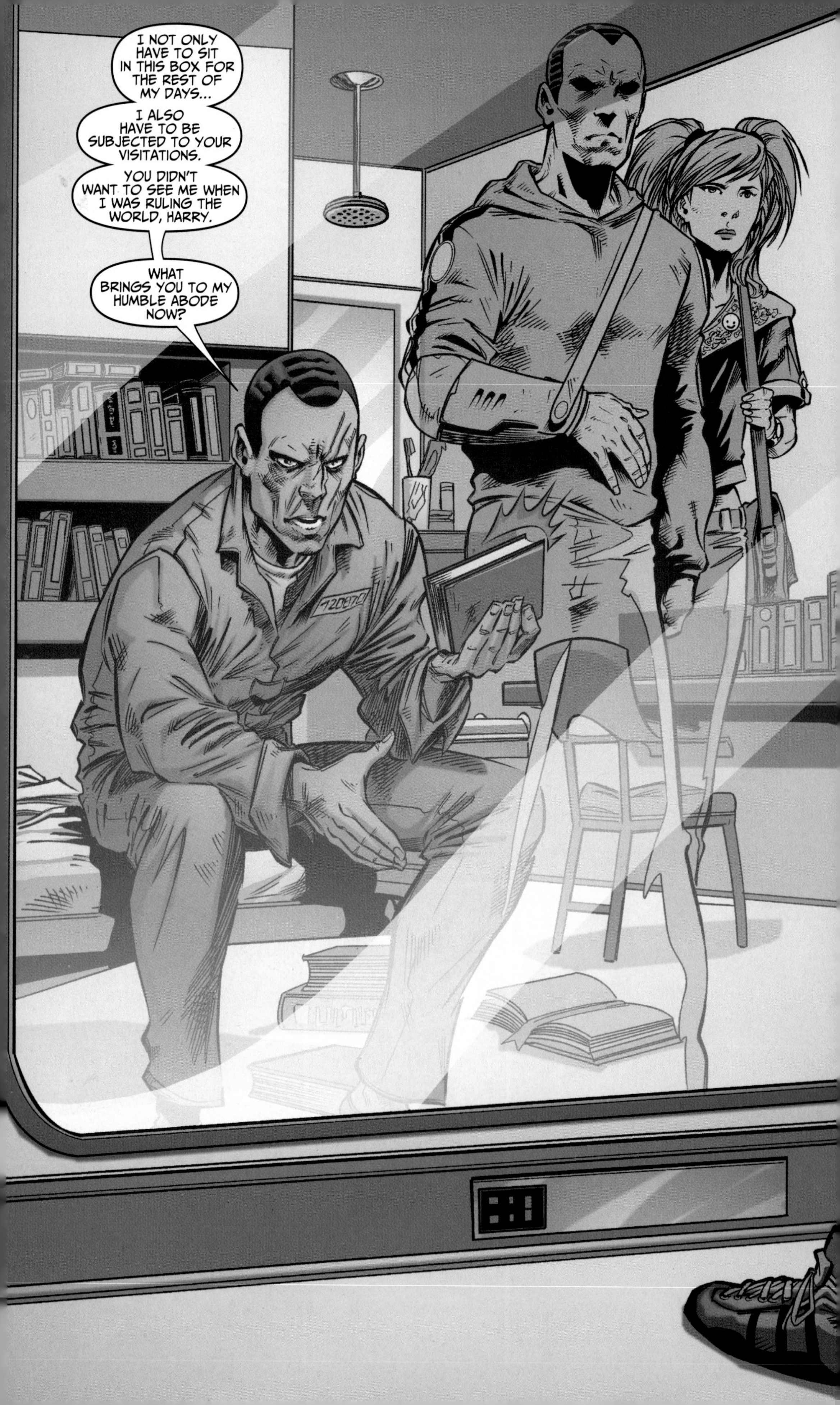
I NOT ONLY HAVE TO SIT IN THIS BOX FOR THE REST OF MY DAYS...
I ALSO HAVE TO BE SUBJECTED TO YOUR VISITATIONS.
YOU DIDN'T WANT TO SEE ME WHEN I WAS RULING THE WORLD, HARRY.
WHAT BRINGS YOU TO MY HUMBLE ABODE NOW?

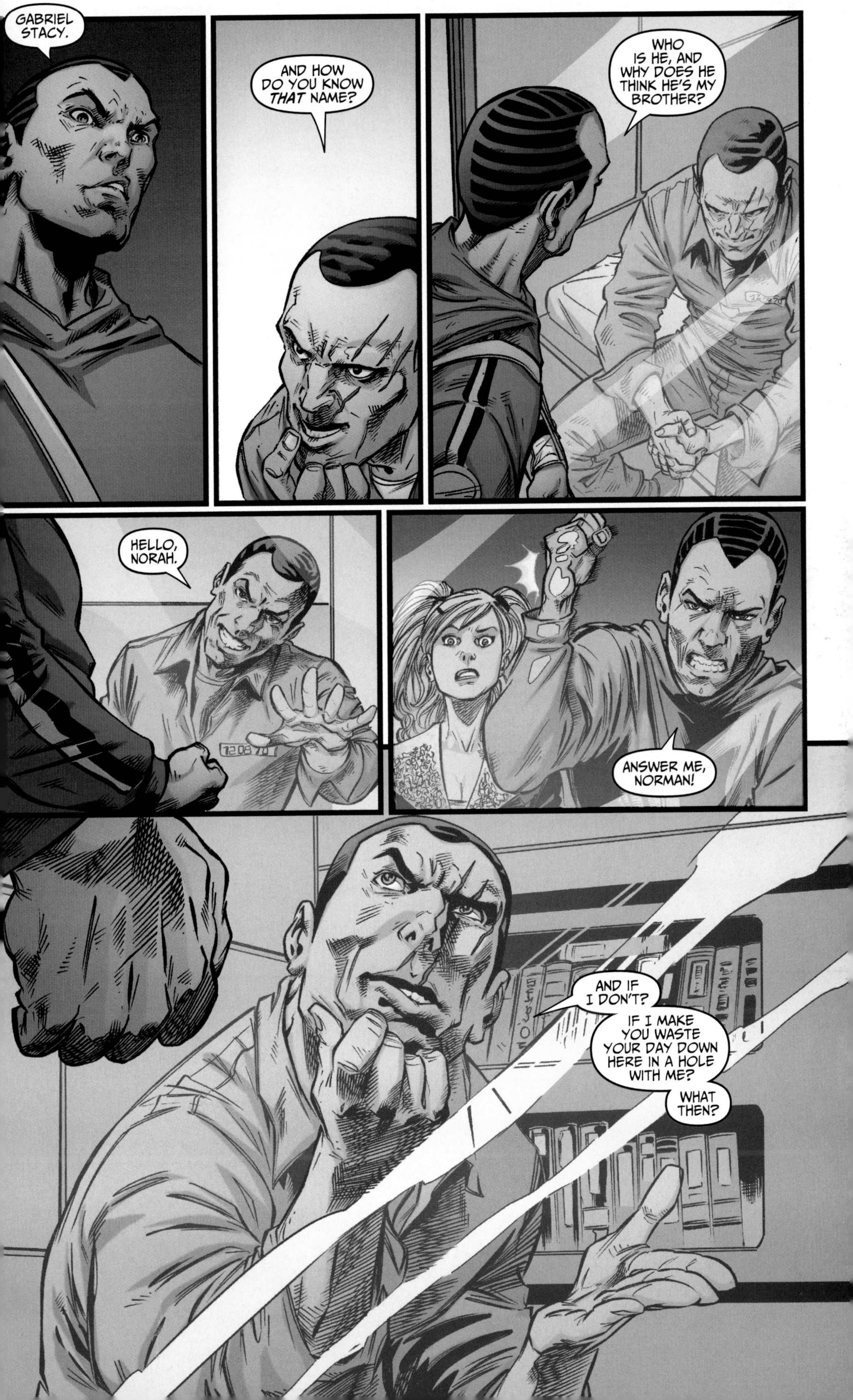
GABRIEL STACY.
AND HOW DO YOU KNOW *THAT* NAME?
WHO IS HE, AND WHY DOES HE THINK HE'S MY BROTHER?
HELLO, NORAH.
ANSWER ME, NORMAN!
AND IF I DON'T?
IF I MAKE YOU WASTE YOUR DAY DOWN HERE IN A HOLE WITH ME?
WHAT THEN?

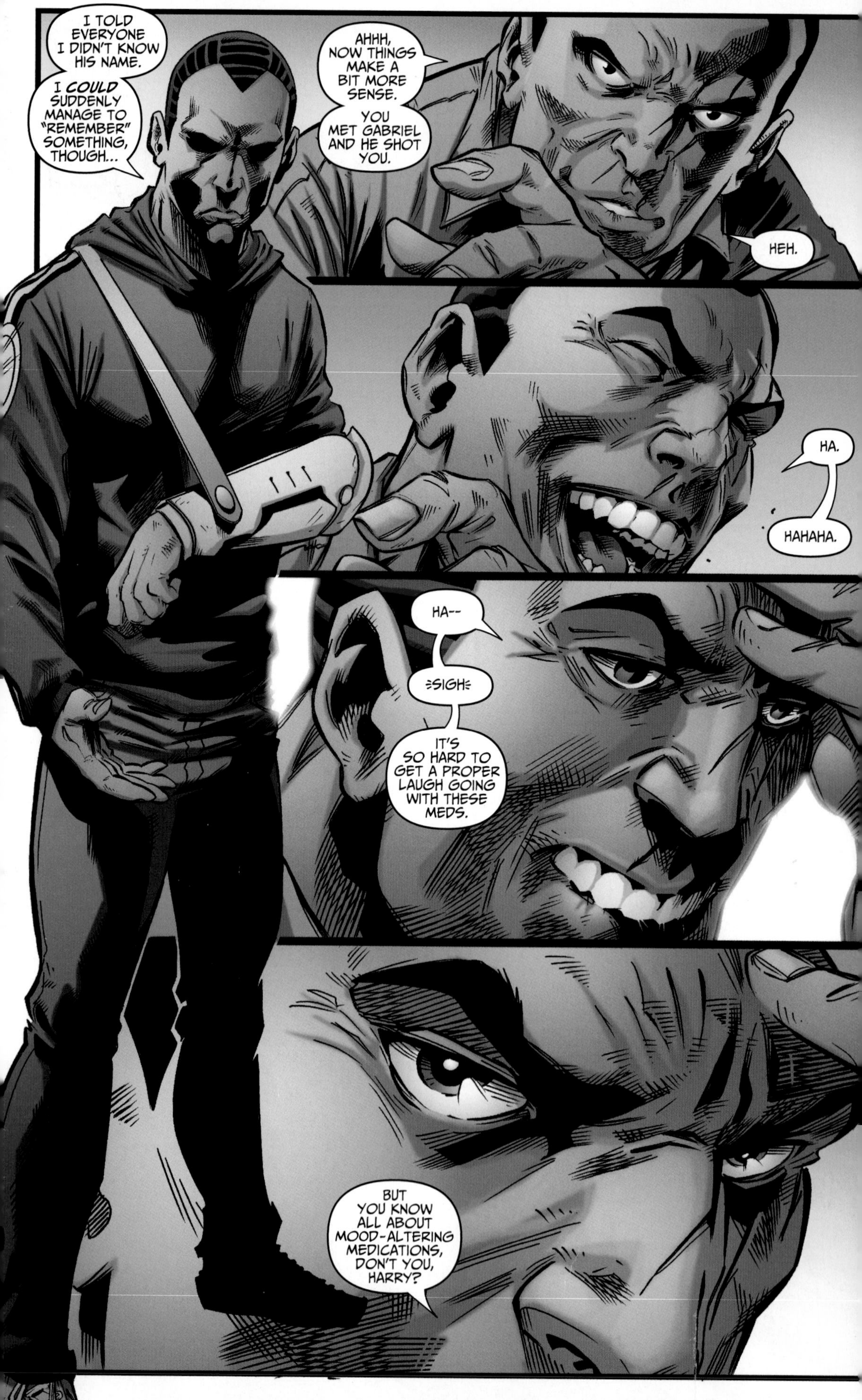
I TOLD EVERYONE I DIDN'T KNOW HIS NAME.
I **COULD** SUDDENLY MANAGE TO "REMEMBER" SOMETHING, THOUGH...
AHHH, NOW THINGS MAKE A BIT MORE SENSE.
YOU MET GABRIEL AND HE SHOT YOU.
HEH.
HA.
HAHAHA.
HA--
≈SIGH≈
IT'S SO HARD TO GET A PROPER LAUGH GOING WITH THESE MEDS.
BUT YOU KNOW ALL ABOUT MOOD-ALTERING MEDICATIONS, DON'T YOU, HARRY?

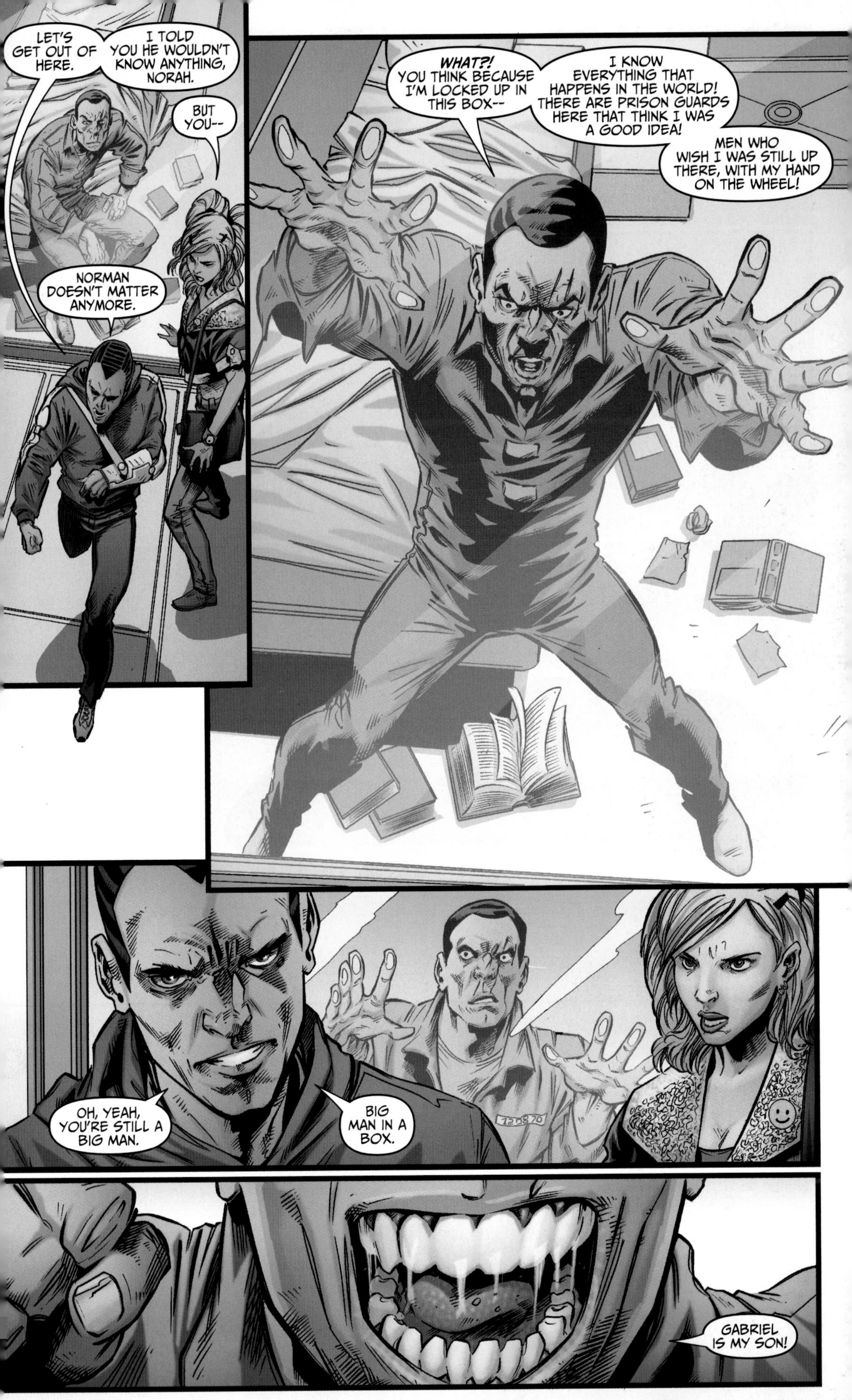

LET'S GET OUT OF HERE.
I TOLD YOU HE WOULDN'T KNOW ANYTHING, NORAH.
BUT YOU--
NORMAN DOESN'T MATTER ANYMORE.
WHAT?! YOU THINK BECAUSE I'M LOCKED UP IN THIS BOX--
I KNOW EVERYTHING THAT HAPPENS IN THE WORLD! THERE ARE PRISON GUARDS HERE THAT THINK I WAS A GOOD IDEA!
MEN WHO WISH I WAS STILL UP THERE, WITH MY HAND ON THE WHEEL!
OH, YEAH, YOU'RE STILL A BIG MAN.
BIG MAN IN A BOX.
GABRIEL IS MY SON!

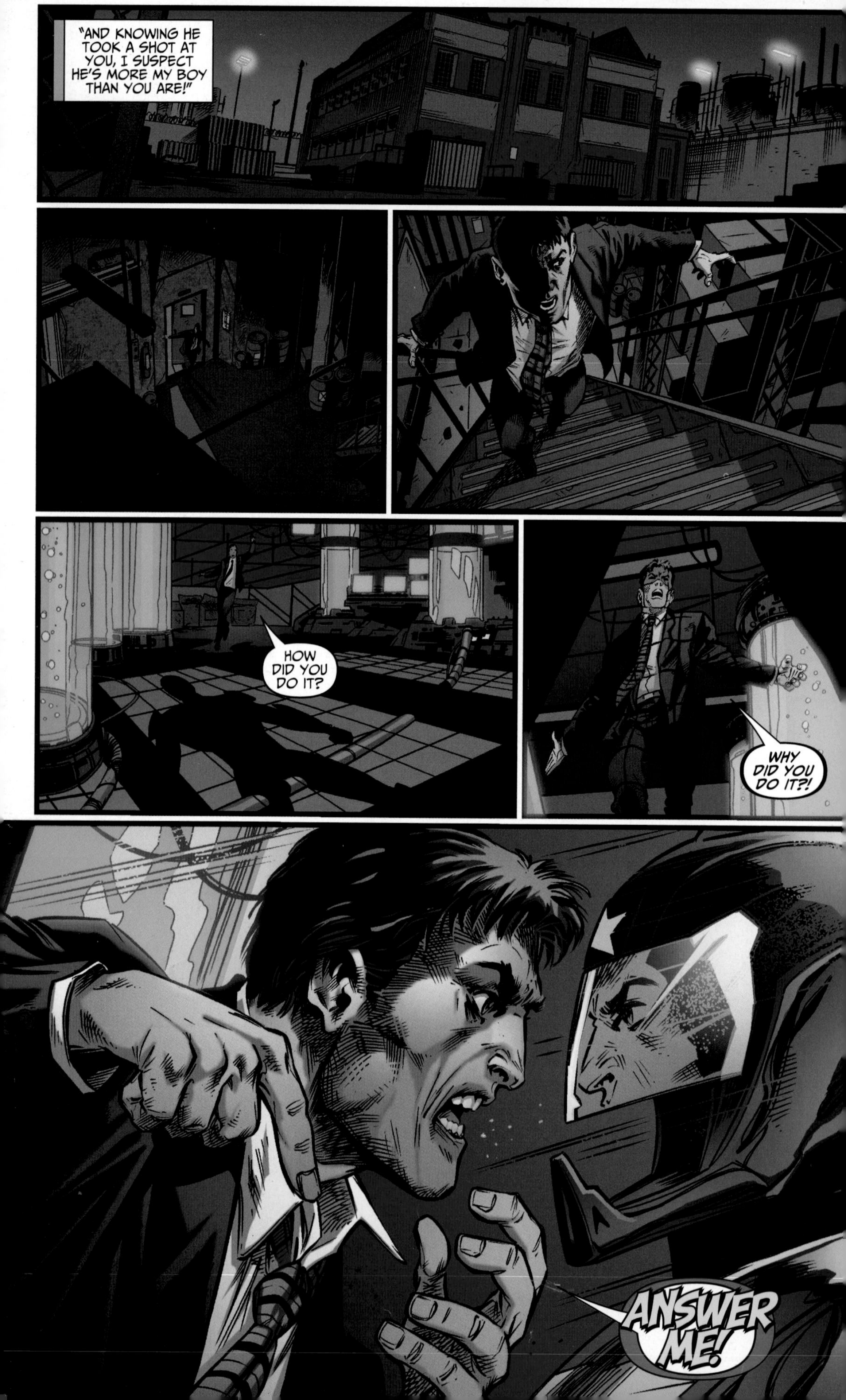
"AND KNOWING HE TOOK A SHOT AT YOU, I SUSPECT HE'S MORE MY BOY THAN YOU ARE!"
HOW DID YOU DO IT?
WHY DID YOU DO IT?!
ANSWER ME!

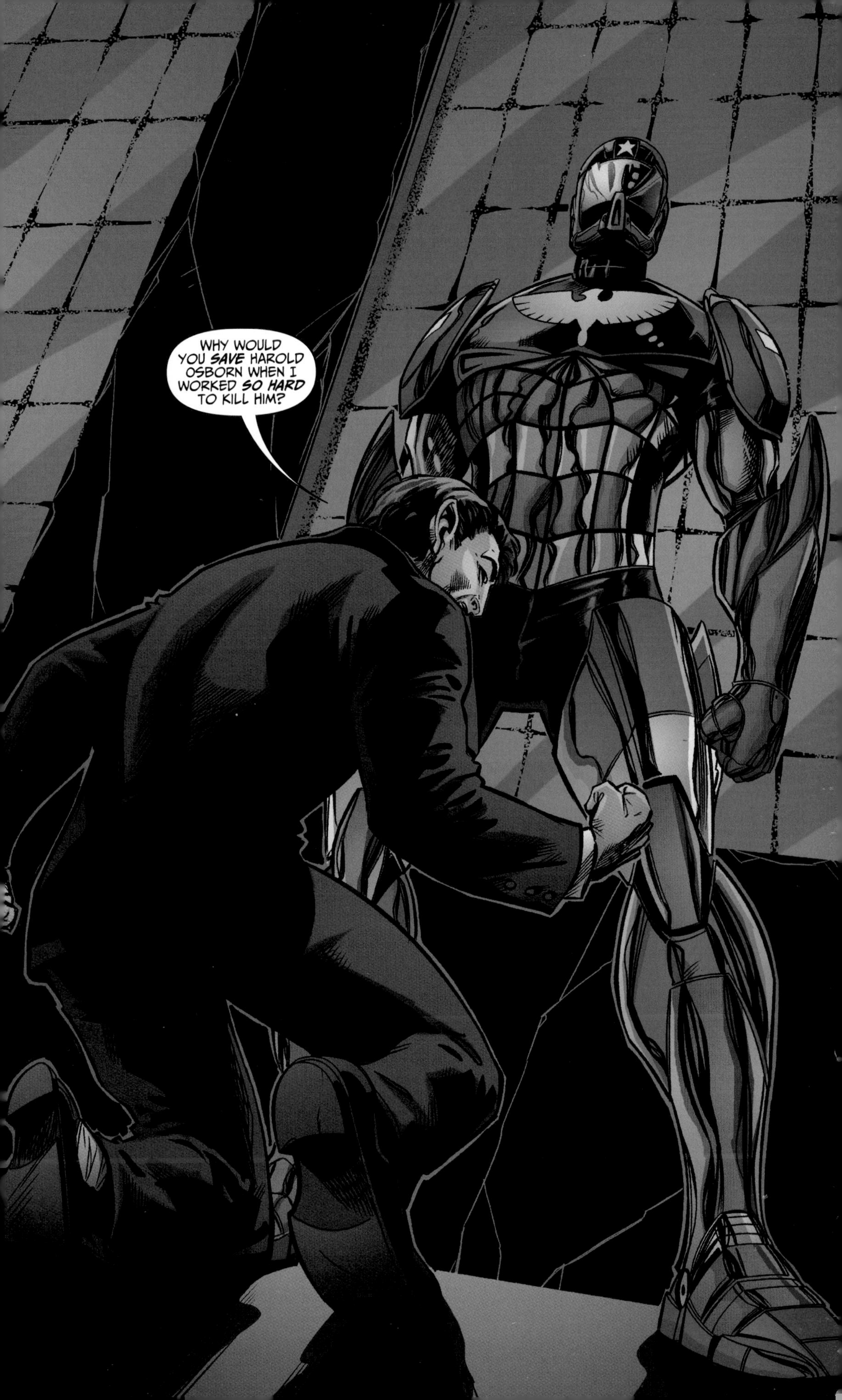
WHY WOULD YOU SAVE HAROLD OSBORN WHEN I WORKED SO HARD TO KILL HIM?

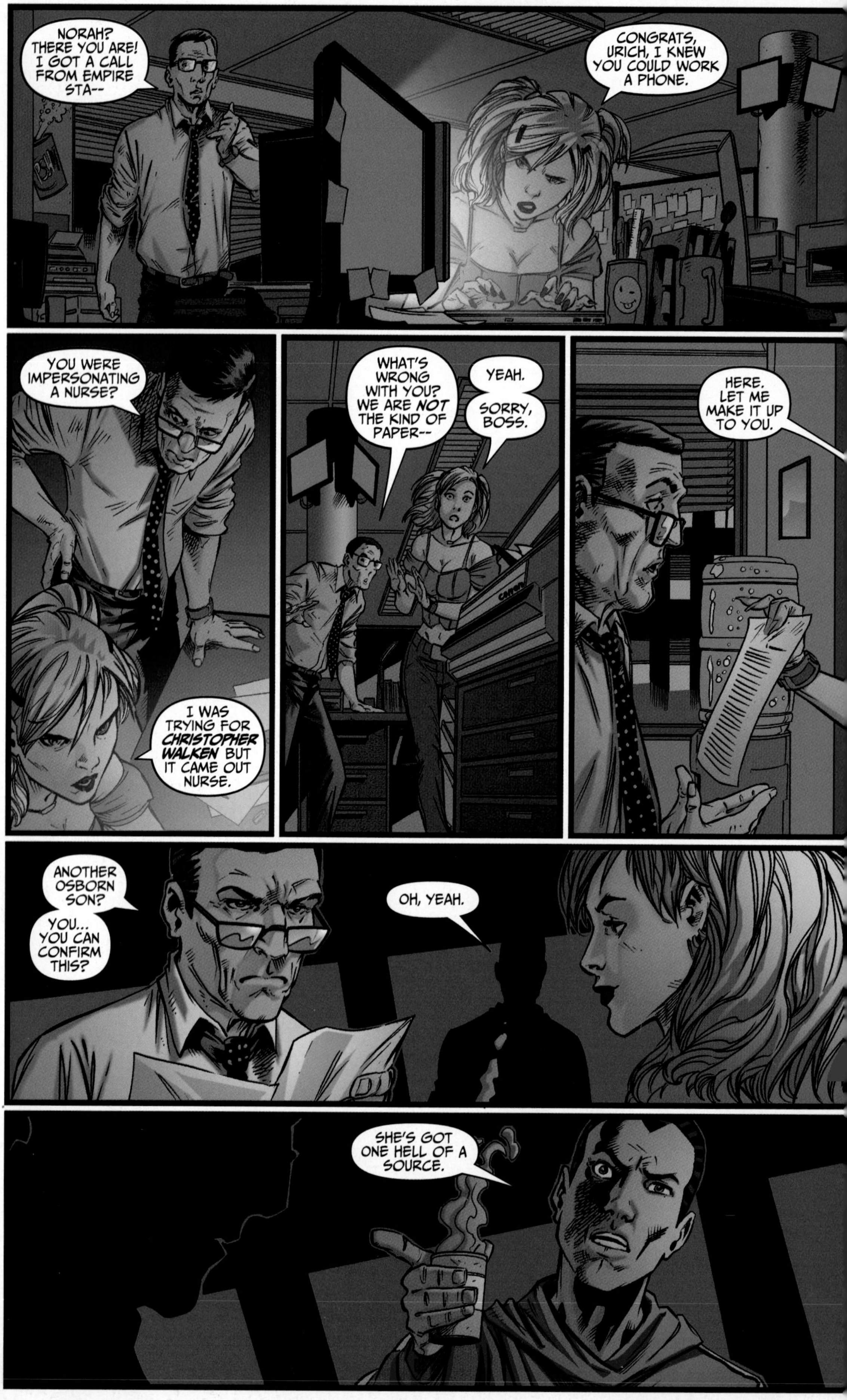
NORAH? THERE YOU ARE! I GOT A CALL FROM EMPIRE STA--
CONGRATS, URICH, I KNEW YOU COULD WORK A PHONE.
YOU WERE IMPERSONATING A NURSE?
I WAS TRYING FOR CHRISTOPHER WALKEN BUT IT CAME OUT NURSE.
WHAT'S WRONG WITH YOU? WE ARE NOT THE KIND OF PAPER--
YEAH.
SORRY, BOSS.
HERE. LET ME MAKE IT UP TO YOU.
ANOTHER OSBORN SON?
YOU... YOU CAN CONFIRM THIS?
OH, YEAH.
SHE'S GOT ONE HELL OF A SOURCE.

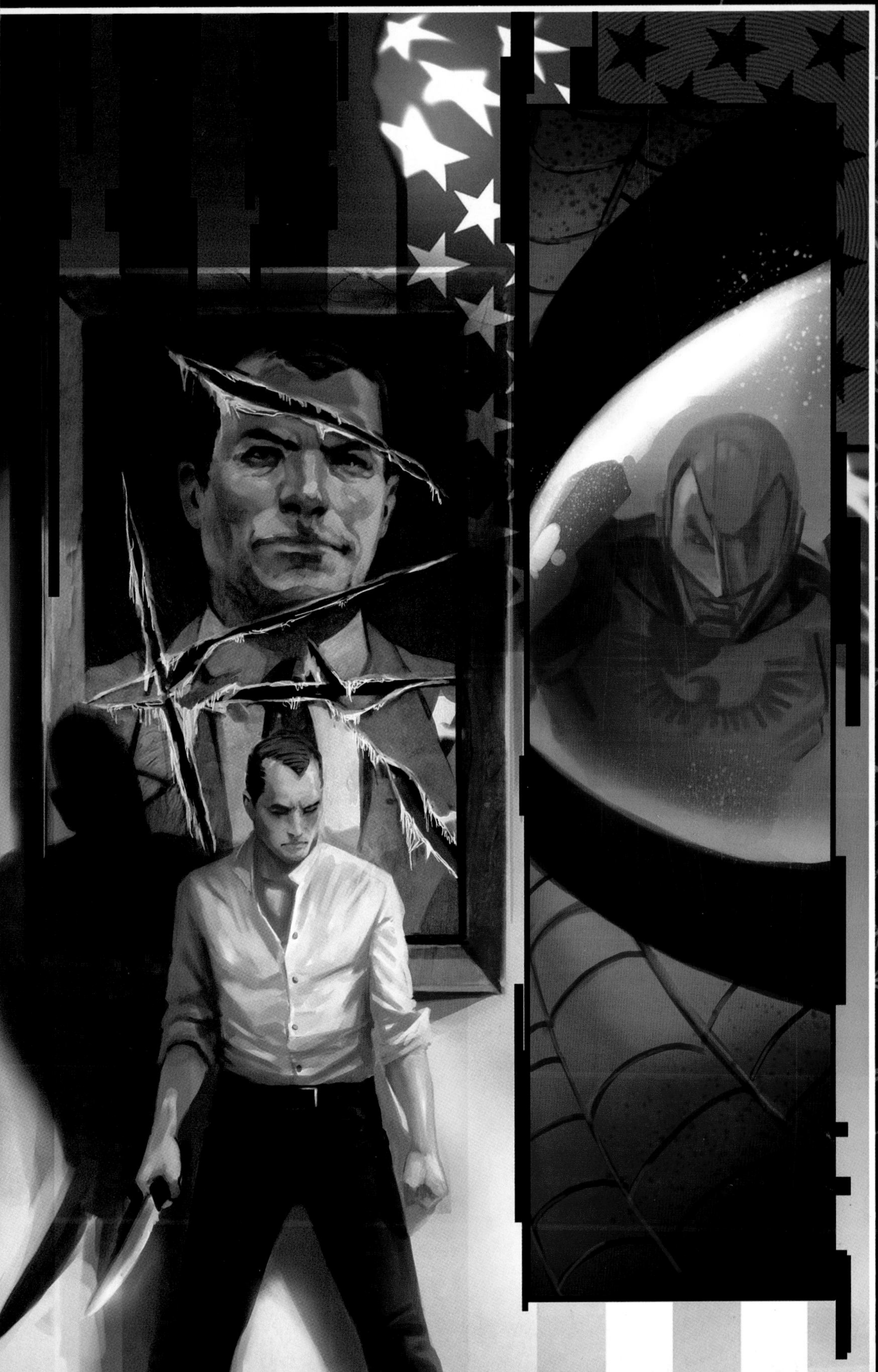

AMAZING SPIDER-MAN PRESENTS: AMERICAN SON #3

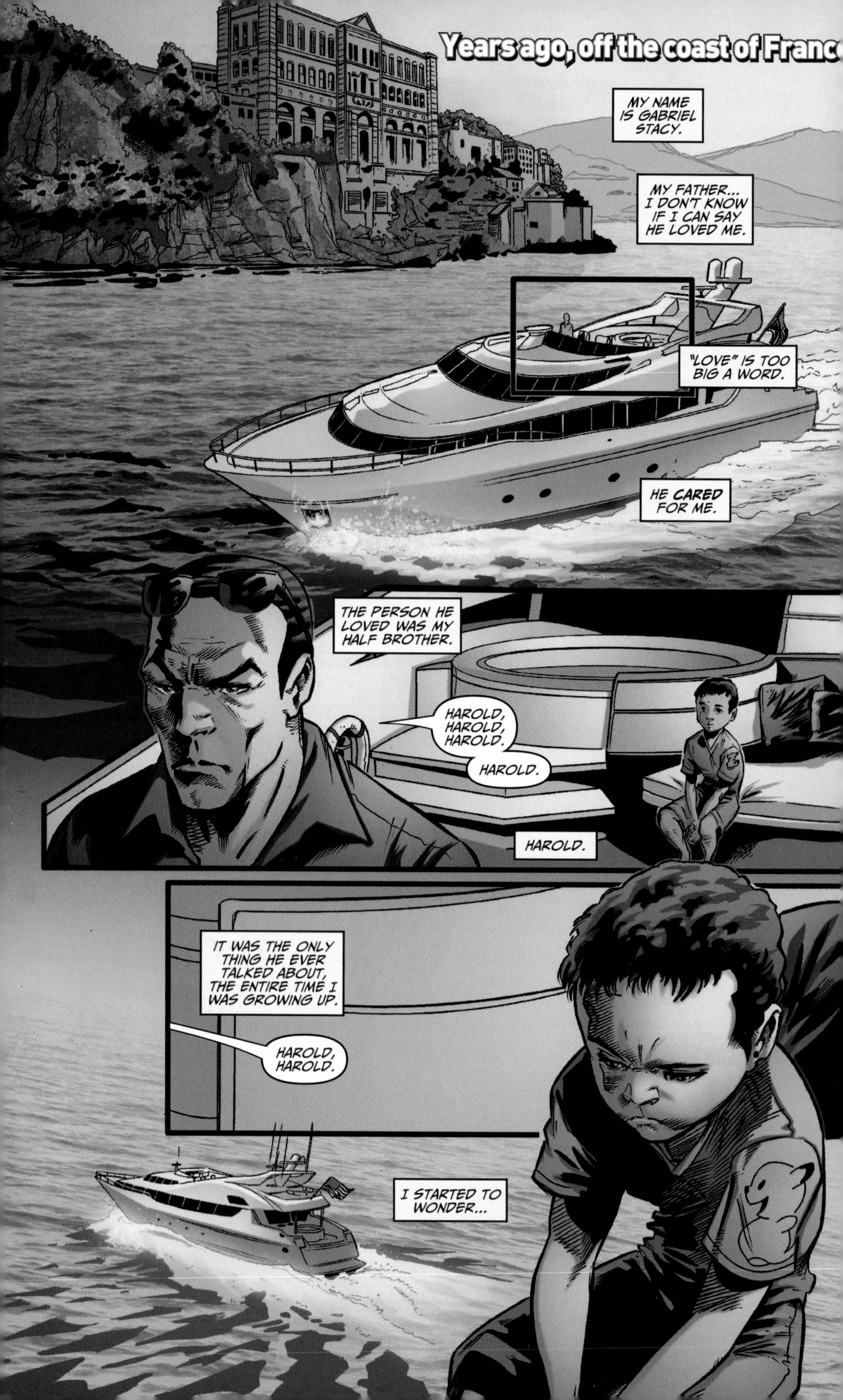
Years ago, off the coast of Franc
MY NAME IS GABRIEL STACY.
MY FATHER... I DON'T KNOW IF I CAN SAY HE LOVED ME.
"LOVE" IS TOO BIG A WORD.
HE **CARED** FOR ME.
THE PERSON HE LOVED WAS MY HALF BROTHER.
HAROLD, HAROLD, HAROLD.
HAROLD.
HAROLD.
IT WAS THE ONLY THING HE EVER TALKED ABOUT, THE ENTIRE TIME I WAS GROWING UP.
HAROLD, HAROLD.
I STARTED TO WONDER...

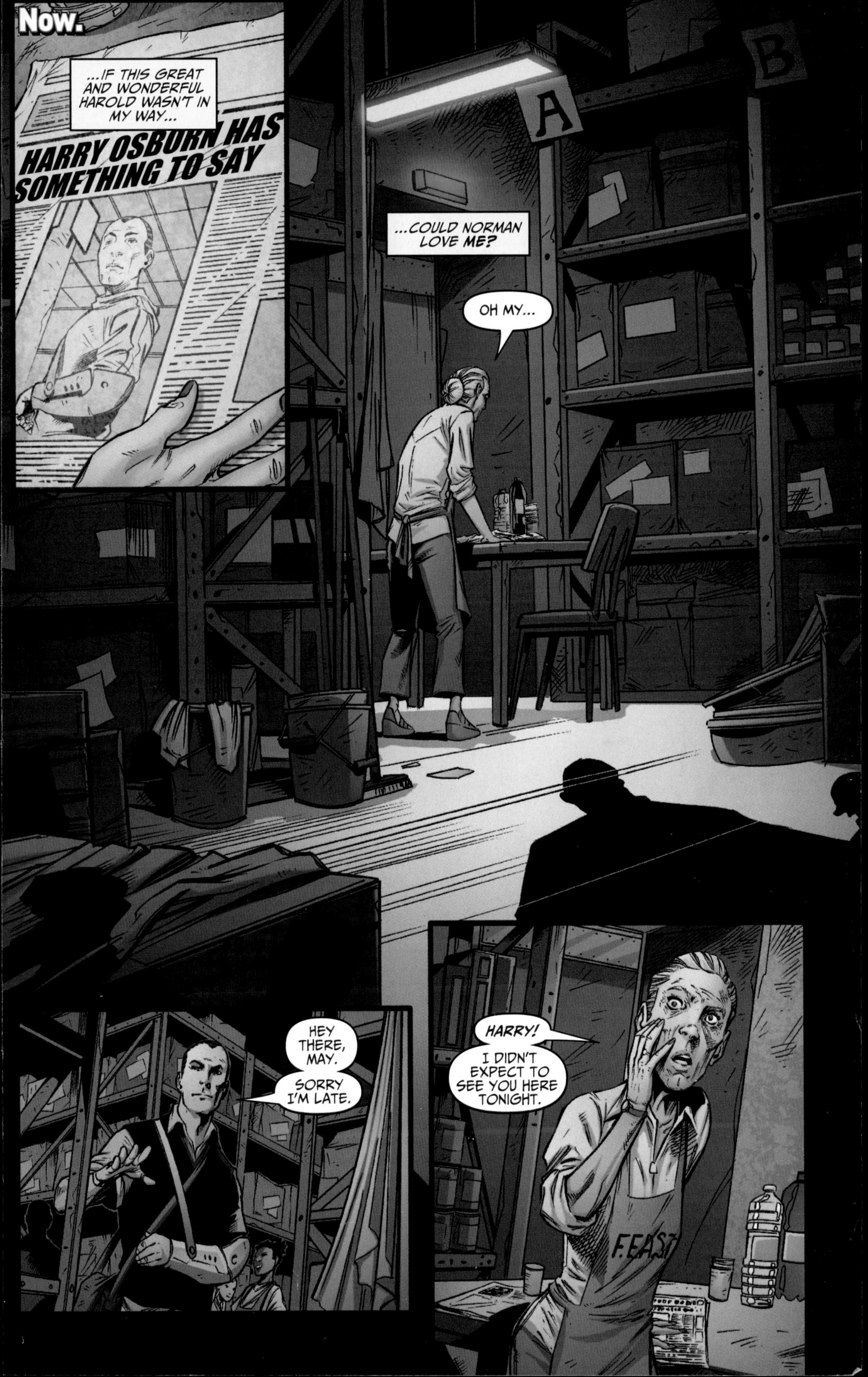
Now.
...IF THIS GREAT AND WONDERFUL HAROLD WASN'T IN MY WAY...
HARRY OSBURN HAS SOMETHING TO SAY
...COULD NORMAN LOVE ME?
OH MY...
HEY THERE, MAY.
SORRY I'M LATE.
HARRY!
I DIDN'T EXPECT TO SEE YOU HERE TONIGHT.
F.E.A.S.T.

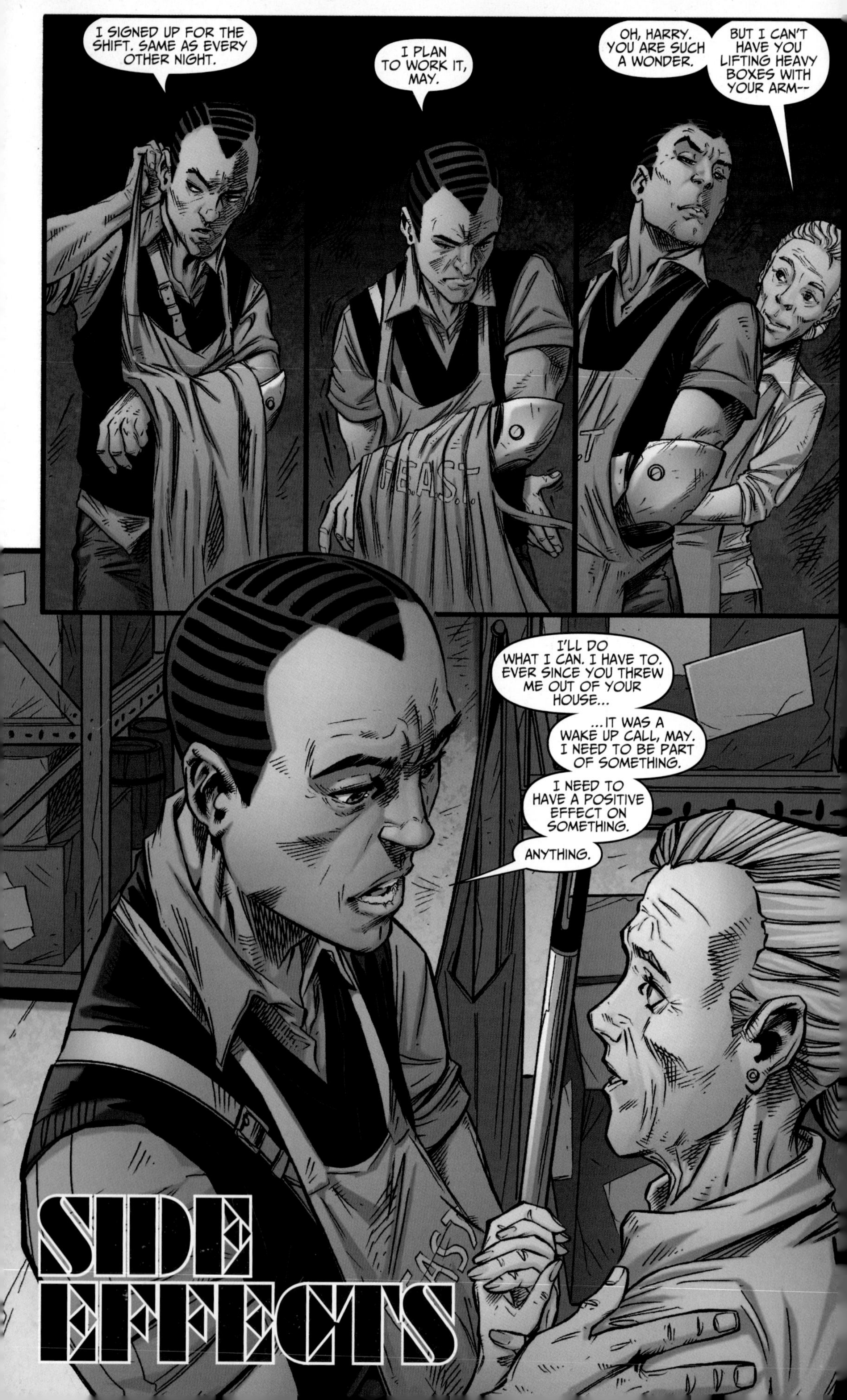

I SIGNED UP FOR THE SHIFT. SAME AS EVERY OTHER NIGHT.
I PLAN TO WORK IT, MAY.
OH, HARRY. YOU ARE SUCH A WONDER.
BUT I CAN'T HAVE YOU LIFTING HEAVY BOXES WITH YOUR ARM--
F.E.A.S.T.
I'LL DO WHAT I CAN. I HAVE TO. EVER SINCE YOU THREW ME OUT OF YOUR HOUSE...
...IT WAS A WAKE UP CALL, MAY. I NEED TO BE PART OF SOMETHING.
I NEED TO HAVE A POSITIVE EFFECT ON SOMETHING.
ANYTHING.
SIDE EFFECTS

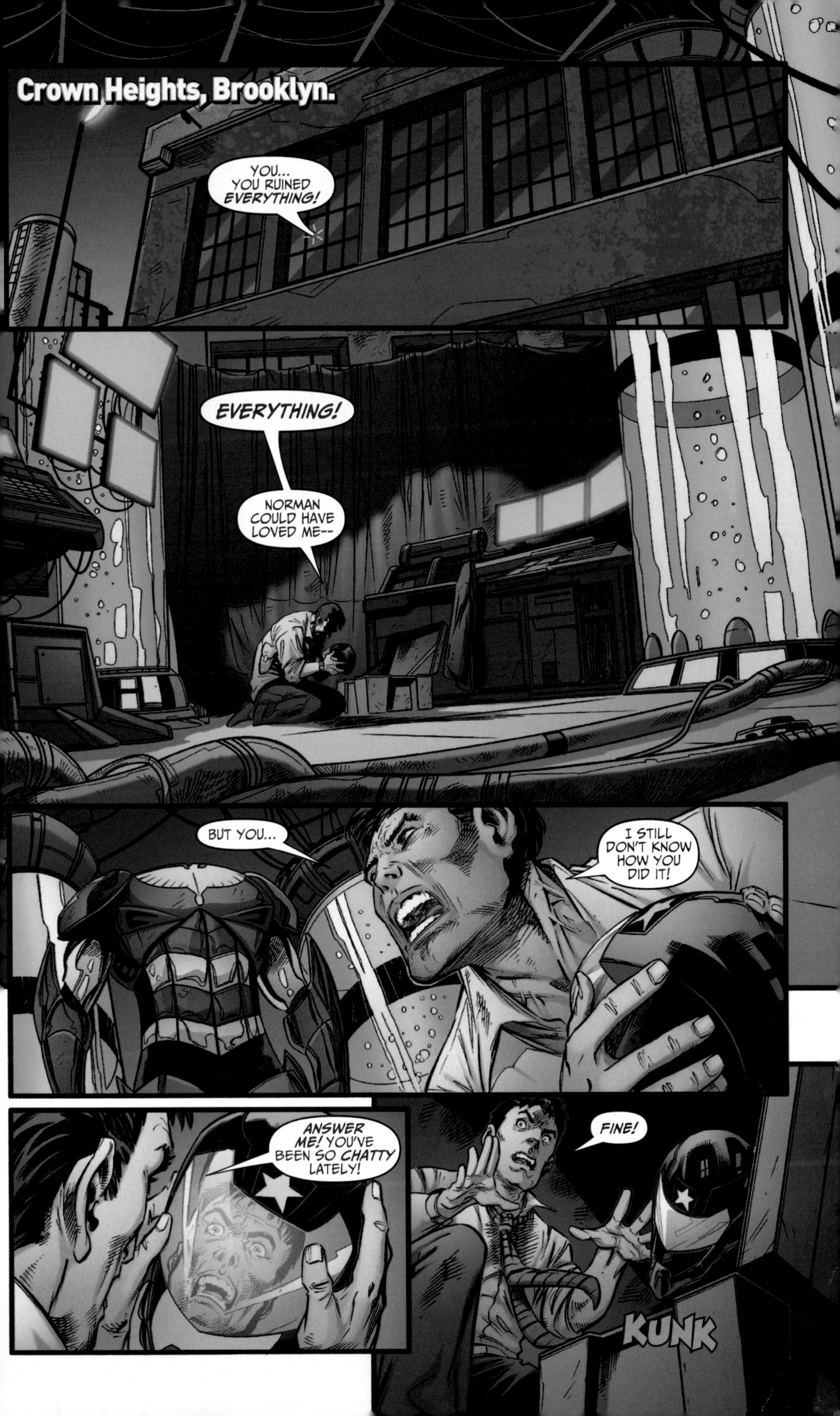
Crown Heights, Brooklyn.
YOU... YOU RUINED EVERYTHING!
EVERYTHING!
NORMAN COULD HAVE LOVED ME--
BUT YOU...
I STILL DON'T KNOW HOW YOU DID IT!
ANSWER ME! YOU'VE BEEN SO CHATTY LATELY!
FINE!
KUNK

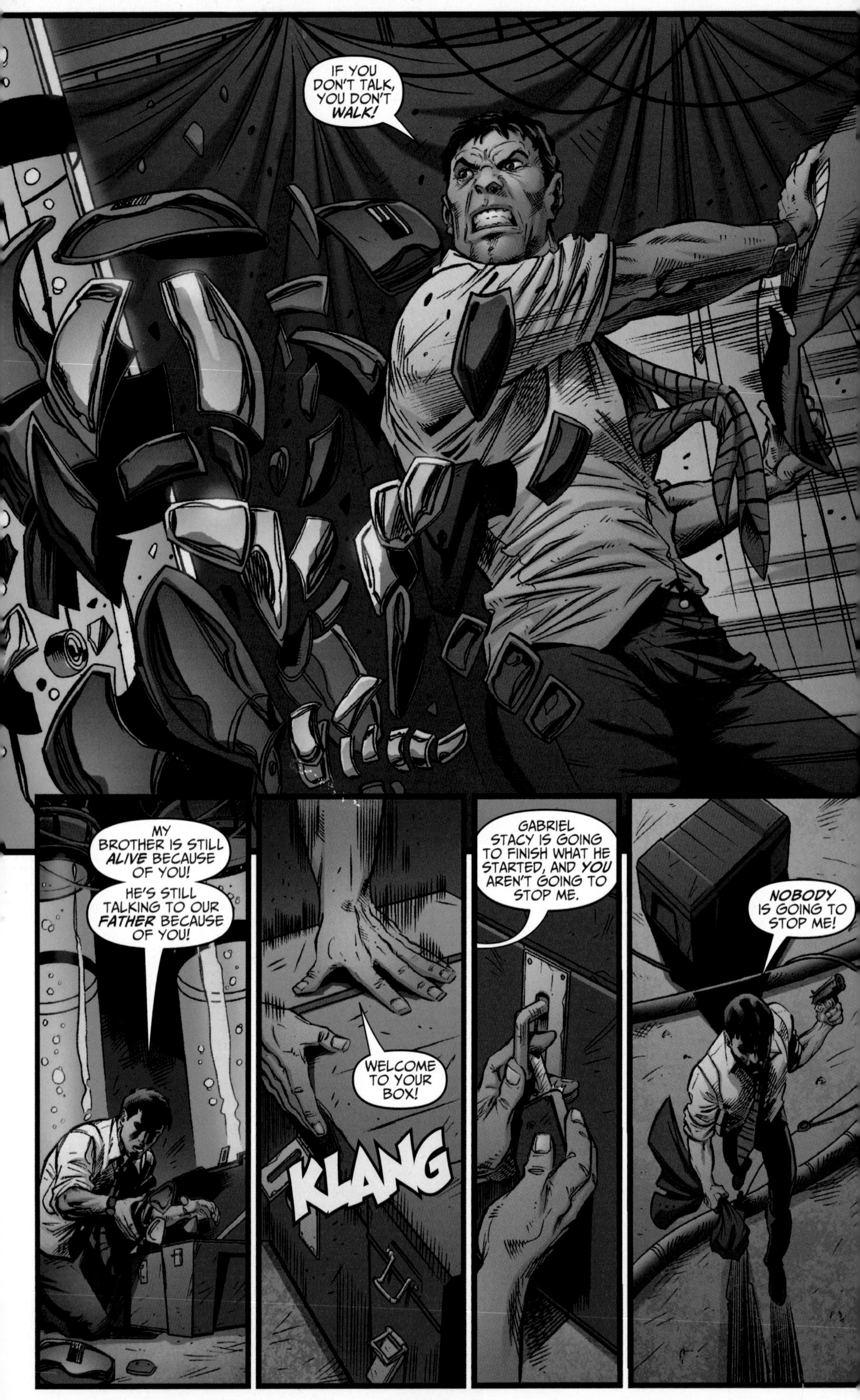
IF YOU DON'T TALK, YOU DON'T WALK!
MY BROTHER IS STILL ALIVE BECAUSE OF YOU!
HE'S STILL TALKING TO OUR FATHER BECAUSE OF YOU!
WELCOME TO YOUR BOX!
KLANG
GABRIEL STACY IS GOING TO FINISH WHAT HE STARTED, AND YOU AREN'T GOING TO STOP ME.
NOBODY IS GOING TO STOP ME!

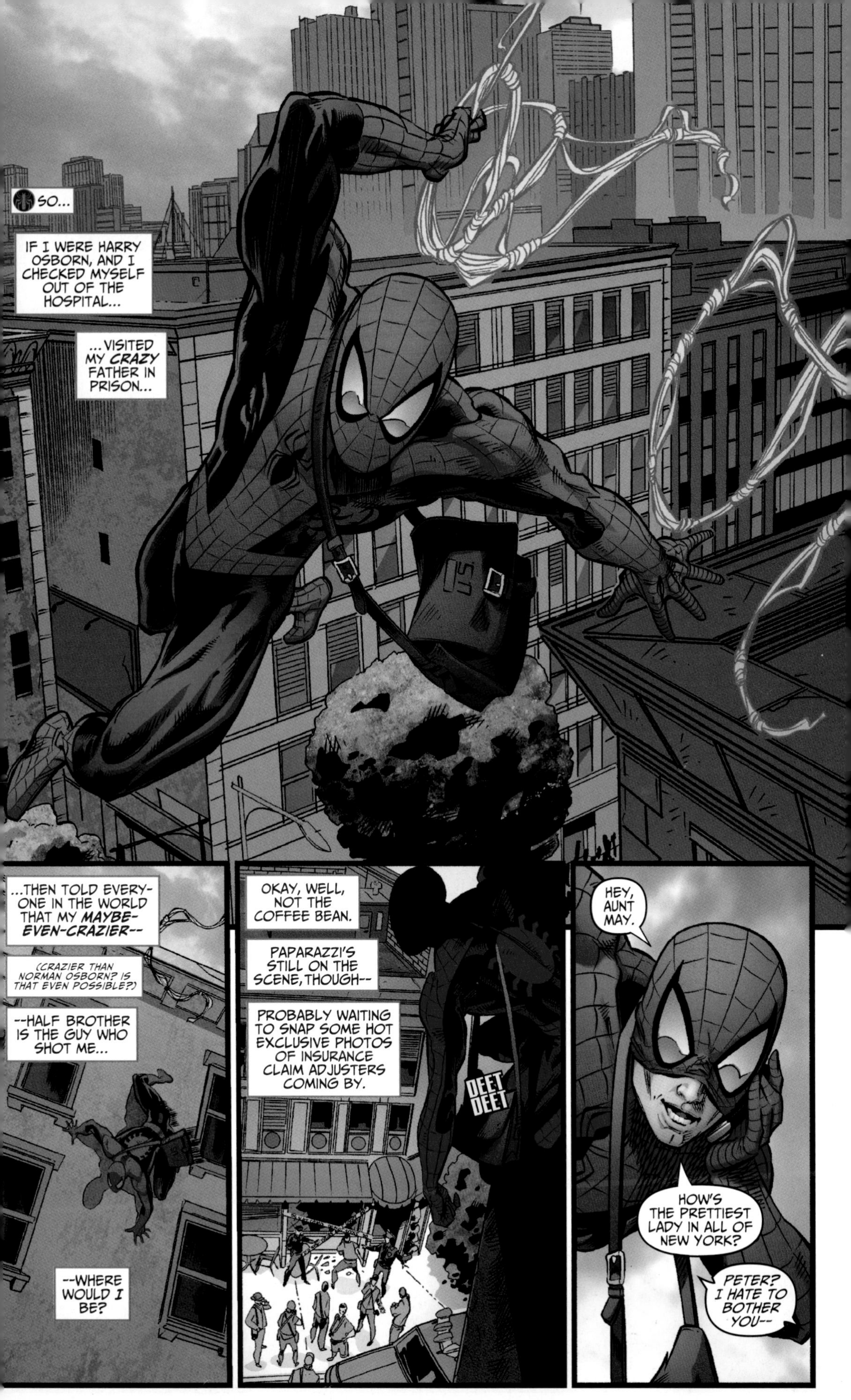
SO...
IF I WERE HARRY OSBORN, AND I CHECKED MYSELF OUT OF THE HOSPITAL...
...VISITED MY CRAZY FATHER IN PRISON...
...THEN TOLD EVERY-ONE IN THE WORLD THAT MY MAYBE-EVEN-CRAZIER--
(CRAZIER THAN NORMAN OSBORN? IS THAT EVEN POSSIBLE?)
--HALF BROTHER IS THE GUY WHO SHOT ME...
--WHERE WOULD I BE?
OKAY, WELL, NOT THE COFFEE BEAN.
PAPARAZZI'S STILL ON THE SCENE, THOUGH--
PROBABLY WAITING TO SNAP SOME HOT EXCLUSIVE PHOTOS OF INSURANCE CLAIM ADJUSTERS COMING BY.
DEET DEET
HEY, AUNT MAY.
HOW'S THE PRETTIEST LADY IN ALL OF NEW YORK?
PETER? I HATE TO BOTHER YOU--

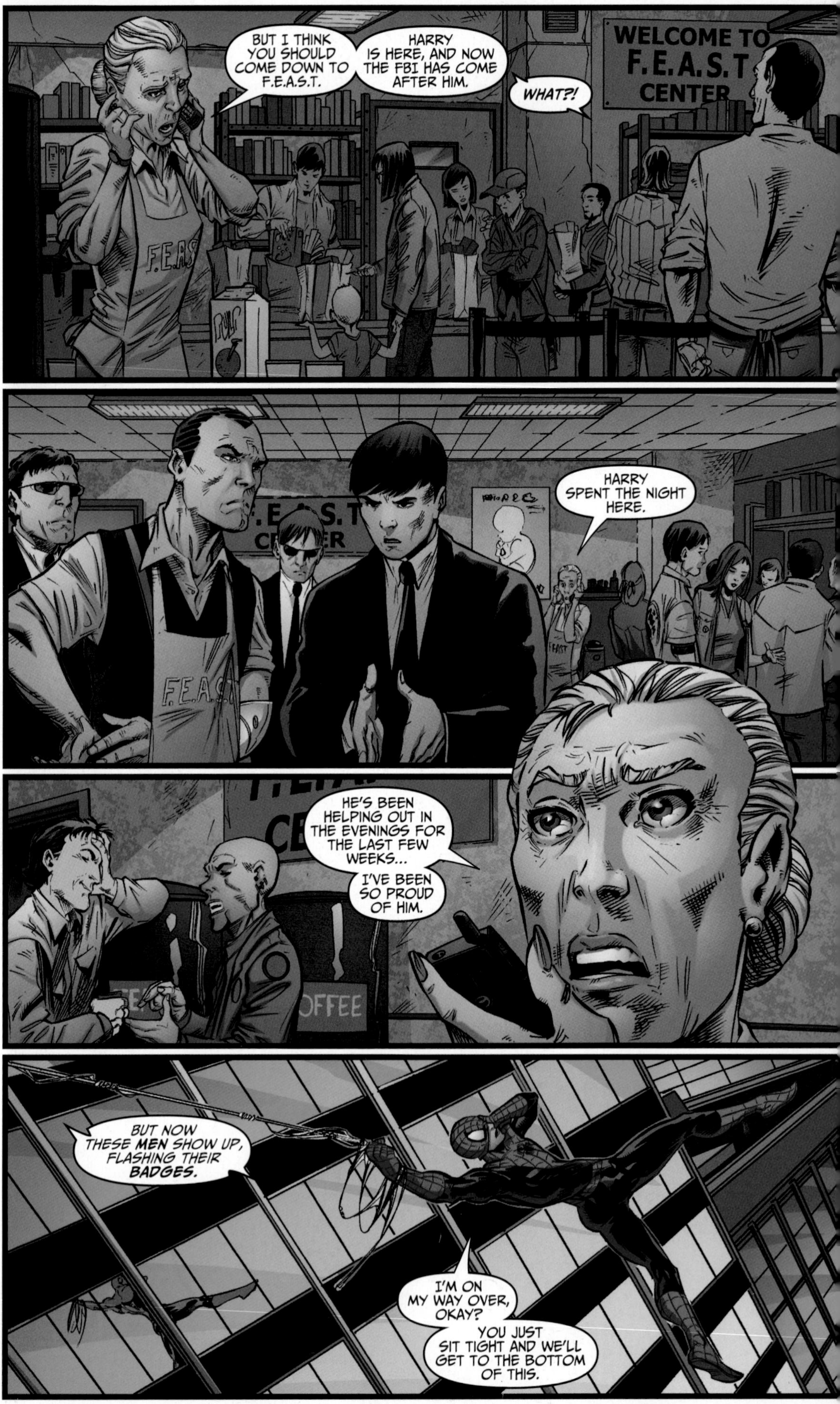
BUT I THINK YOU SHOULD COME DOWN TO F.E.A.S.T.
HARRY IS HERE, AND NOW THE FBI HAS COME AFTER HIM.
WHAT?!
WELCOME TO F.E.A.S.T CENTER
F.E.A.S.T
HARRY SPENT THE NIGHT HERE.
HE'S BEEN HELPING OUT IN THE EVENINGS FOR THE LAST FEW WEEKS...
I'VE BEEN SO PROUD OF HIM.
OFFEE
BUT NOW THESE MEN SHOW UP, FLASHING THEIR BADGES.
I'M ON MY WAY OVER, OKAY?
YOU JUST SIT TIGHT AND WE'LL GET TO THE BOTTOM OF THIS.

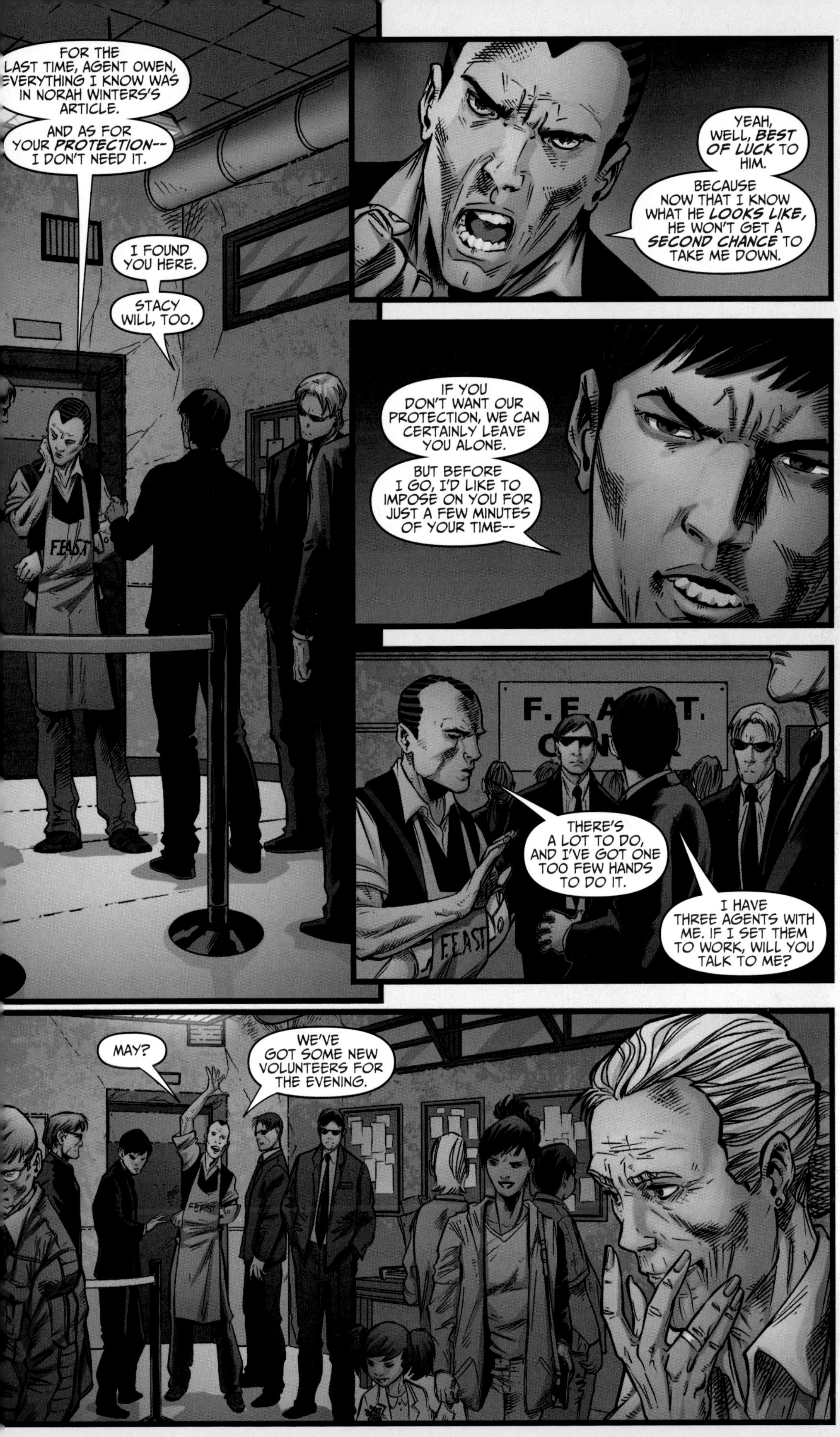

FOR THE LAST TIME, AGENT OWEN, EVERYTHING I KNOW WAS IN NORAH WINTERS'S ARTICLE.
AND AS FOR YOUR *PROTECTION*-- I DON'T NEED IT.
I FOUND YOU HERE.
STACY WILL, TOO.
YEAH, WELL, *BEST OF LUCK* TO HIM.
BECAUSE NOW THAT I KNOW WHAT HE *LOOKS LIKE,* HE WON'T GET A *SECOND CHANCE* TO TAKE ME DOWN.
IF YOU DON'T WANT OUR PROTECTION, WE CAN CERTAINLY LEAVE YOU ALONE.
BUT BEFORE I GO, I'D LIKE TO IMPOSE ON YOU FOR JUST A FEW MINUTES OF YOUR TIME--
THERE'S A LOT TO DO, AND I'VE GOT ONE TOO FEW HANDS TO DO IT.
I HAVE THREE AGENTS WITH ME. IF I SET THEM TO WORK, WILL YOU TALK TO ME?
MAY?
WE'VE GOT SOME NEW VOLUNTEERS FOR THE EVENING.

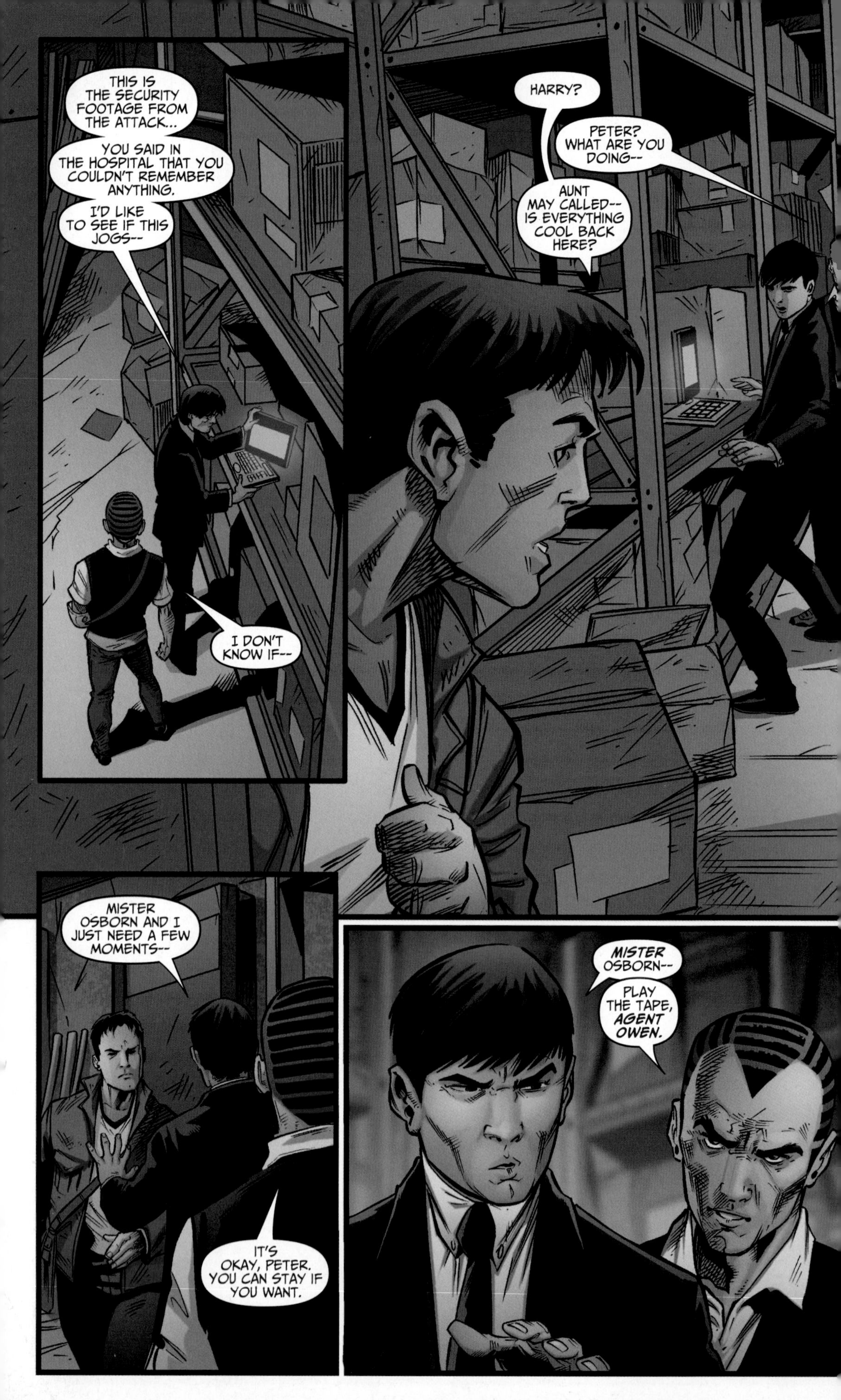
THIS IS THE SECURITY FOOTAGE FROM THE ATTACK...
YOU SAID IN THE HOSPITAL THAT YOU COULDN'T REMEMBER ANYTHING.
I'D LIKE TO SEE IF THIS JOGS--
I DON'T KNOW IF--
HARRY?
PETER? WHAT ARE YOU DOING--
AUNT MAY CALLED-- IS EVERYTHING COOL BACK HERE?
MISTER OSBORN AND I JUST NEED A FEW MOMENTS--
IT'S OKAY, PETER. YOU CAN STAY IF YOU WANT.
MISTER OSBORN--
PLAY THE TAPE, *AGENT OWEN.*

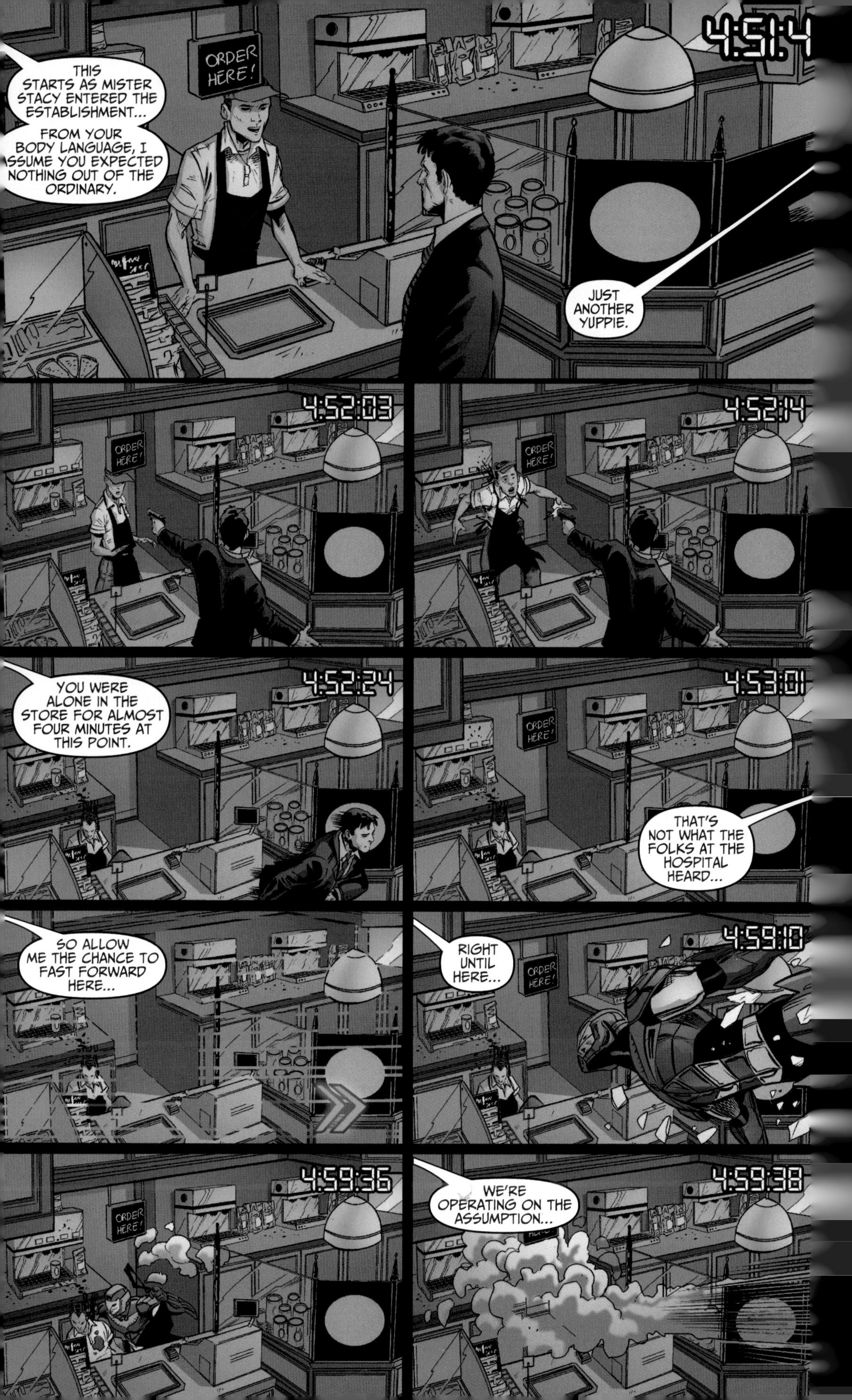
4:51:14
ORDER HERE!
THIS STARTS AS MISTER STACY ENTERED THE ESTABLISHMENT...
FROM YOUR BODY LANGUAGE, I ASSUME YOU EXPECTED NOTHING OUT OF THE ORDINARY.
JUST ANOTHER YUPPIE.
4:52:03
ORDER HERE!
4:52:14
ORDER HERE!
YOU WERE ALONE IN THE STORE FOR ALMOST FOUR MINUTES AT THIS POINT.
4:52:24
4:53:01
ORDER HERE!
THAT'S NOT WHAT THE FOLKS AT THE HOSPITAL HEARD...
SO ALLOW ME THE CHANCE TO FAST FORWARD HERE...
RIGHT UNTIL HERE...
4:59:10
ORDER HERE!
4:59:36
ORDER HERE!
WE'RE OPERATING ON THE ASSUMPTION...
4:59:38

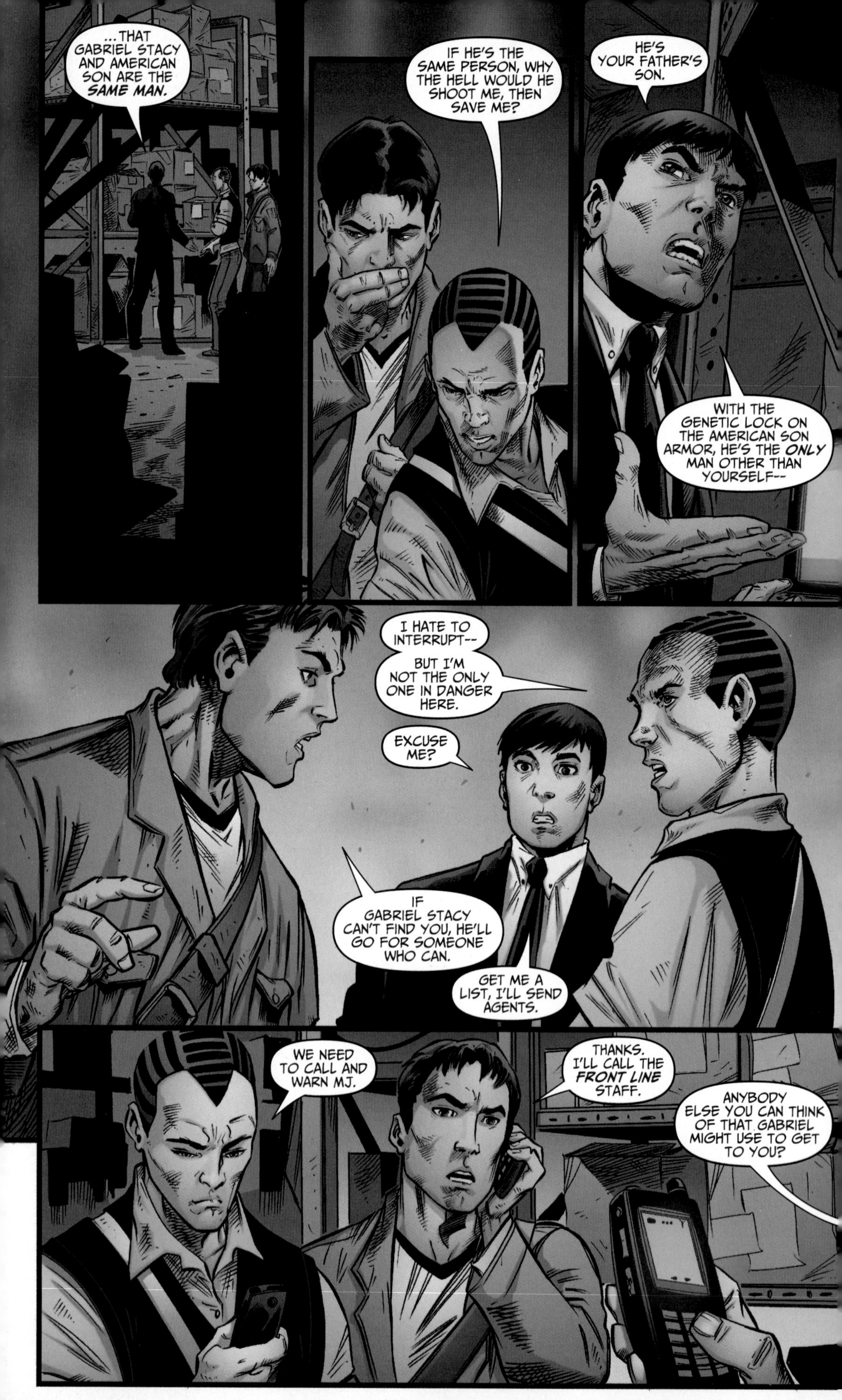
...THAT GABRIEL STACY AND AMERICAN SON ARE THE SAME MAN.
IF HE'S THE SAME PERSON, WHY THE HELL WOULD HE SHOOT ME, THEN SAVE ME?
HE'S YOUR FATHER'S SON.
WITH THE GENETIC LOCK ON THE AMERICAN SON ARMOR, HE'S THE ONLY MAN OTHER THAN YOURSELF--
I HATE TO INTERRUPT--
BUT I'M NOT THE ONLY ONE IN DANGER HERE.
EXCUSE ME?
IF GABRIEL STACY CAN'T FIND YOU, HE'LL GO FOR SOMEONE WHO CAN.
GET ME A LIST, I'LL SEND AGENTS.
WE NEED TO CALL AND WARN MJ.
THANKS. I'LL CALL THE FRONT LINE STAFF.
ANYBODY ELSE YOU CAN THINK OF THAT GABRIEL MIGHT USE TO GET TO YOU?

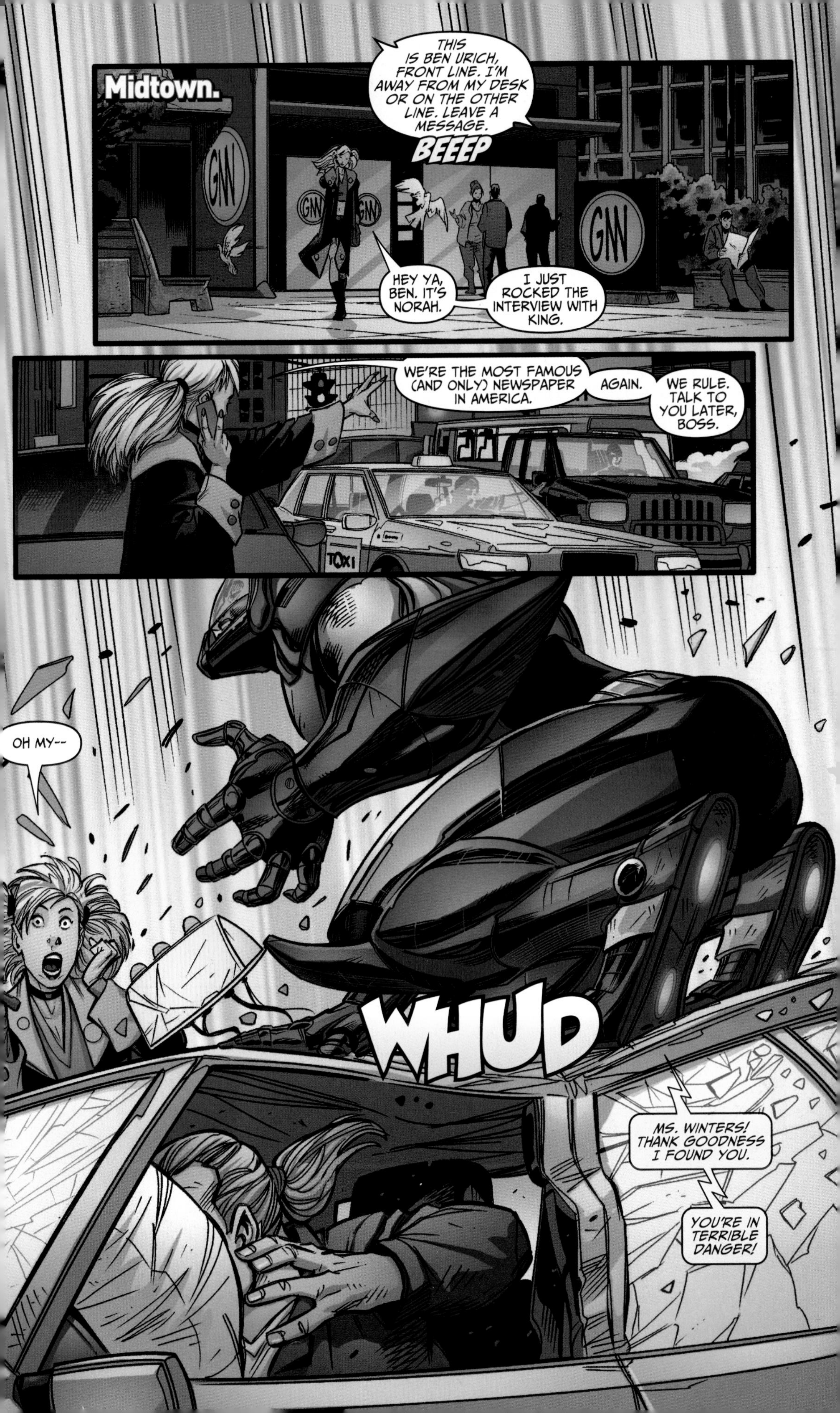
Midtown.
THIS IS BEN URICH, FRONT LINE. I'M AWAY FROM MY DESK OR ON THE OTHER LINE. LEAVE A MESSAGE.
BEEEP
GNN
HEY YA, BEN. IT'S NORAH.
I JUST ROCKED THE INTERVIEW WITH KING.
WE'RE THE MOST FAMOUS (AND ONLY) NEWSPAPER IN AMERICA.
AGAIN.
WE RULE. TALK TO YOU LATER, BOSS.
TAXI
OH MY--
WHUD
MS. WINTERS! THANK GOODNESS I FOUND YOU.
YOU'RE IN TERRIBLE DANGER!

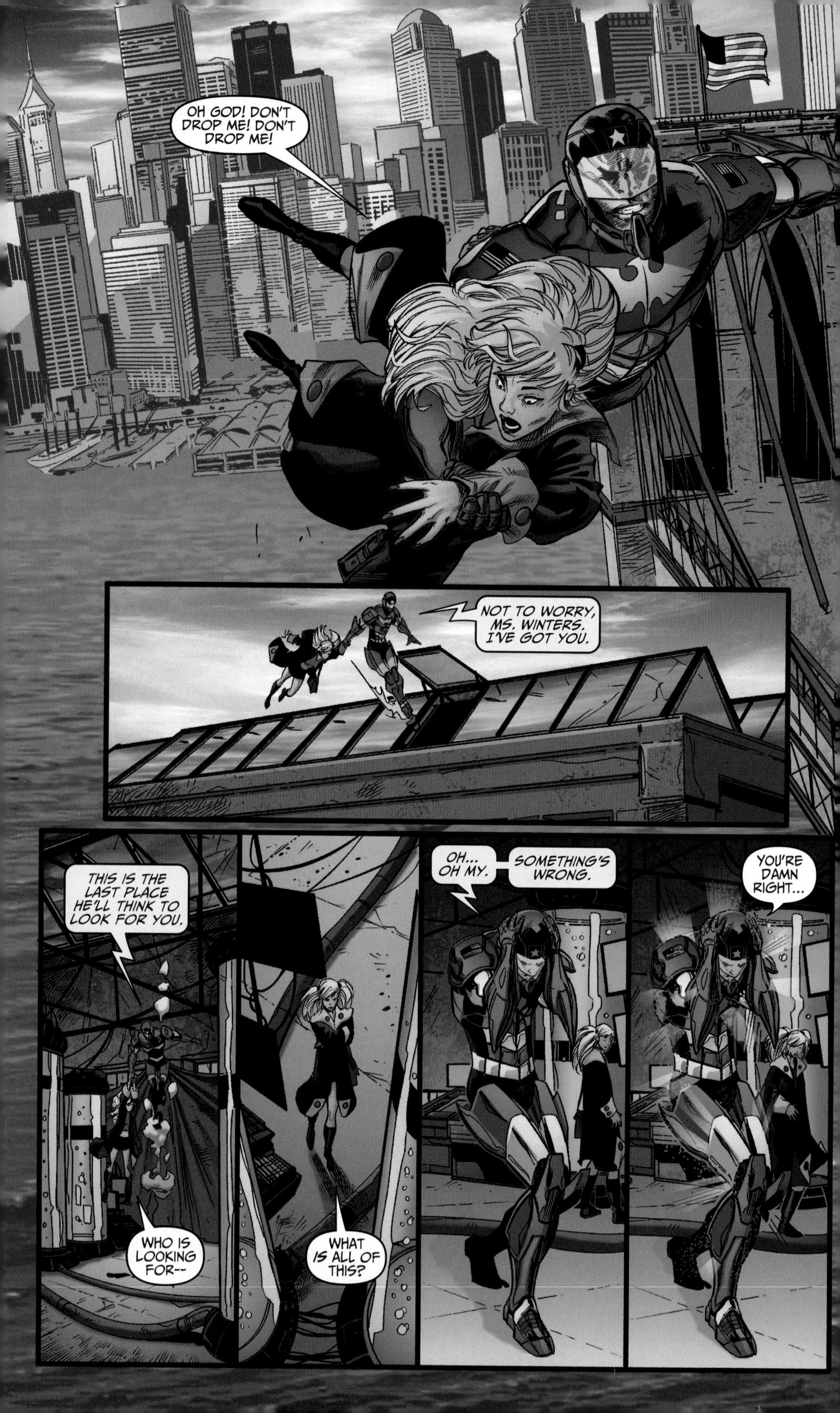
OH GOD! DON'T DROP ME! DON'T DROP ME!
NOT TO WORRY, MS. WINTERS. I'VE GOT YOU.
THIS IS THE LAST PLACE HE'LL THINK TO LOOK FOR YOU.
WHO IS LOOKING FOR--
WHAT IS ALL OF THIS?
OH... OH MY.
SOMETHING'S WRONG.
YOU'RE DAMN RIGHT...

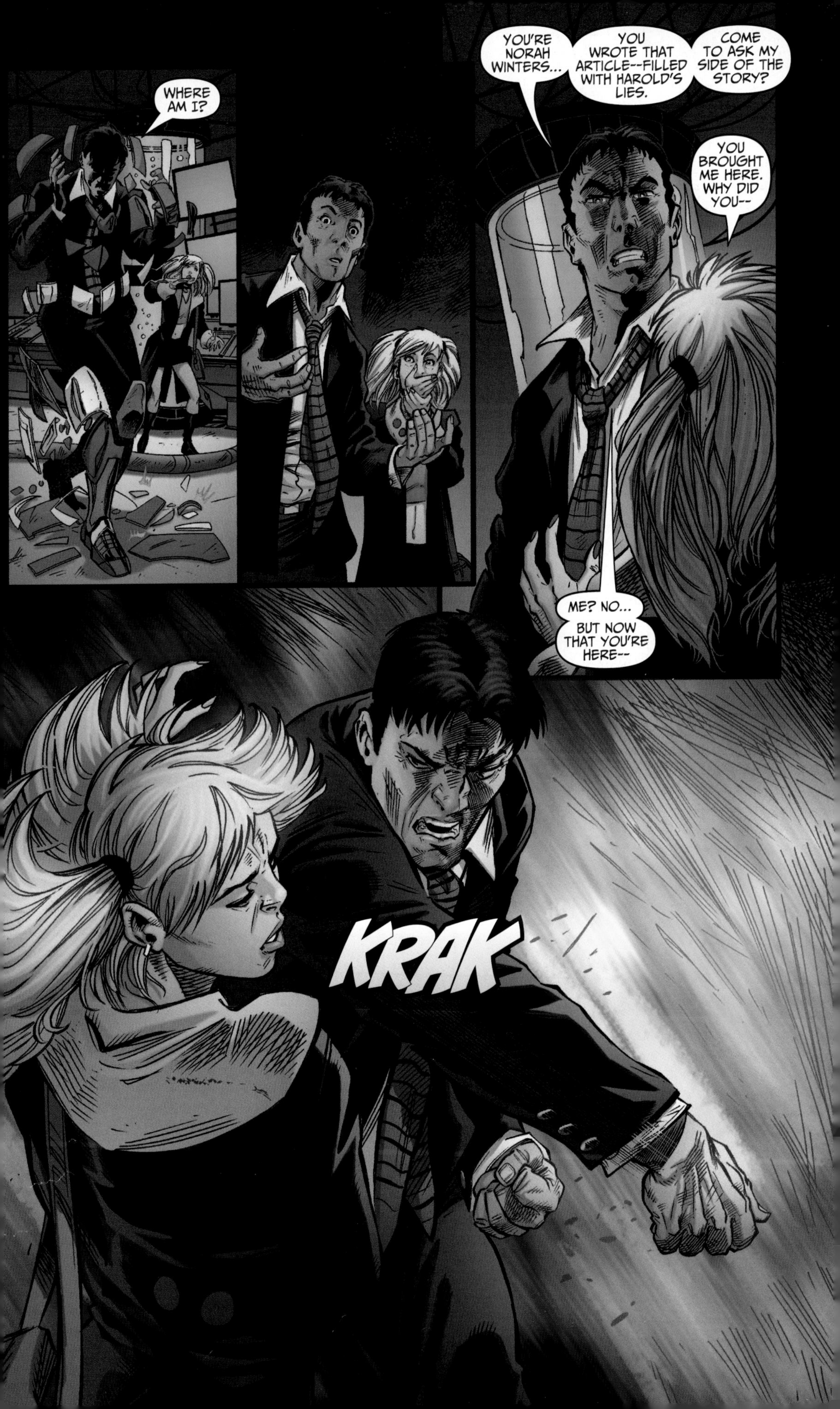
WHERE AM I?
YOU'RE NORAH WINTERS...
YOU WROTE THAT ARTICLE--FILLED WITH HAROLD'S LIES.
COME TO ASK MY SIDE OF THE STORY?
YOU BROUGHT ME HERE. WHY DID YOU--
ME? NO...
BUT NOW THAT YOU'RE HERE--
KRAK

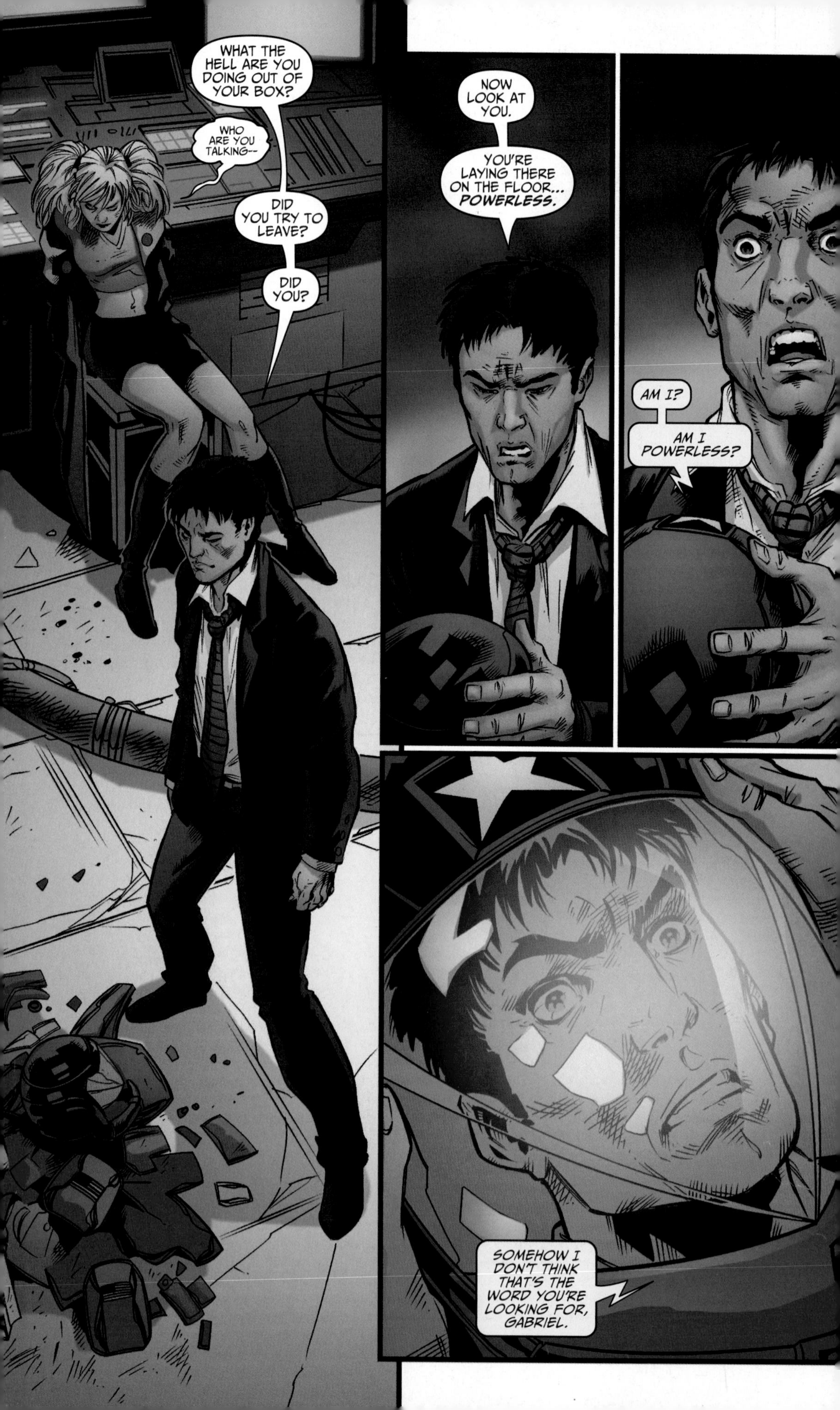
WHAT THE HELL ARE YOU DOING OUT OF YOUR BOX?
WHO ARE YOU TALKING--
DID YOU TRY TO LEAVE?
DID YOU?
NOW LOOK AT YOU.
YOU'RE LAYING THERE ON THE FLOOR... POWERLESS.
AM I?
AM I POWERLESS?
SOMEHOW I DON'T THINK THAT'S THE WORD YOU'RE LOOKING FOR, GABRIEL.

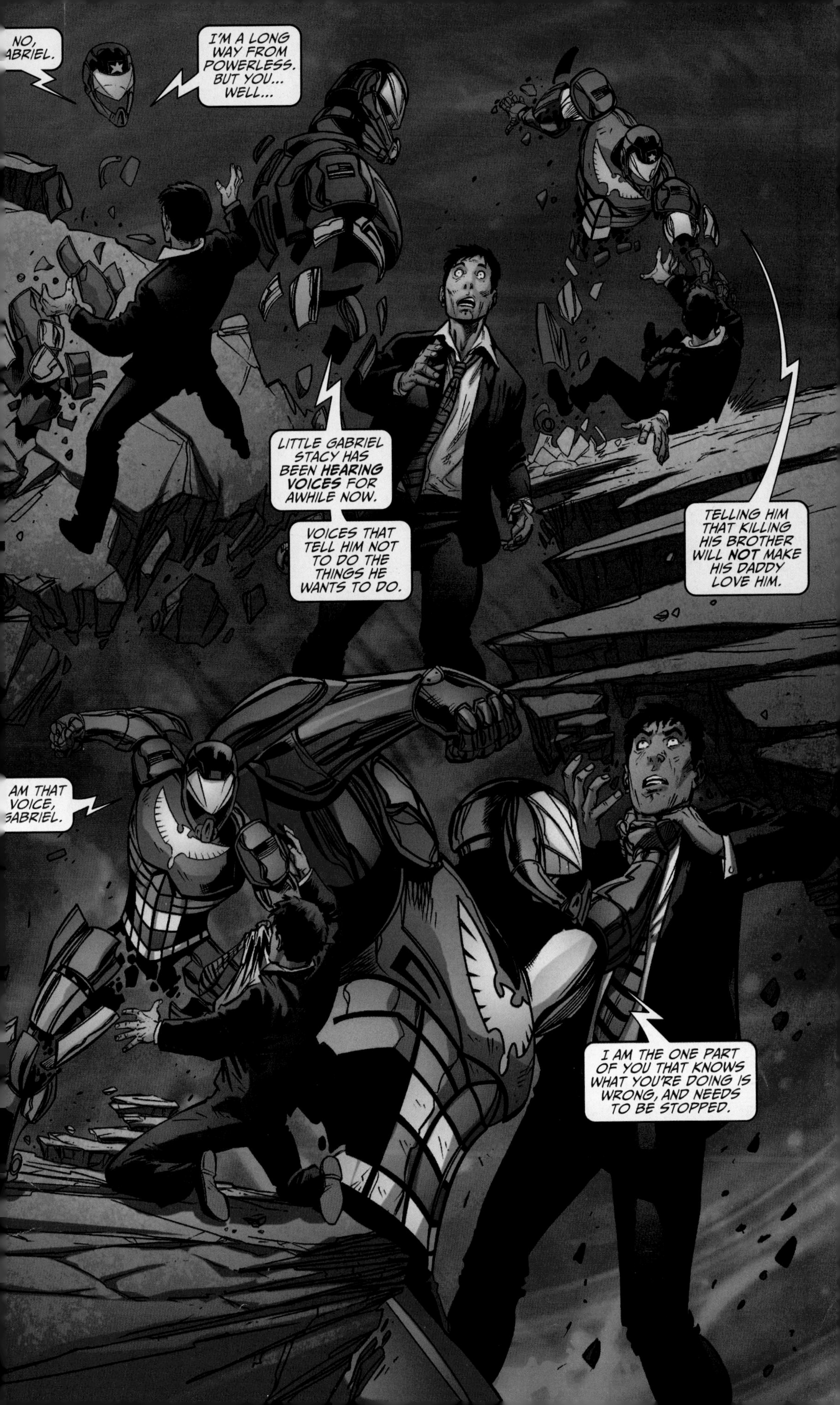

NO, GABRIEL.
I'M A LONG WAY FROM POWERLESS. BUT YOU... WELL...
LITTLE GABRIEL STACY HAS BEEN HEARING VOICES FOR AWHILE NOW.
VOICES THAT TELL HIM NOT TO DO THE THINGS HE WANTS TO DO.
TELLING HIM THAT KILLING HIS BROTHER WILL NOT MAKE HIS DADDY LOVE HIM.
AM THAT VOICE, GABRIEL.
I AM THE ONE PART OF YOU THAT KNOWS WHAT YOU'RE DOING IS WRONG, AND NEEDS TO BE STOPPED.

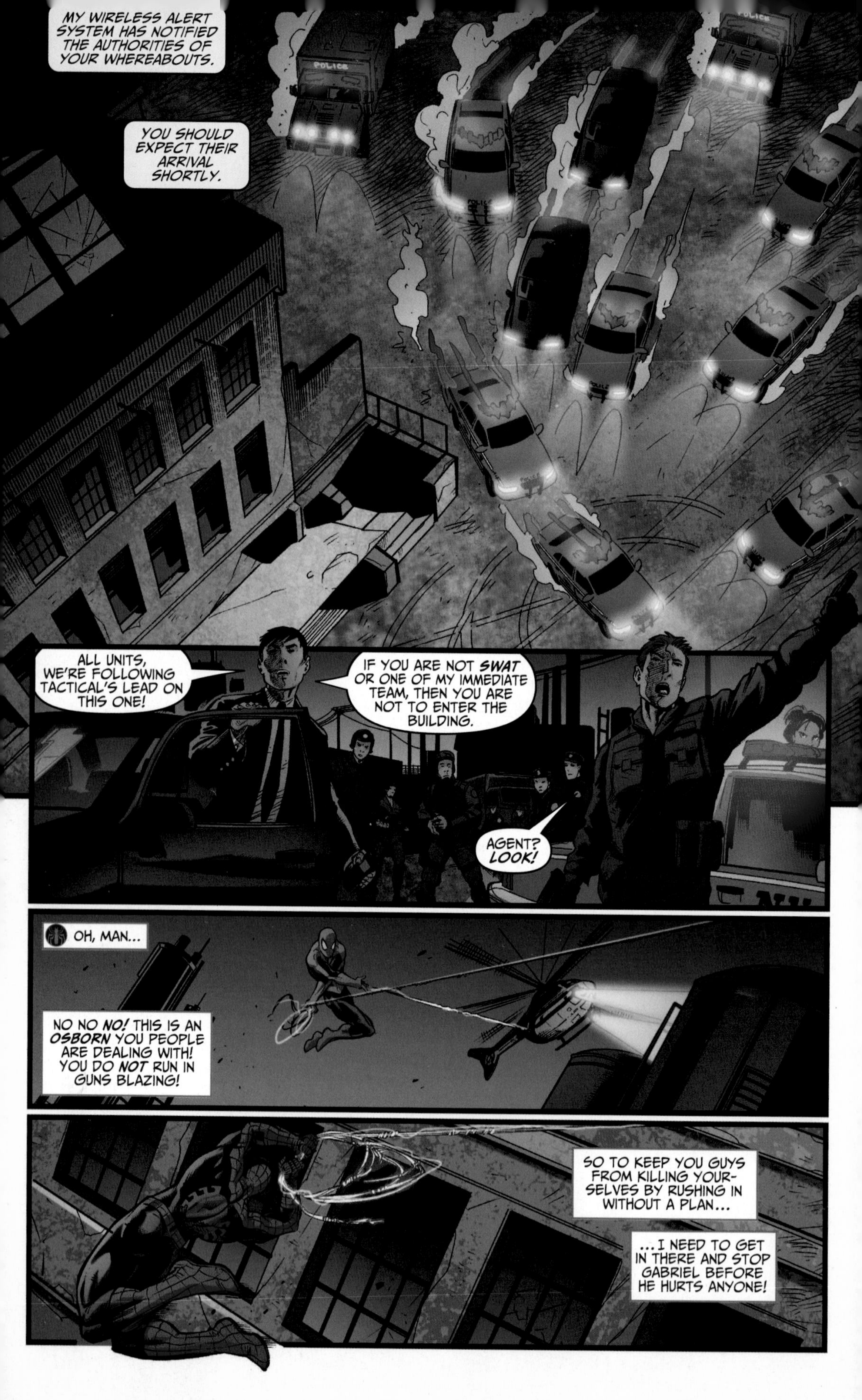
MY WIRELESS ALERT SYSTEM HAS NOTIFIED THE AUTHORITIES OF YOUR WHEREABOUTS.
YOU SHOULD EXPECT THEIR ARRIVAL SHORTLY.
ALL UNITS, WE'RE FOLLOWING TACTICAL'S LEAD ON THIS ONE!
IF YOU ARE NOT SWAT OR ONE OF MY IMMEDIATE TEAM, THEN YOU ARE NOT TO ENTER THE BUILDING.
AGENT? LOOK!
OH, MAN...
NO NO NO! THIS IS AN OSBORN YOU PEOPLE ARE DEALING WITH! YOU DO NOT RUN IN GUNS BLAZING!
SO TO KEEP YOU GUYS FROM KILLING YOURSELVES BY RUSHING IN WITHOUT A PLAN...
...I NEED TO GET IN THERE AND STOP GABRIEL BEFORE HE HURTS ANYONE!

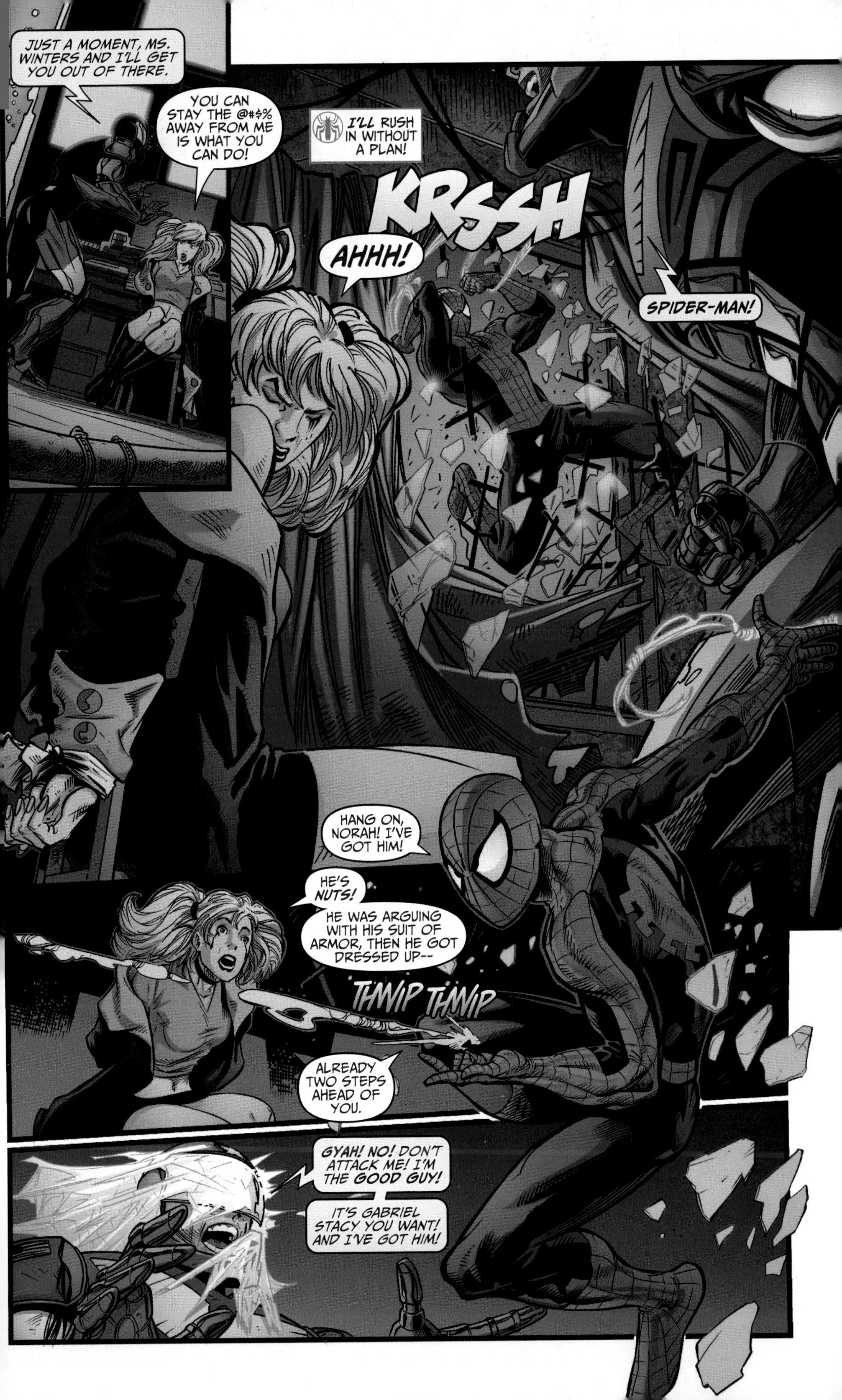

JUST A MOMENT, MS. WINTERS AND I'LL GET YOU OUT OF THERE.
YOU CAN STAY THE @#$% AWAY FROM ME IS WHAT YOU CAN DO!
I'LL RUSH IN WITHOUT A PLAN!
KRSSH
AHHH!
SPIDER-MAN!
HANG ON, NORAH! I'VE GOT HIM!
HE'S NUTS!
HE WAS ARGUING WITH HIS SUIT OF ARMOR, THEN HE GOT DRESSED UP--
THWIP THWIP
ALREADY TWO STEPS AHEAD OF YOU.
GYAH! NO! DON'T ATTACK ME! I'M THE GOOD GUY!
IT'S GABRIEL STACY YOU WANT! AND I'VE GOT HIM!

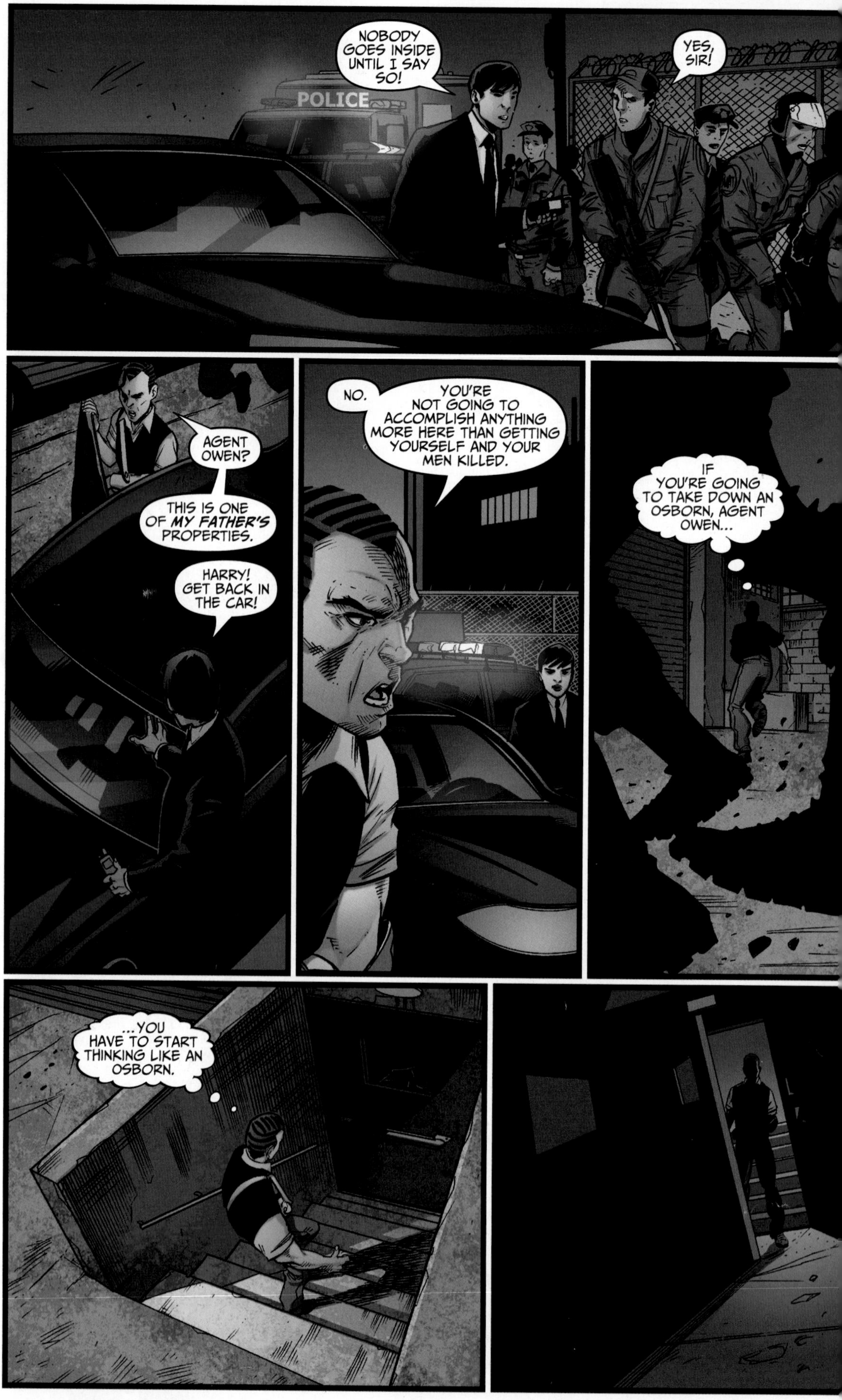
NOBODY GOES INSIDE UNTIL I SAY SO!
YES, SIR!
POLICE
AGENT OWEN?
THIS IS ONE OF MY FATHER'S PROPERTIES.
HARRY! GET BACK IN THE CAR!
NO.
YOU'RE NOT GOING TO ACCOMPLISH ANYTHING MORE HERE THAN GETTING YOURSELF AND YOUR MEN KILLED.
IF YOU'RE GOING TO TAKE DOWN AN OSBORN, AGENT OWEN...
...YOU HAVE TO START THINKING LIKE AN OSBORN.

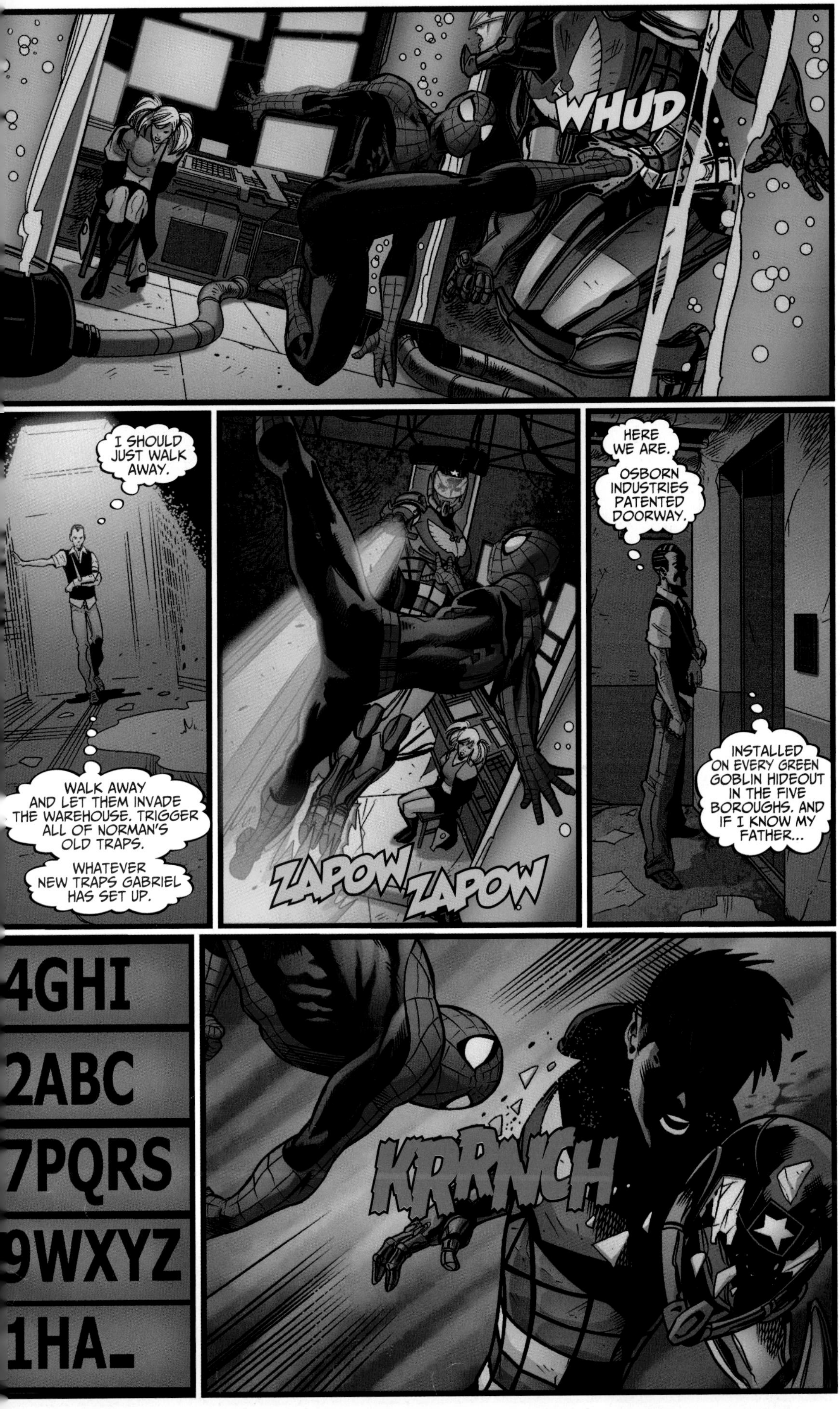

WHUD
I SHOULD JUST WALK AWAY.
WALK AWAY AND LET THEM INVADE THE WAREHOUSE. TRIGGER ALL OF NORMAN'S OLD TRAPS.
WHATEVER NEW TRAPS GABRIEL HAS SET UP.
ZAPOW
ZAPOW
HERE WE ARE.
OSBORN INDUSTRIES PATENTED DOORWAY.
INSTALLED ON EVERY GREEN GOBLIN HIDEOUT IN THE FIVE BOROUGHS. AND IF I KNOW MY FATHER...
4GHI
2ABC
7PQRS
9WXYZ
1HA_
KRRNCH

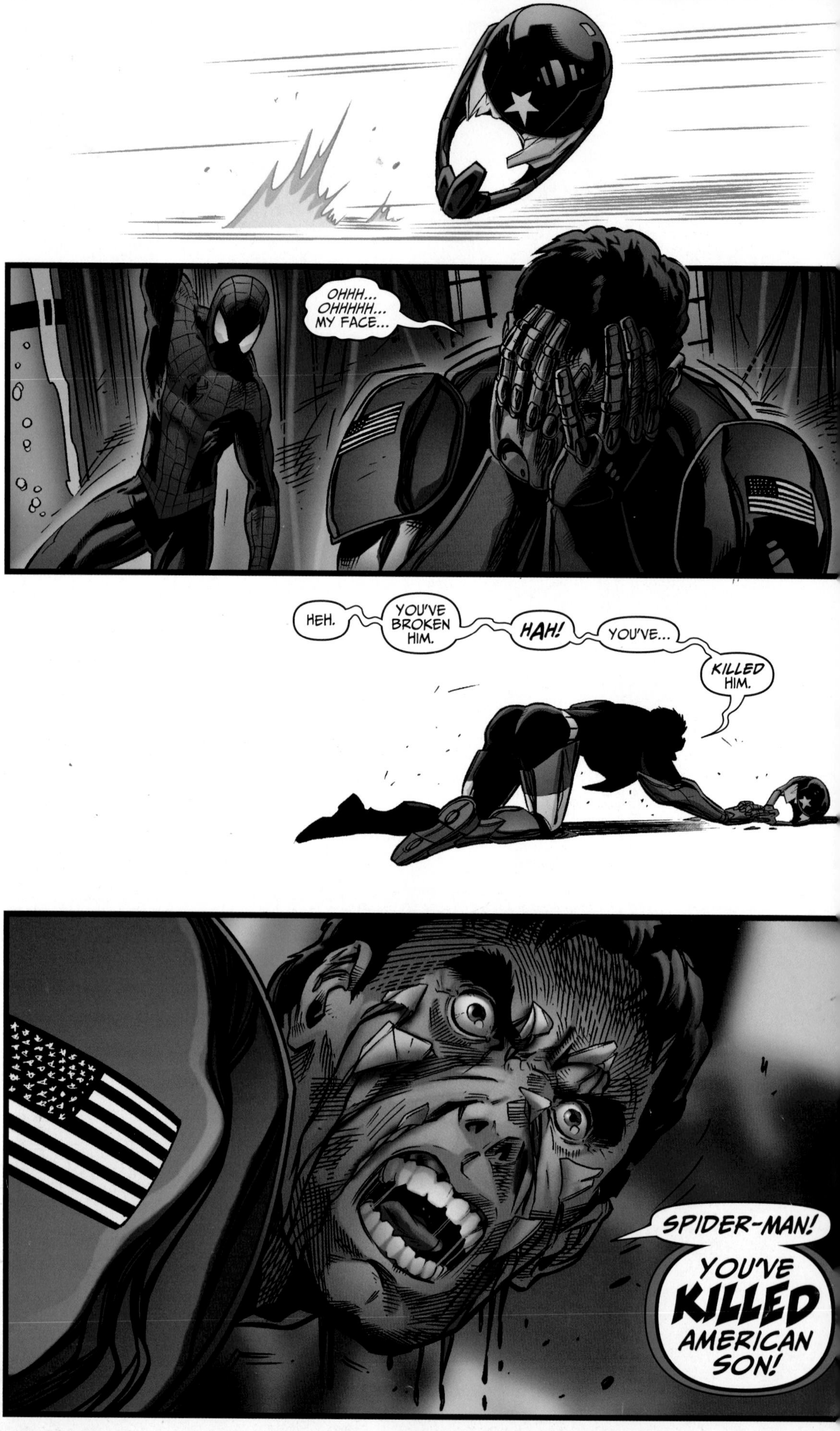
OHHH... OHHHHH... MY FACE...
HEH.
YOU'VE BROKEN HIM.
HAH!
YOU'VE...
KILLED HIM.
SPIDER-MAN!
YOU'VE KILLED AMERICAN SON!

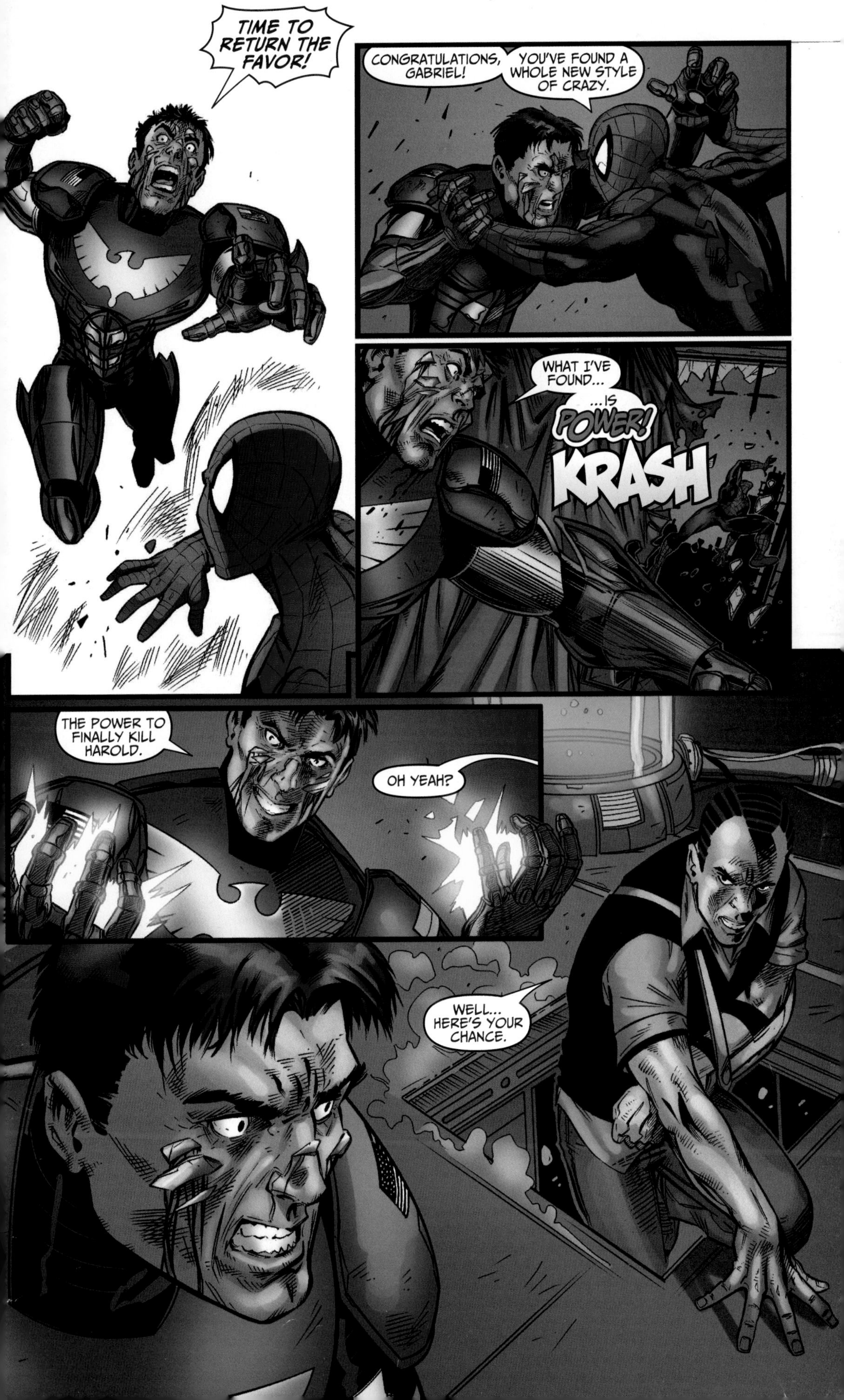
TIME TO RETURN THE FAVOR!
CONGRATULATIONS, GABRIEL!
YOU'VE FOUND A WHOLE NEW STYLE OF CRAZY.
WHAT I'VE FOUND...
...IS POWER!
KRASH
THE POWER TO FINALLY KILL HAROLD.
OH YEAH?
WELL... HERE'S YOUR CHANCE.

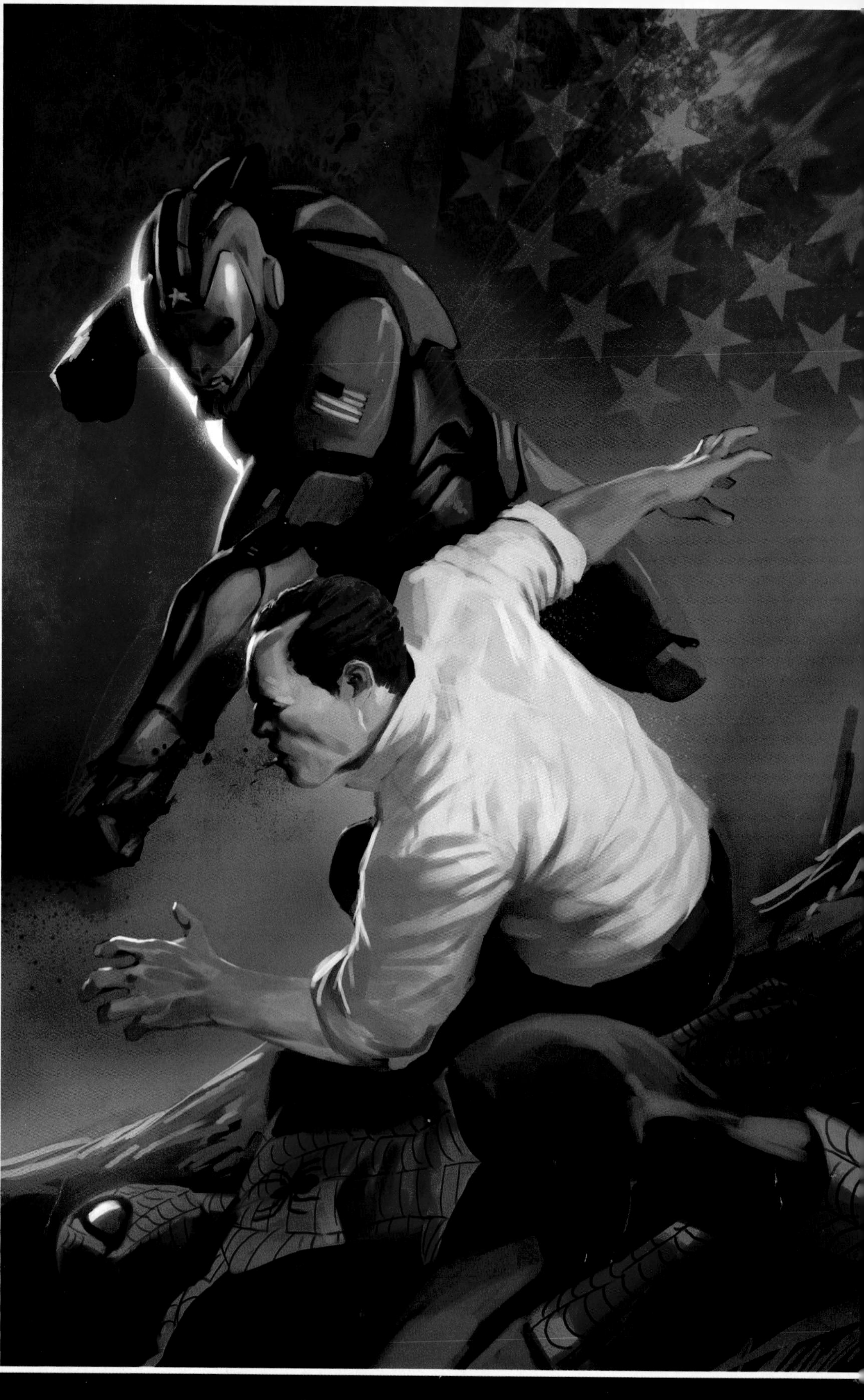

AMAZING SPIDER-MAN PRESENTS: AMERICAN SON #4

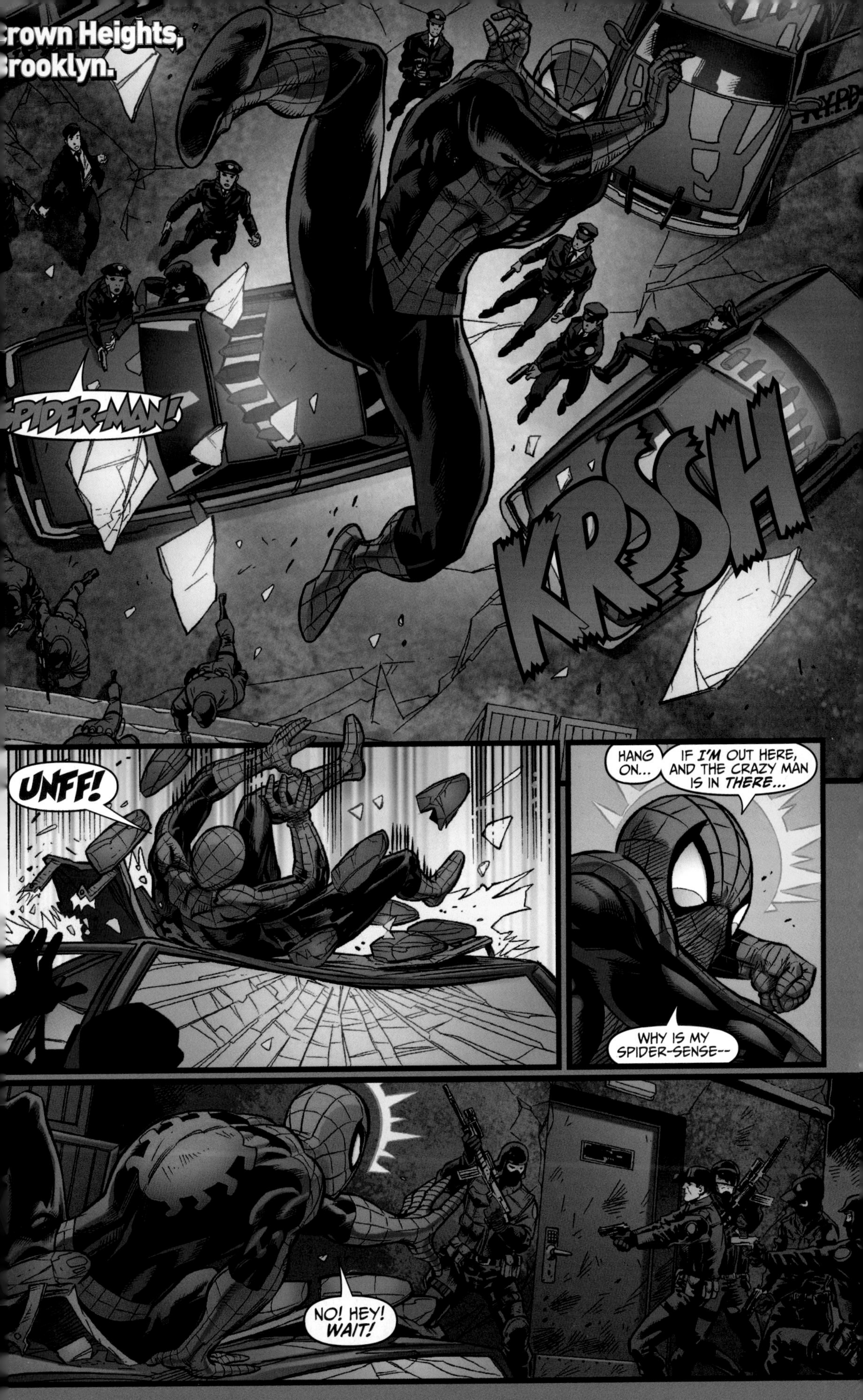
rown Heights,
rooklyn.
N.Y.P.D.
SPIDER-MAN!
KRSH
UNFF!
HANG ON...
IF I'M OUT HERE, AND THE CRAZY MAN IS IN THERE...
WHY IS MY SPIDER-SENSE--
NO! HEY! WAIT!

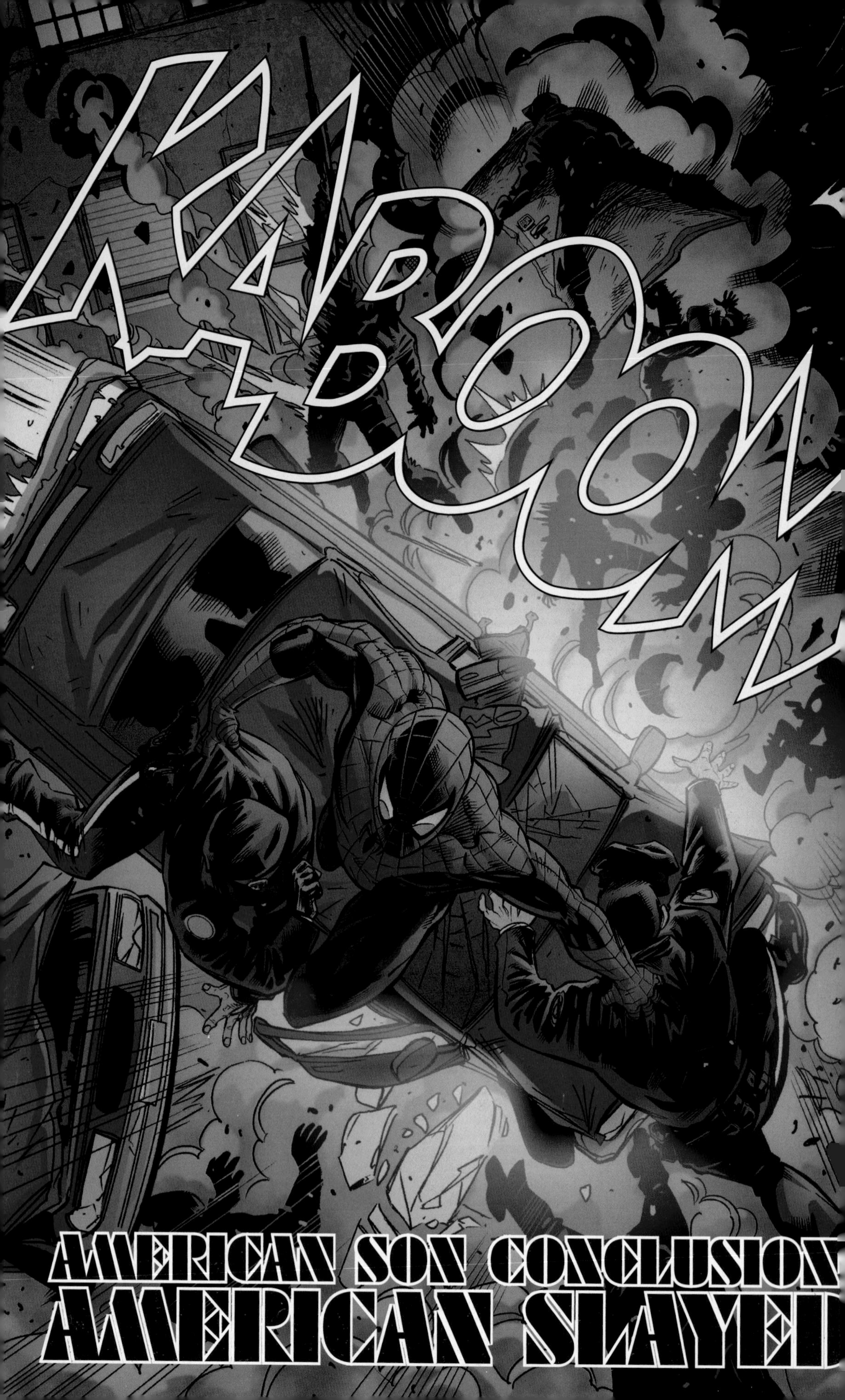
KABOOM
AMERICAN SON CONCLUSION
AMERICAN SLAYED

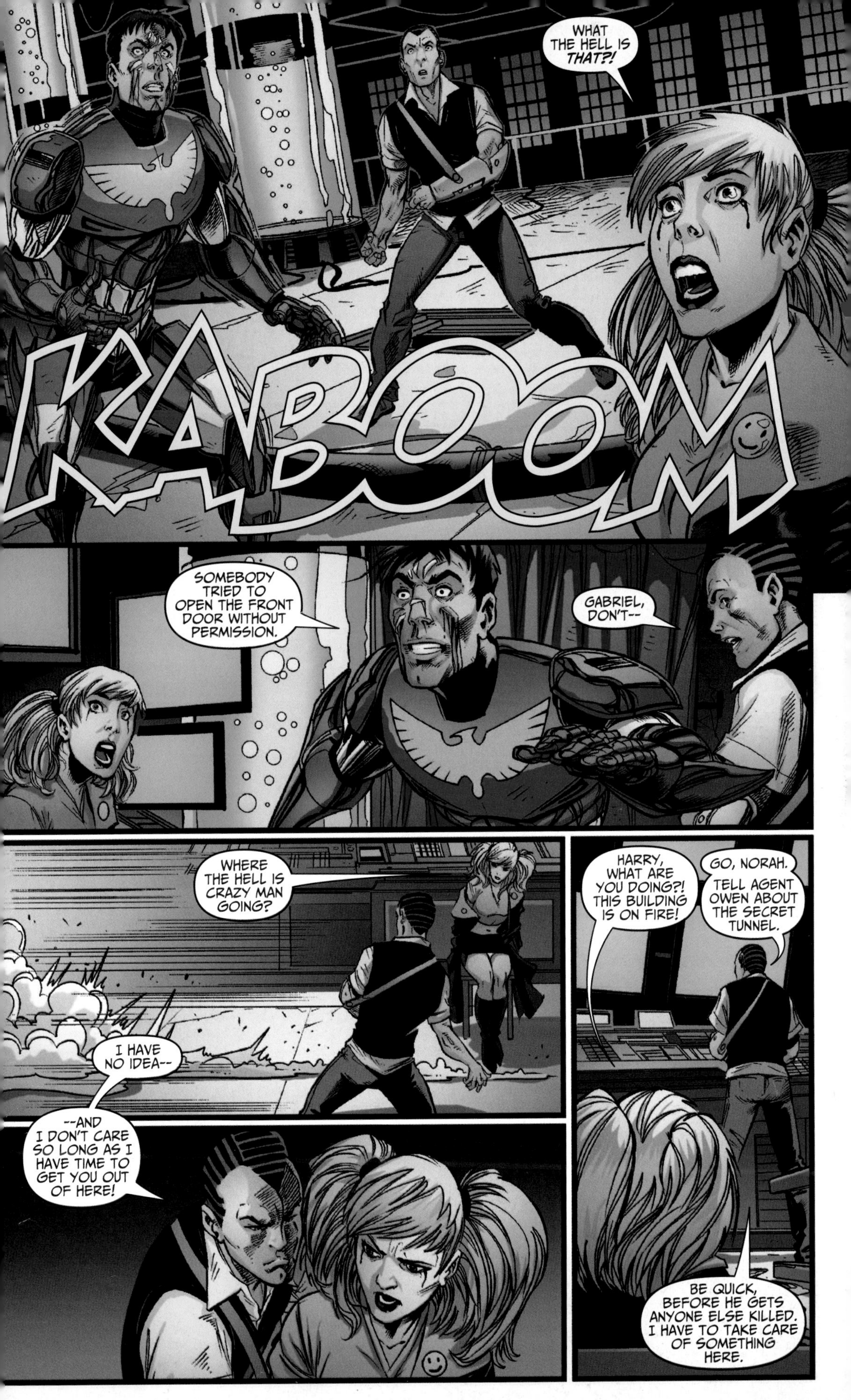
WHAT THE HELL IS *THAT?!*
KABOOM
SOMEBODY TRIED TO OPEN THE FRONT DOOR WITHOUT PERMISSION.
GABRIEL, DON'T--
WHERE THE HELL IS CRAZY MAN GOING?
I HAVE NO IDEA--
--AND I DON'T CARE SO LONG AS I HAVE TIME TO GET YOU OUT OF HERE!
HARRY, WHAT ARE YOU DOING?! THIS BUILDING IS ON FIRE!
GO, NORAH.
TELL AGENT OWEN ABOUT THE SECRET TUNNEL.
BE QUICK, BEFORE HE GETS ANYONE ELSE KILLED. I HAVE TO TAKE CARE OF SOMETHING HERE.

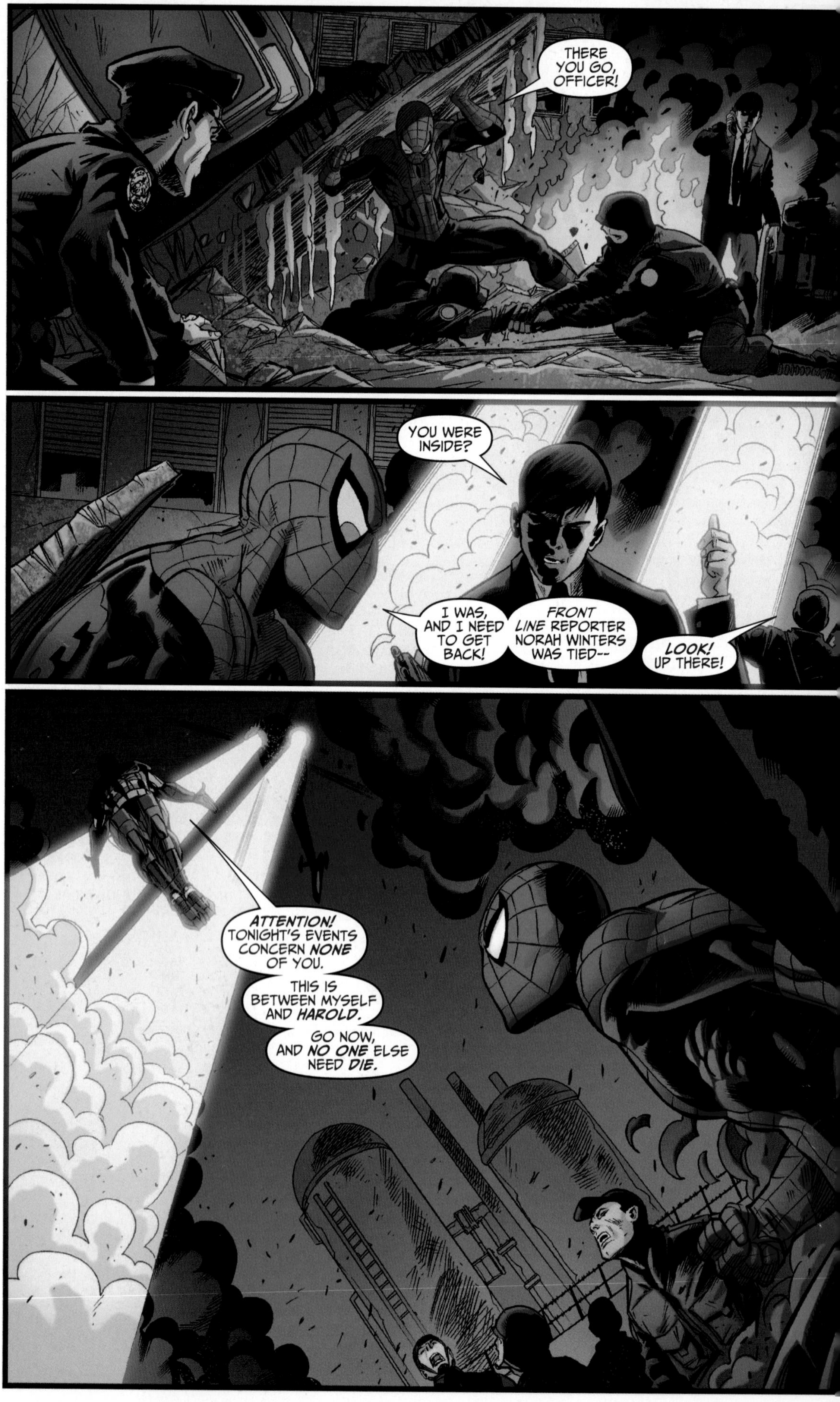

THERE YOU GO, OFFICER!
YOU WERE INSIDE?
I WAS, AND I NEED TO GET BACK!
FRONT LINE REPORTER NORAH WINTERS WAS TIED--
LOOK! UP THERE!
ATTENTION! TONIGHT'S EVENTS CONCERN NONE OF YOU.
THIS IS BETWEEN MYSELF AND HAROLD.
GO NOW, AND NO ONE ELSE NEED DIE.

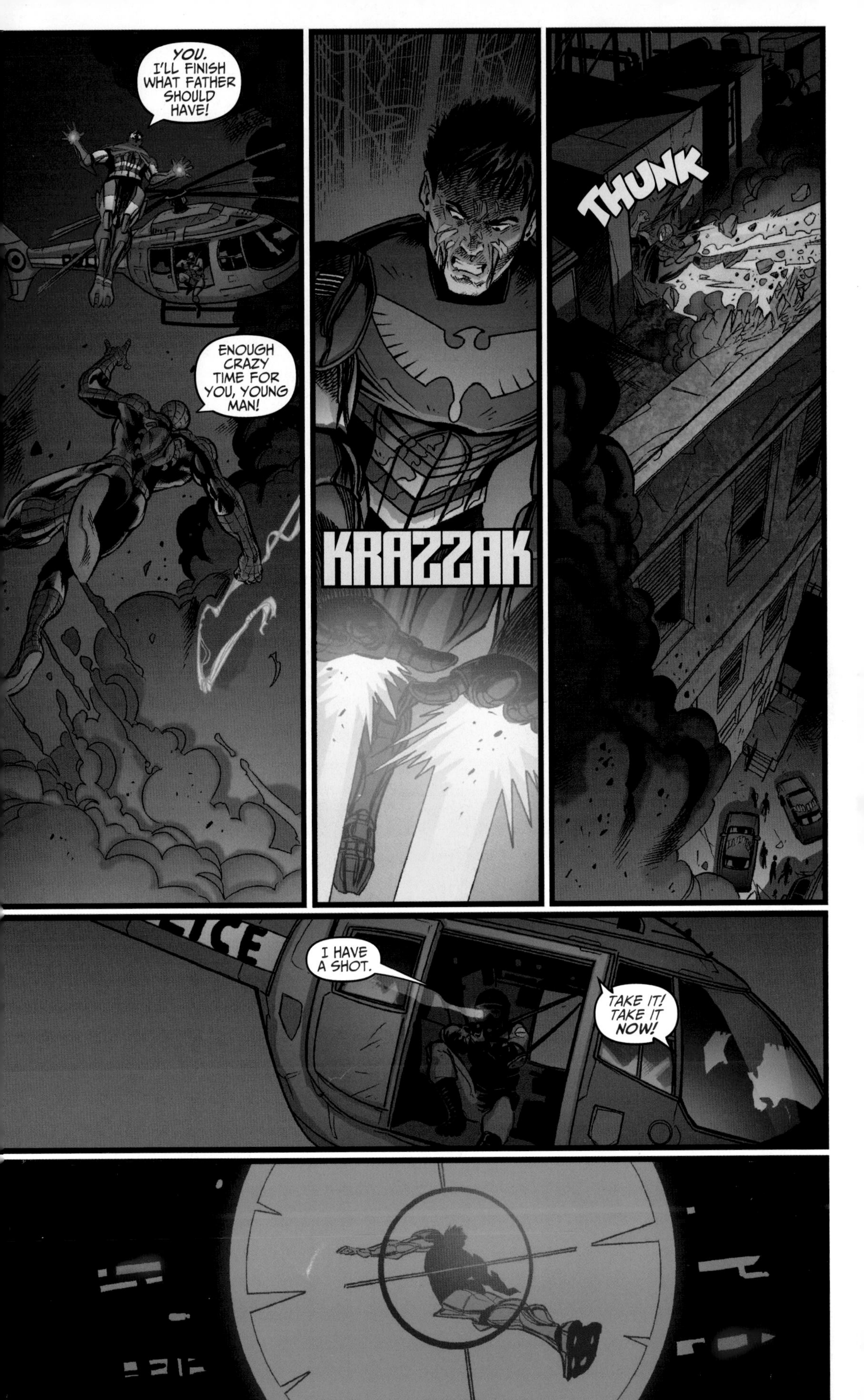
YOU. I'LL FINISH WHAT FATHER SHOULD HAVE!
ENOUGH CRAZY TIME FOR YOU, YOUNG MAN!
KRAZZAK
THUNK
I HAVE A SHOT.
TAKE IT! TAKE IT NOW!

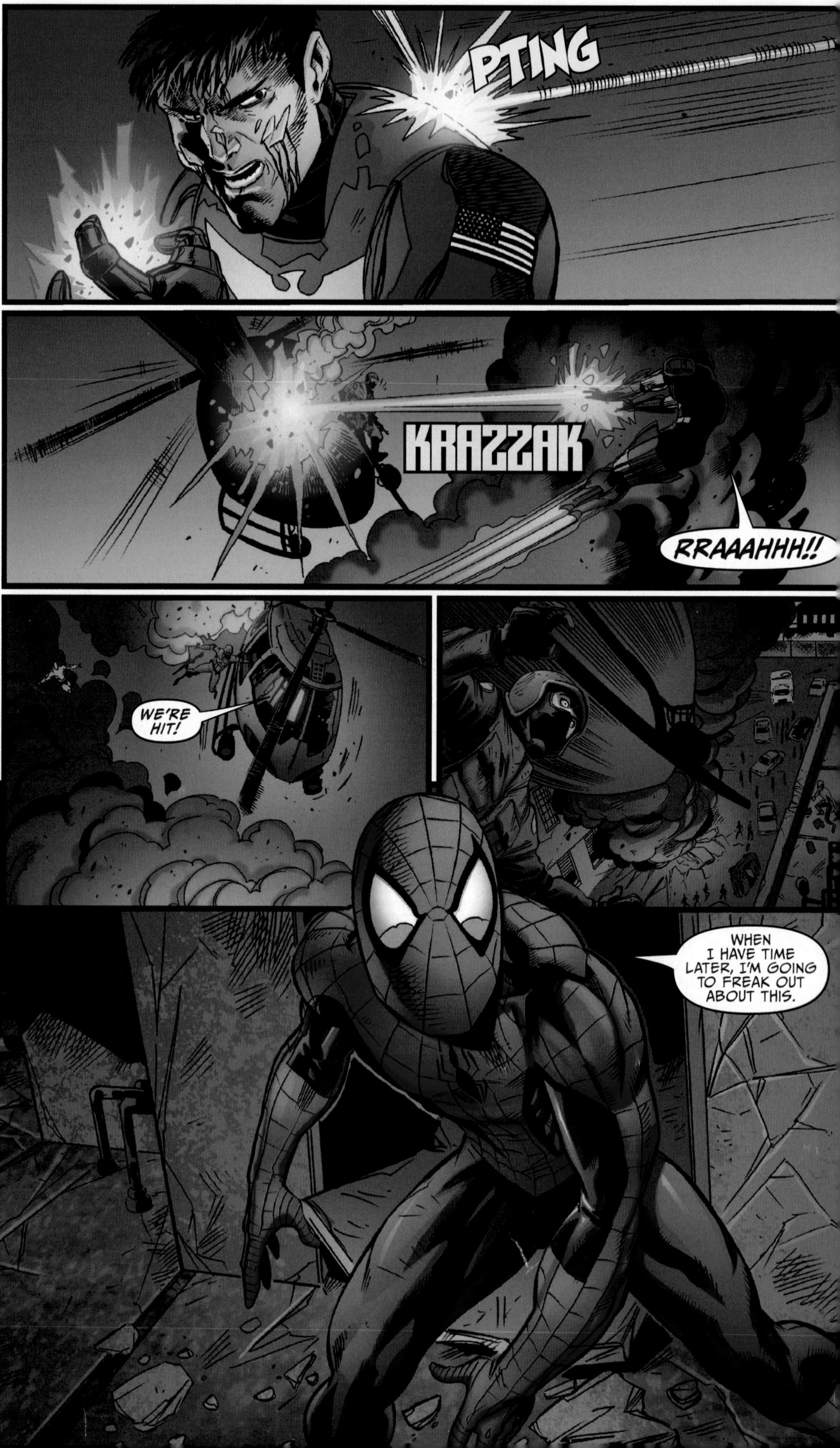
PTING
KRAZZAK
RRAAAHHH!!
WE'RE HIT!
WHEN I HAVE TIME LATER, I'M GOING TO FREAK OUT ABOUT THIS.

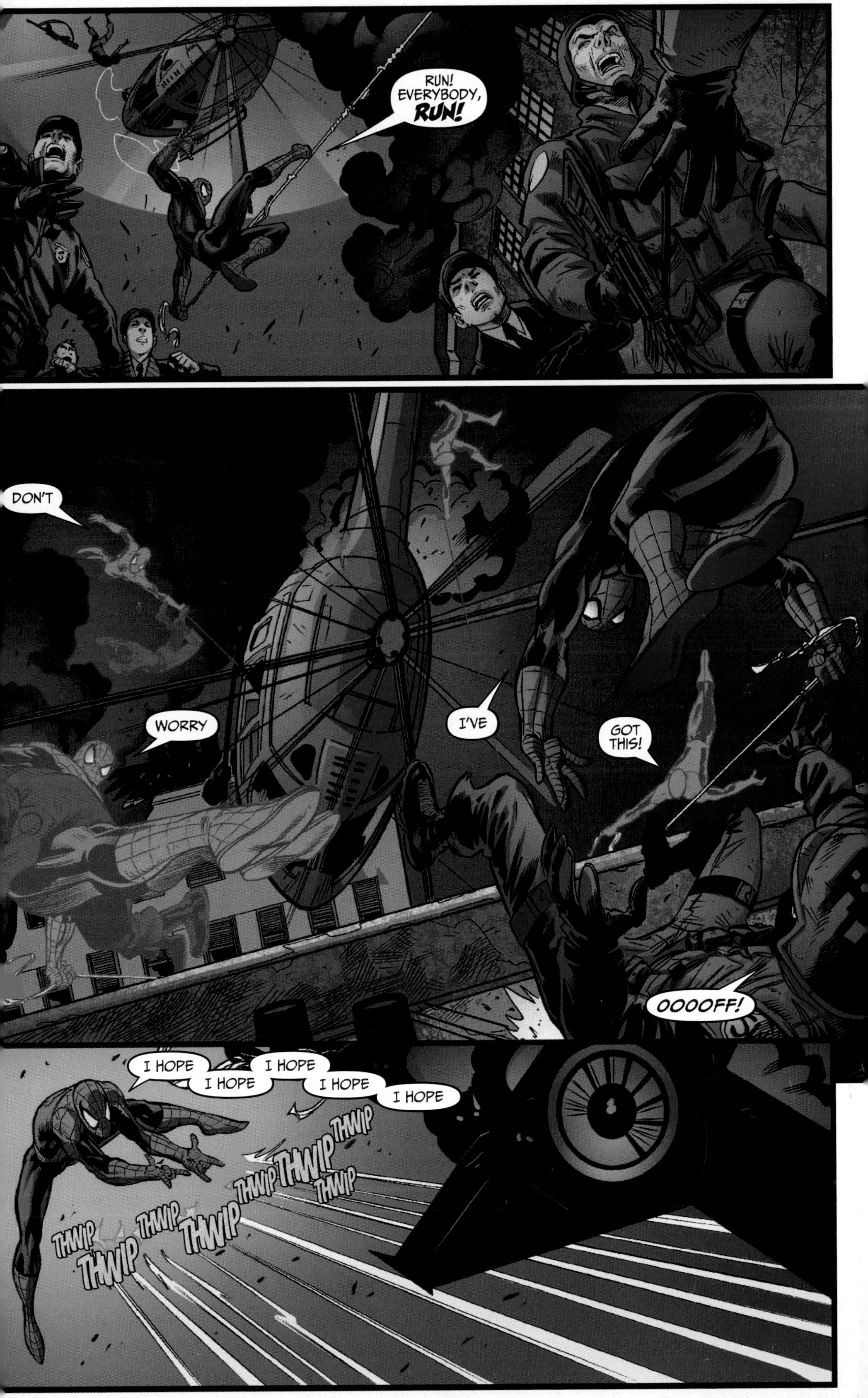
RUN! EVERYBODY, RUN!
DON'T
WORRY
I'VE
GOT THIS!
OOOOFF!
I HOPE
I HOPE
I HOPE
I HOPE
I HOPE
THWIP
THWIP
THWIP
THWIP
THWIP
THWIP
THWIP
THWIP
THWIP

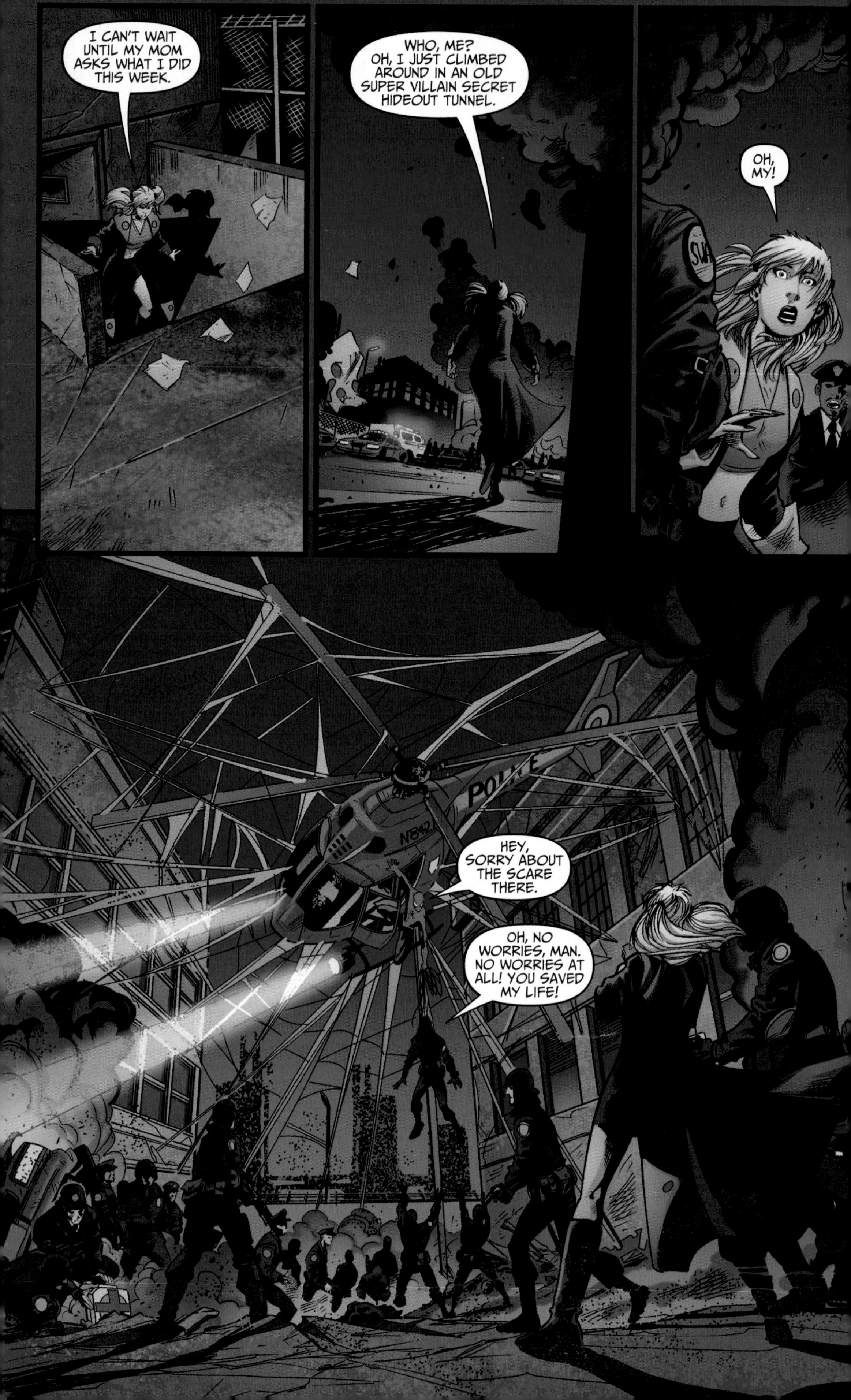
I CAN'T WAIT UNTIL MY MOM ASKS WHAT I DID THIS WEEK.
WHO, ME? OH, I JUST CLIMBED AROUND IN AN OLD SUPER VILLAIN SECRET HIDEOUT TUNNEL.
OH, MY!
POLICE
N842
HEY, SORRY ABOUT THE SCARE THERE.
OH, NO WORRIES, MAN. NO WORRIES AT ALL! YOU SAVED MY LIFE!

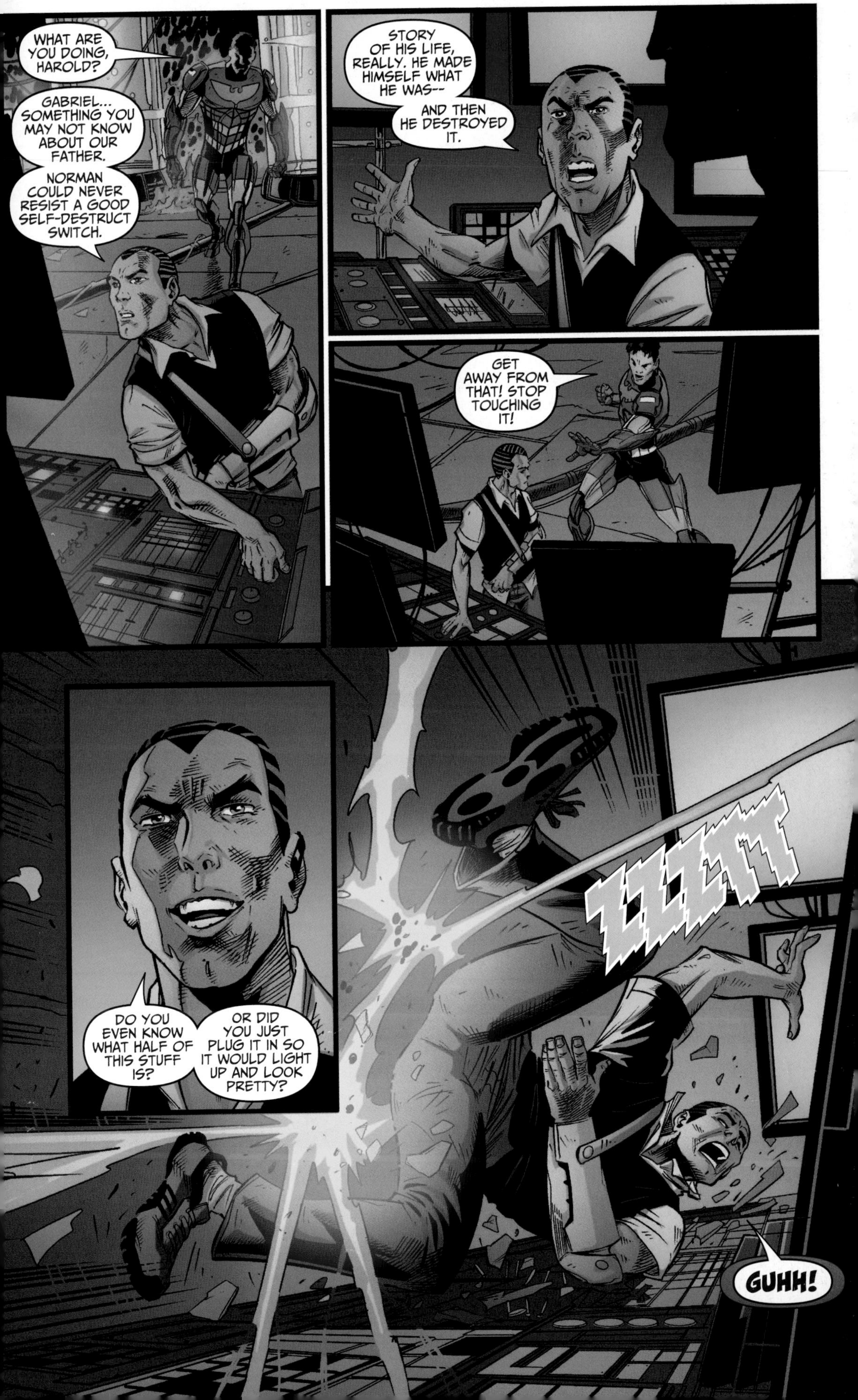
WHAT ARE YOU DOING, HAROLD?
GABRIEL... SOMETHING YOU MAY NOT KNOW ABOUT OUR FATHER.
NORMAN COULD NEVER RESIST A GOOD SELF-DESTRUCT SWITCH.
STORY OF HIS LIFE, REALLY. HE MADE HIMSELF WHAT HE WAS--
AND THEN HE DESTROYED IT.
GET AWAY FROM THAT! STOP TOUCHING IT!
DO YOU EVEN KNOW WHAT HALF OF THIS STUFF IS?
OR DID YOU JUST PLUG IT IN SO IT WOULD LIGHT UP AND LOOK PRETTY?
ZZZTT
GUHH!

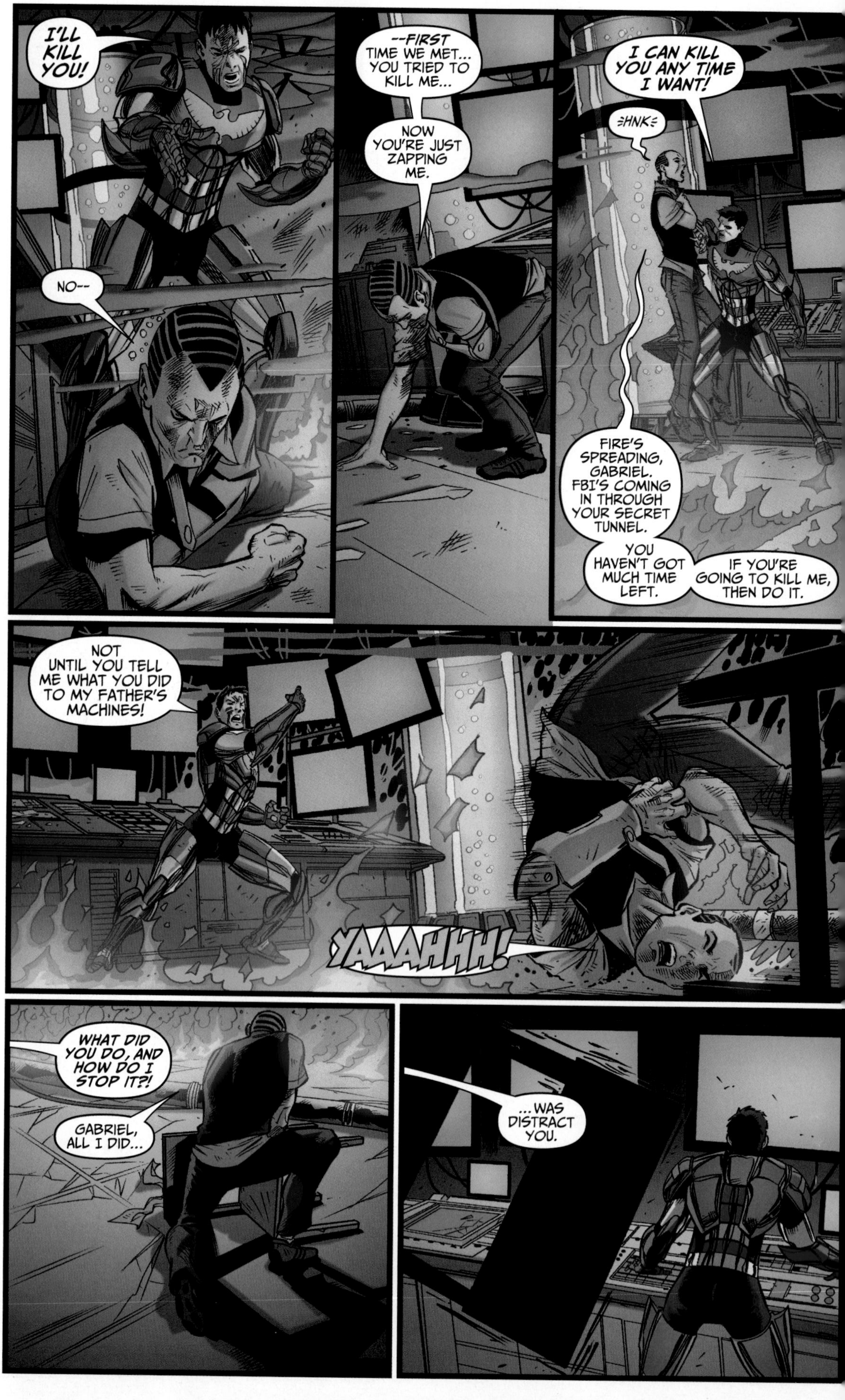
I'LL KILL YOU!
NO--
--FIRST TIME WE MET... YOU TRIED TO KILL ME...
NOW YOU'RE JUST ZAPPING ME.
I CAN KILL YOU ANY TIME I WANT!
HNK
FIRE'S SPREADING, GABRIEL. FBI'S COMING IN THROUGH YOUR SECRET TUNNEL.
YOU HAVEN'T GOT MUCH TIME LEFT.
IF YOU'RE GOING TO KILL ME, THEN DO IT.
NOT UNTIL YOU TELL ME WHAT YOU DID TO MY FATHER'S MACHINES!
YAAAHHH!
WHAT DID YOU DO, AND HOW DO I STOP IT?!
GABRIEL, ALL I DID...
...WAS DISTRACT YOU.

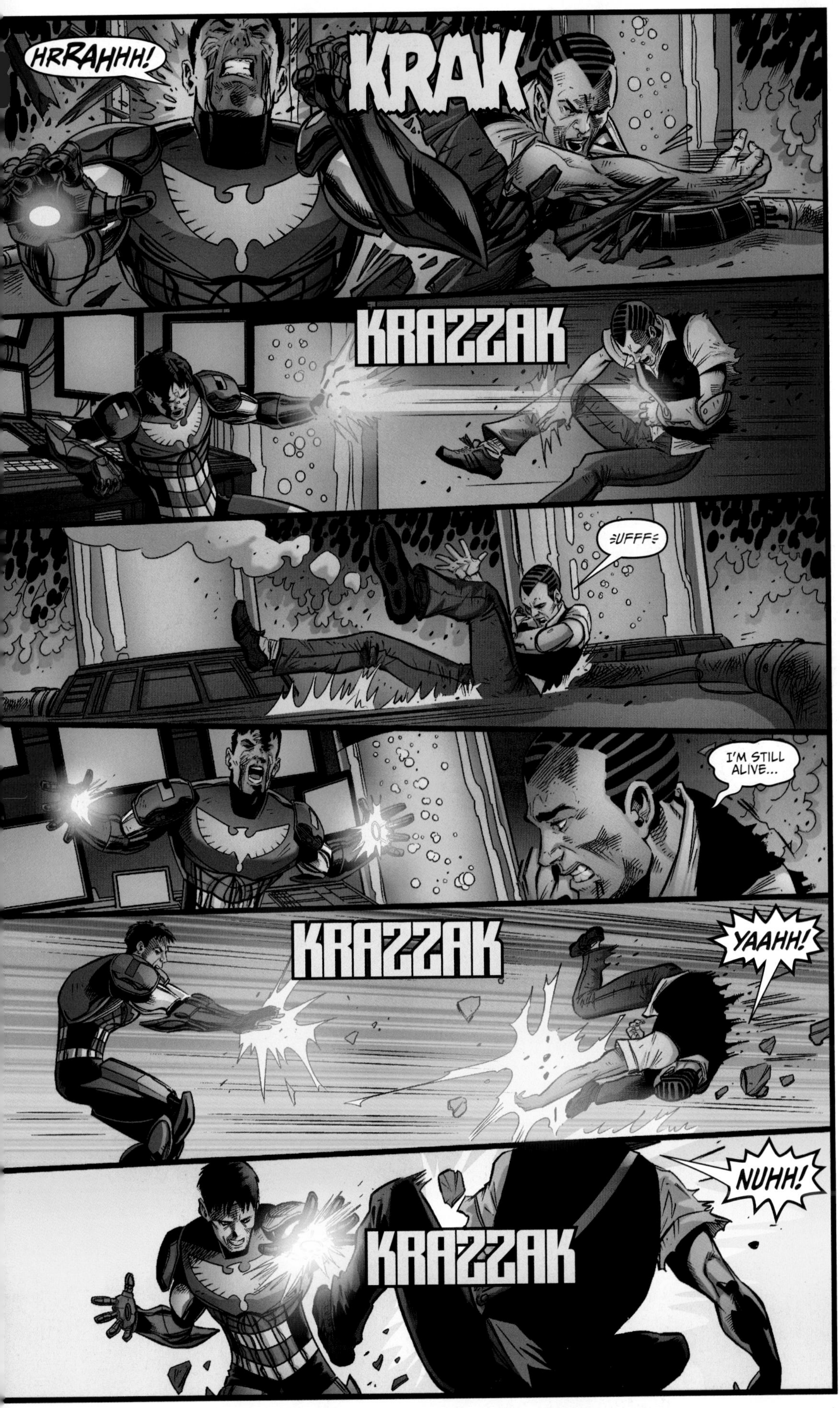
HRRAHHH!
KRAK
KRAZZAK
UFFF
I'M STILL ALIVE...
KRAZZAK
YAAHH!
NUHH!
KRAZZAK

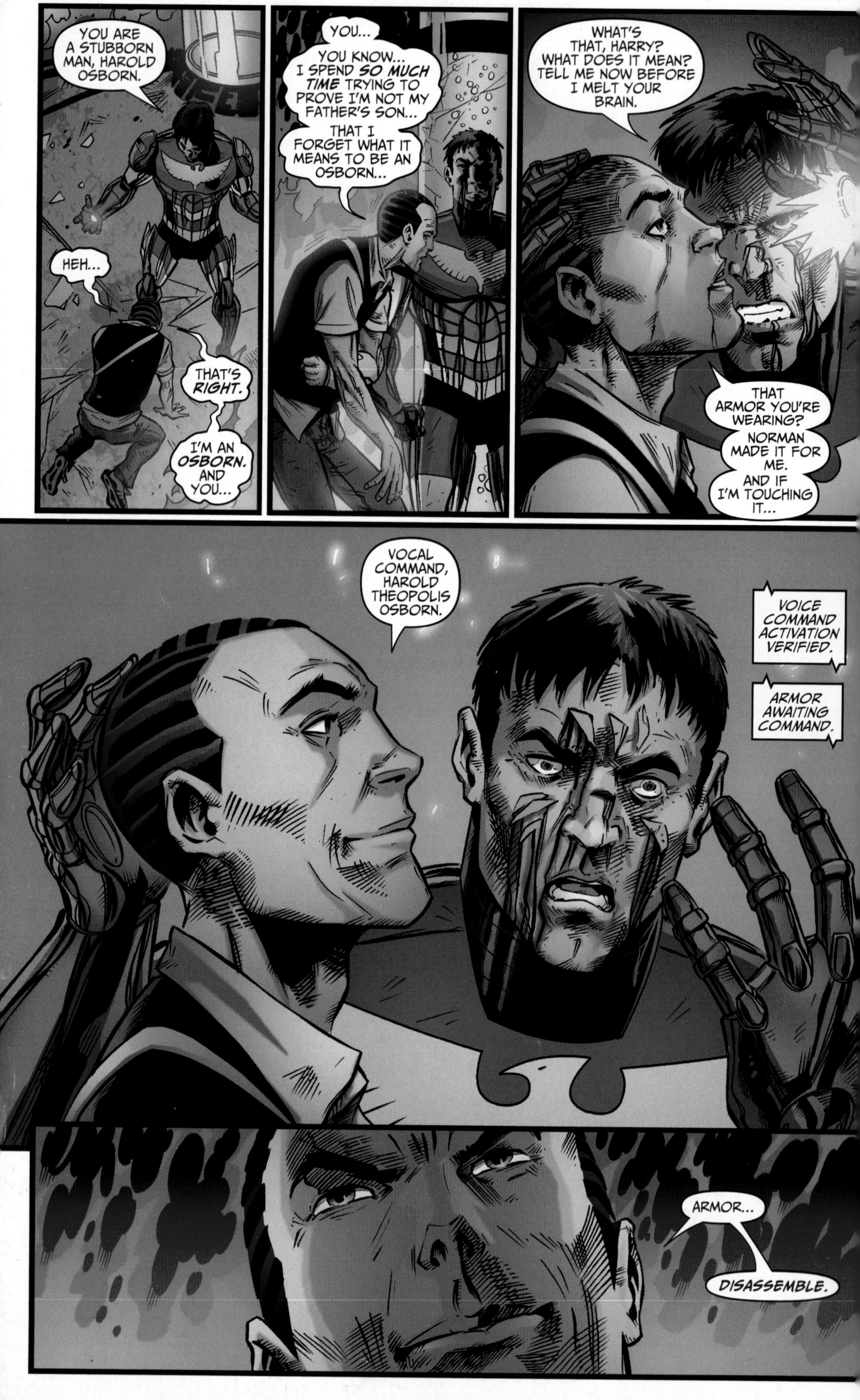

YOU ARE A STUBBORN MAN, HAROLD OSBORN.
HEH...
THAT'S *RIGHT*.
I'M AN *OSBORN*. AND YOU...
YOU...
YOU KNOW... I SPEND ***SO MUCH TIME*** TRYING TO PROVE I'M NOT MY FATHER'S SON...
THAT I FORGET WHAT IT MEANS TO BE AN OSBORN...
WHAT'S THAT, HARRY? WHAT DOES IT MEAN? TELL ME NOW BEFORE I MELT YOUR BRAIN.
THAT ARMOR YOU'RE WEARING?
NORMAN MADE IT FOR ME.
AND IF I'M TOUCHING IT...
VOCAL COMMAND, HAROLD THEOPOLIS OSBORN.
VOICE COMMAND ACTIVATION VERIFIED.
ARMOR AWAITING COMMAND.
ARMOR...
DISASSEMBLE.

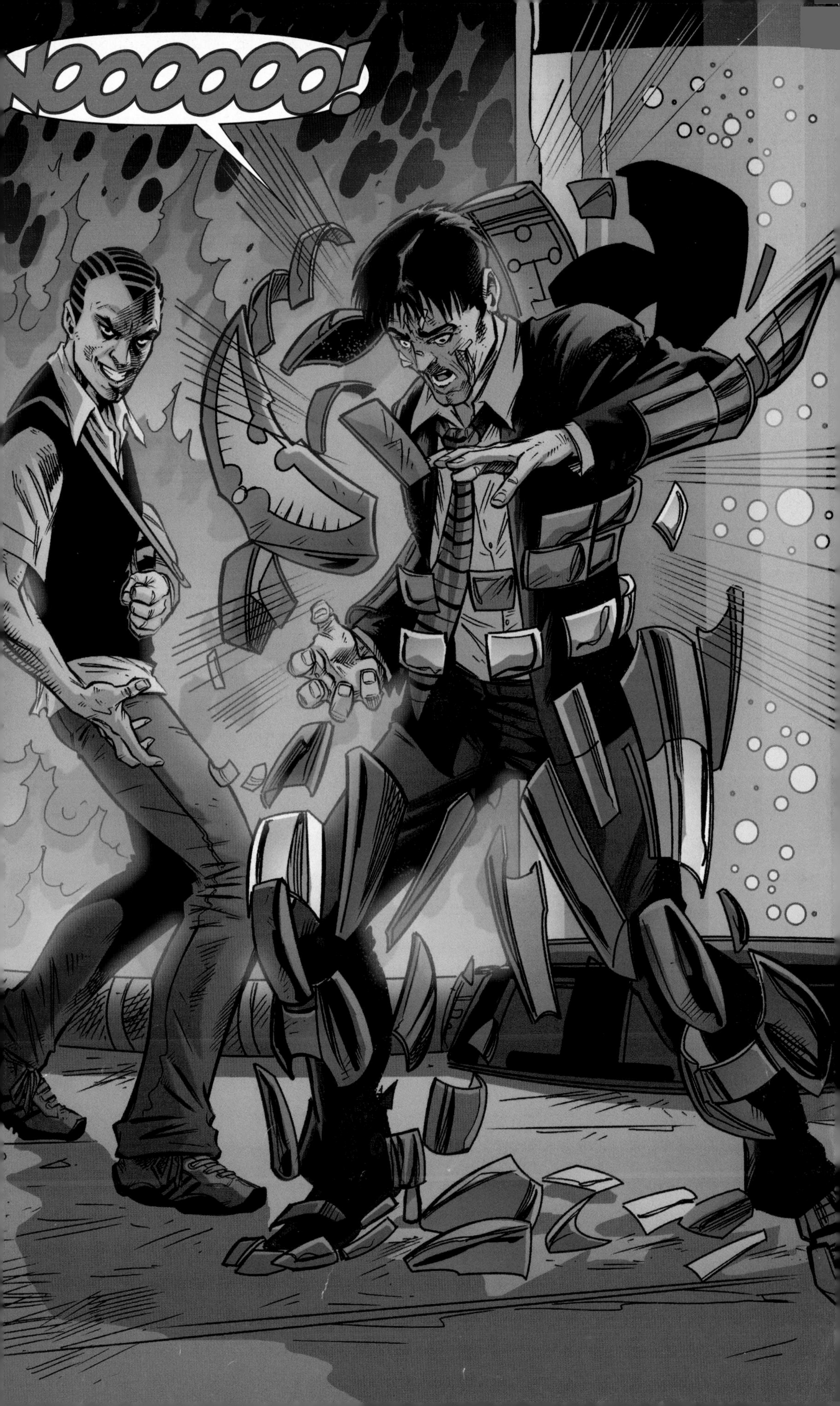
NOOOOOOO!

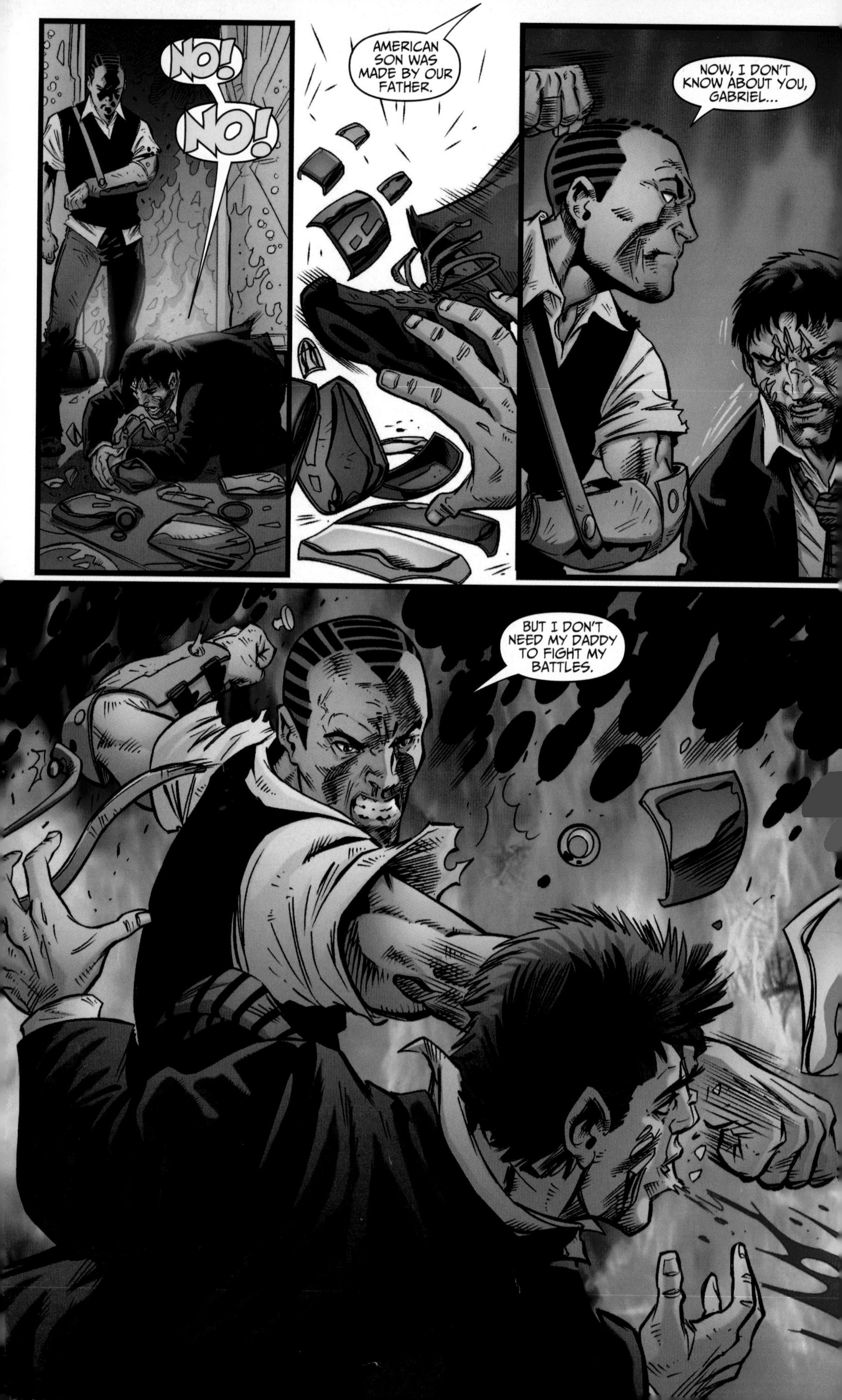
NO! NO!
AMERICAN SON WAS MADE BY OUR FATHER.
NOW, I DON'T KNOW ABOUT YOU, GABRIEL...
BUT I DON'T NEED MY DADDY TO FIGHT MY BATTLES.

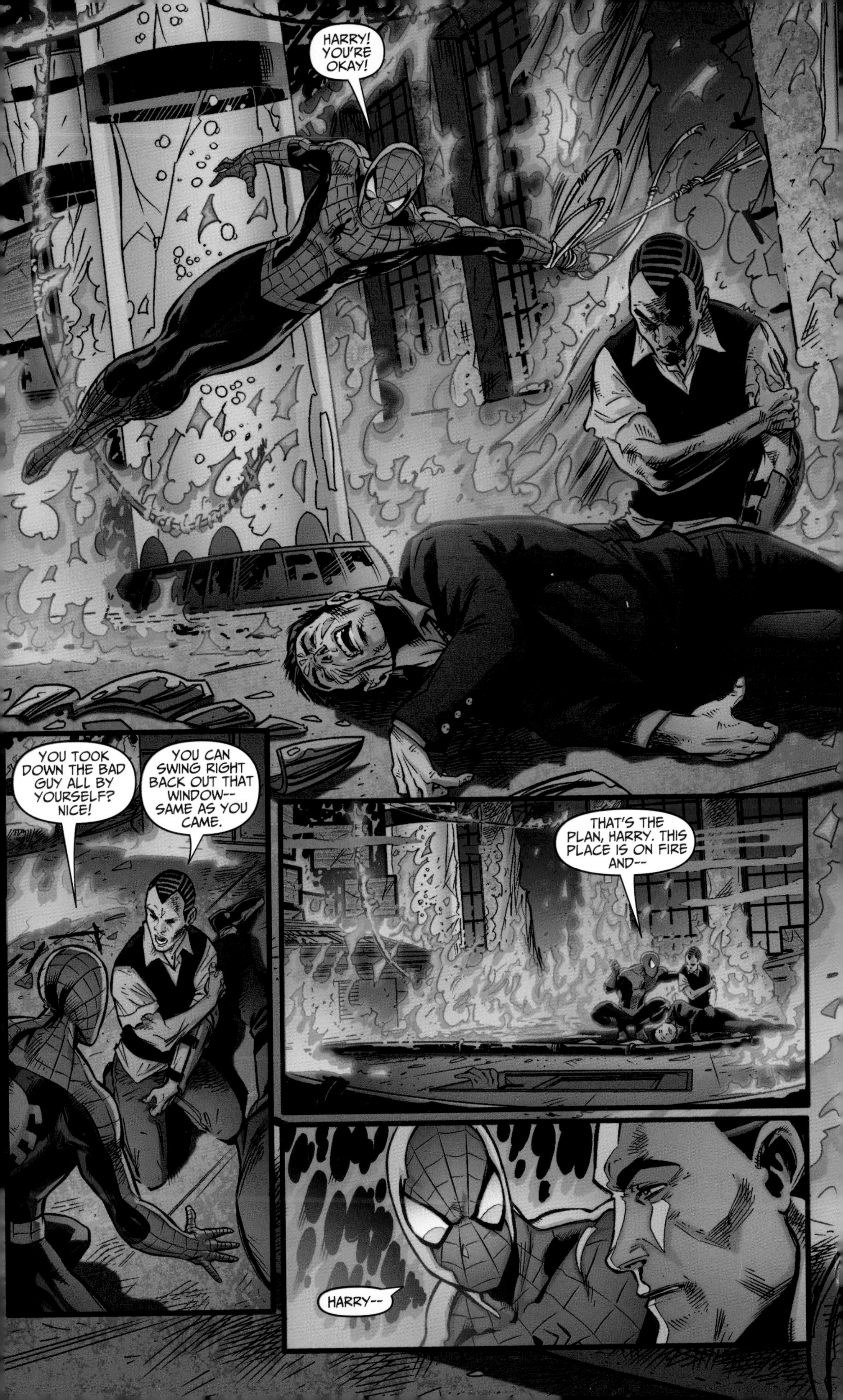
HARRY! YOU'RE OKAY!
YOU TOOK DOWN THE BAD GUY ALL BY YOURSELF? NICE!
YOU CAN SWING RIGHT BACK OUT THAT WINDOW-- SAME AS YOU CAME.
THAT'S THE PLAN, HARRY. THIS PLACE IS ON FIRE AND--
HARRY--

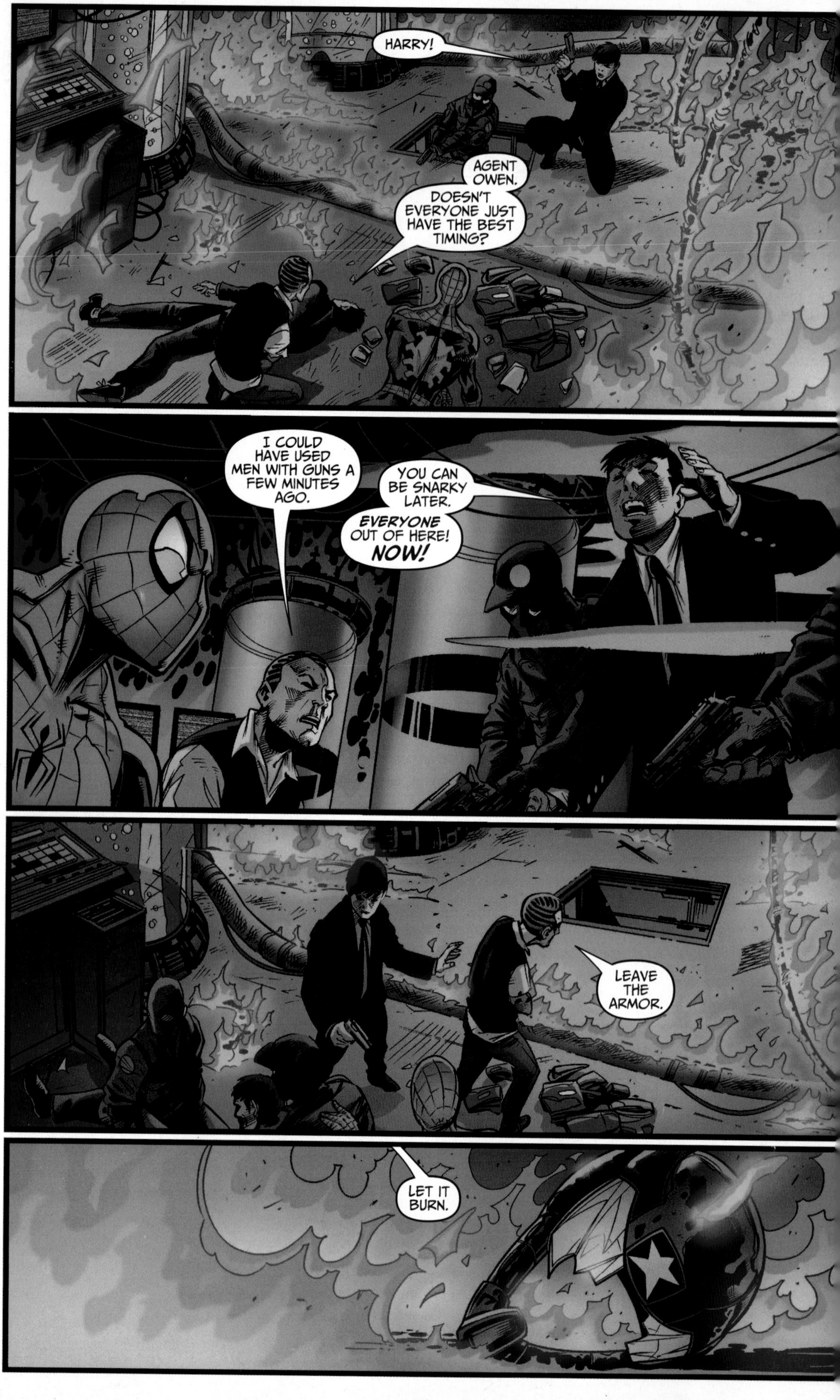
HARRY!
AGENT OWEN.
DOESN'T EVERYONE JUST HAVE THE BEST TIMING?
I COULD HAVE USED MEN WITH GUNS A FEW MINUTES AGO.
YOU CAN BE SNARKY LATER.
EVERYONE OUT OF HERE! NOW!
LEAVE THE ARMOR.
LET IT BURN.

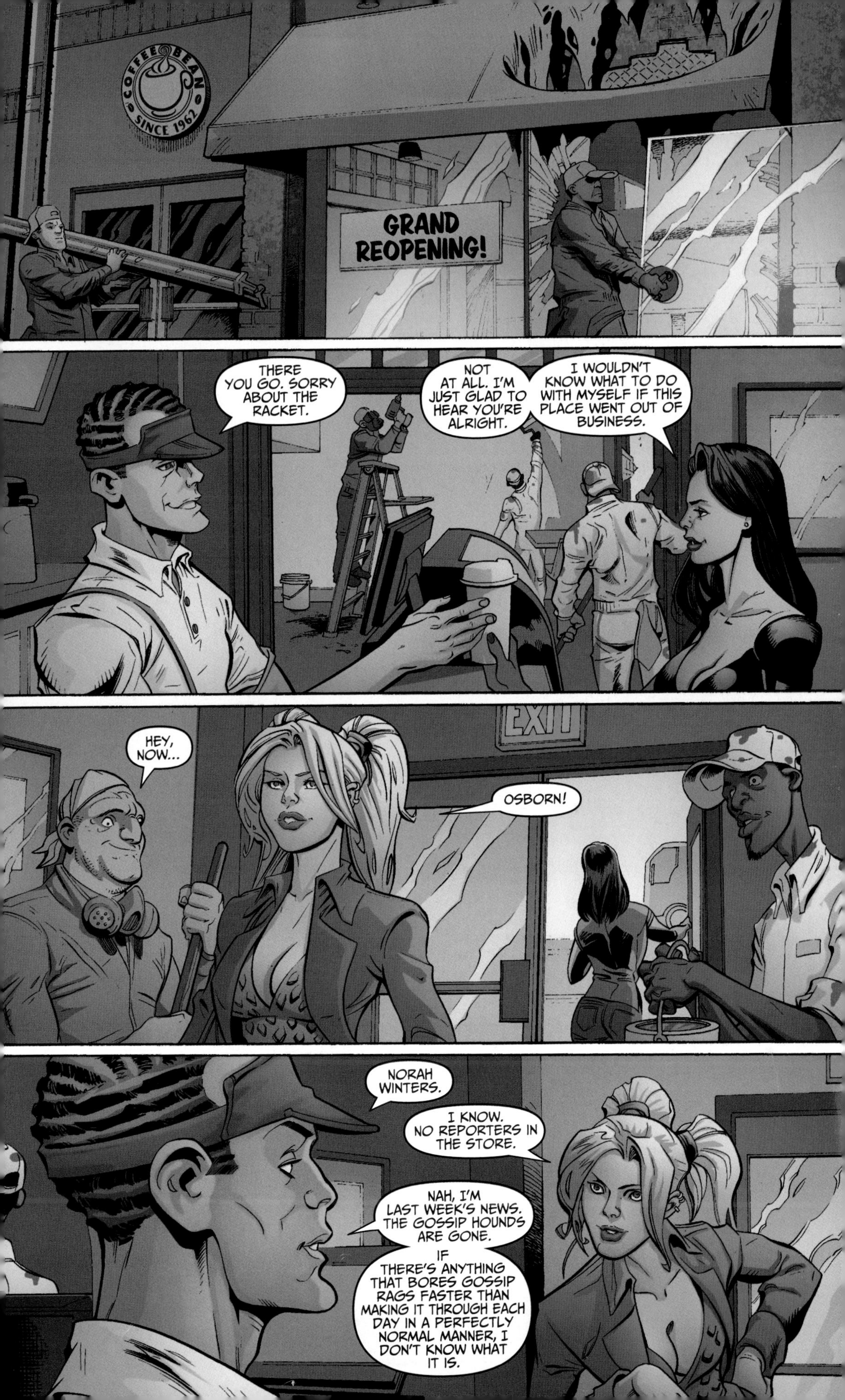

COFFEE BEAN SINCE 1962
GRAND REOPENING!
THERE YOU GO. SORRY ABOUT THE RACKET.
NOT AT ALL. I'M JUST GLAD TO HEAR YOU'RE ALRIGHT.
I WOULDN'T KNOW WHAT TO DO WITH MYSELF IF THIS PLACE WENT OUT OF BUSINESS.
HEY, NOW...
EXIT
OSBORN!
NORAH WINTERS.
I KNOW. NO REPORTERS IN THE STORE.
NAH, I'M LAST WEEK'S NEWS. THE GOSSIP HOUNDS ARE GONE.
IF THERE'S ANYTHING THAT BORES GOSSIP RAGS FASTER THAN MAKING IT THROUGH EACH DAY IN A PERFECTLY NORMAL MANNER, I DON'T KNOW WHAT IT IS.

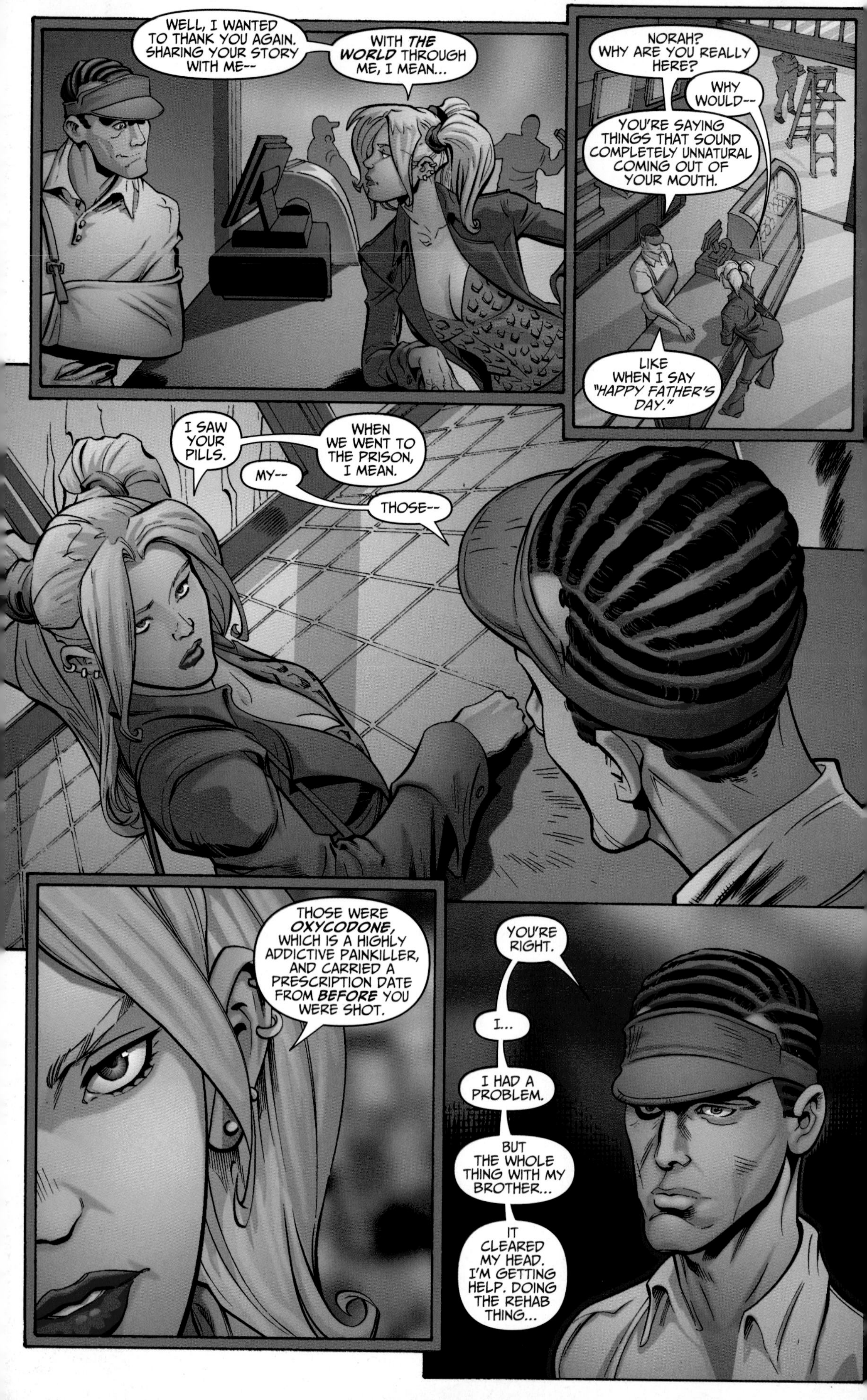
WELL, I WANTED TO THANK YOU AGAIN. SHARING YOUR STORY WITH ME--
WITH *THE WORLD* THROUGH ME, I MEAN...
NORAH? WHY ARE YOU REALLY HERE?
WHY WOULD--
YOU'RE SAYING THINGS THAT SOUND COMPLETELY UNNATURAL COMING OUT OF YOUR MOUTH.
LIKE WHEN I SAY *"HAPPY FATHER'S DAY."*
I SAW YOUR PILLS.
WHEN WE WENT TO THE PRISON, I MEAN.
MY--
THOSE--
THOSE WERE ***OXYCODONE,*** WHICH IS A HIGHLY ADDICTIVE PAINKILLER, AND CARRIED A PRESCRIPTION DATE FROM ***BEFORE*** YOU WERE SHOT.
YOU'RE RIGHT.
I...
I HAD A PROBLEM.
BUT THE WHOLE THING WITH MY BROTHER...
IT CLEARED MY HEAD. I'M GETTING HELP. DOING THE REHAB THING...

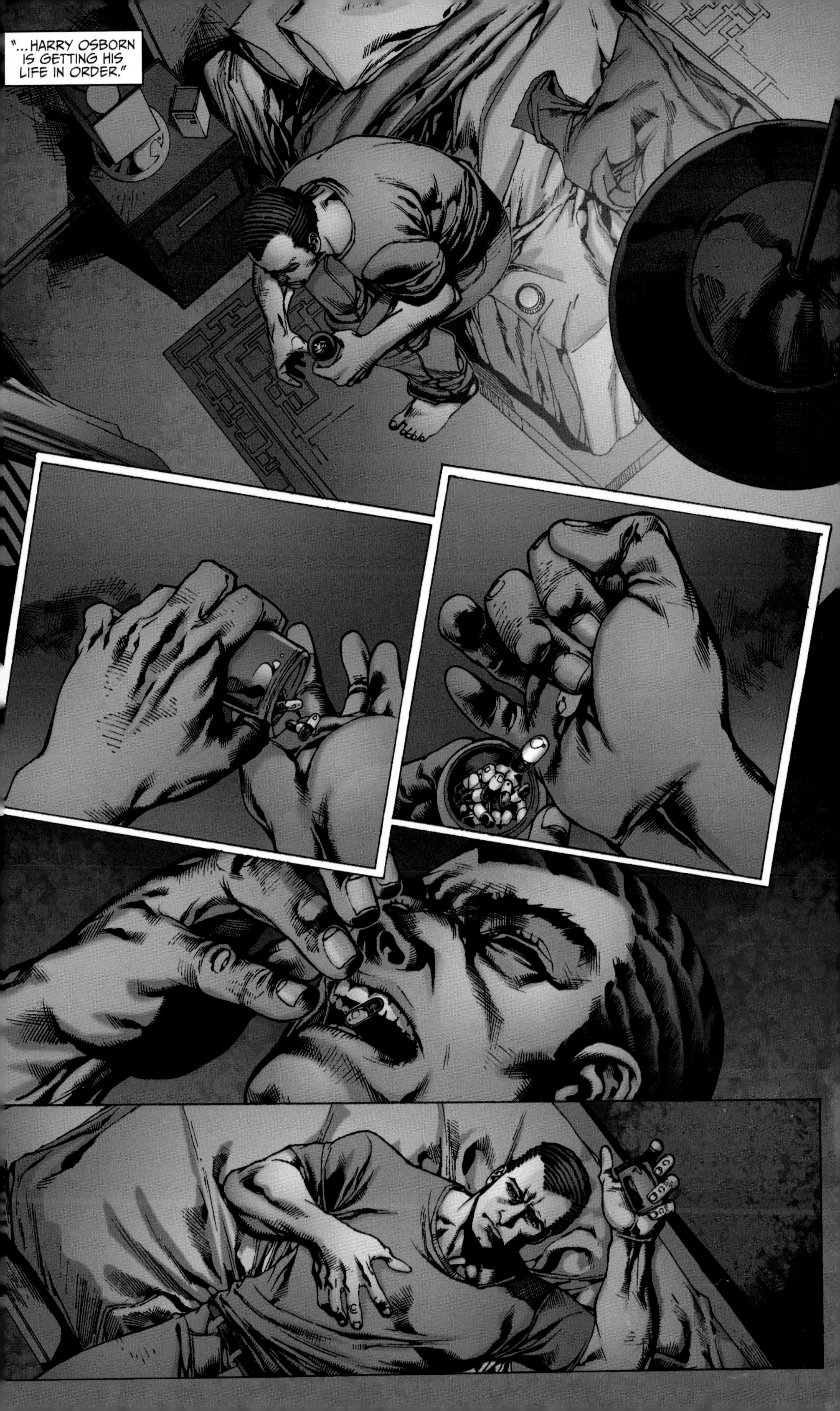
"...HARRY OSBORN IS GETTING HIS LIFE IN ORDER."

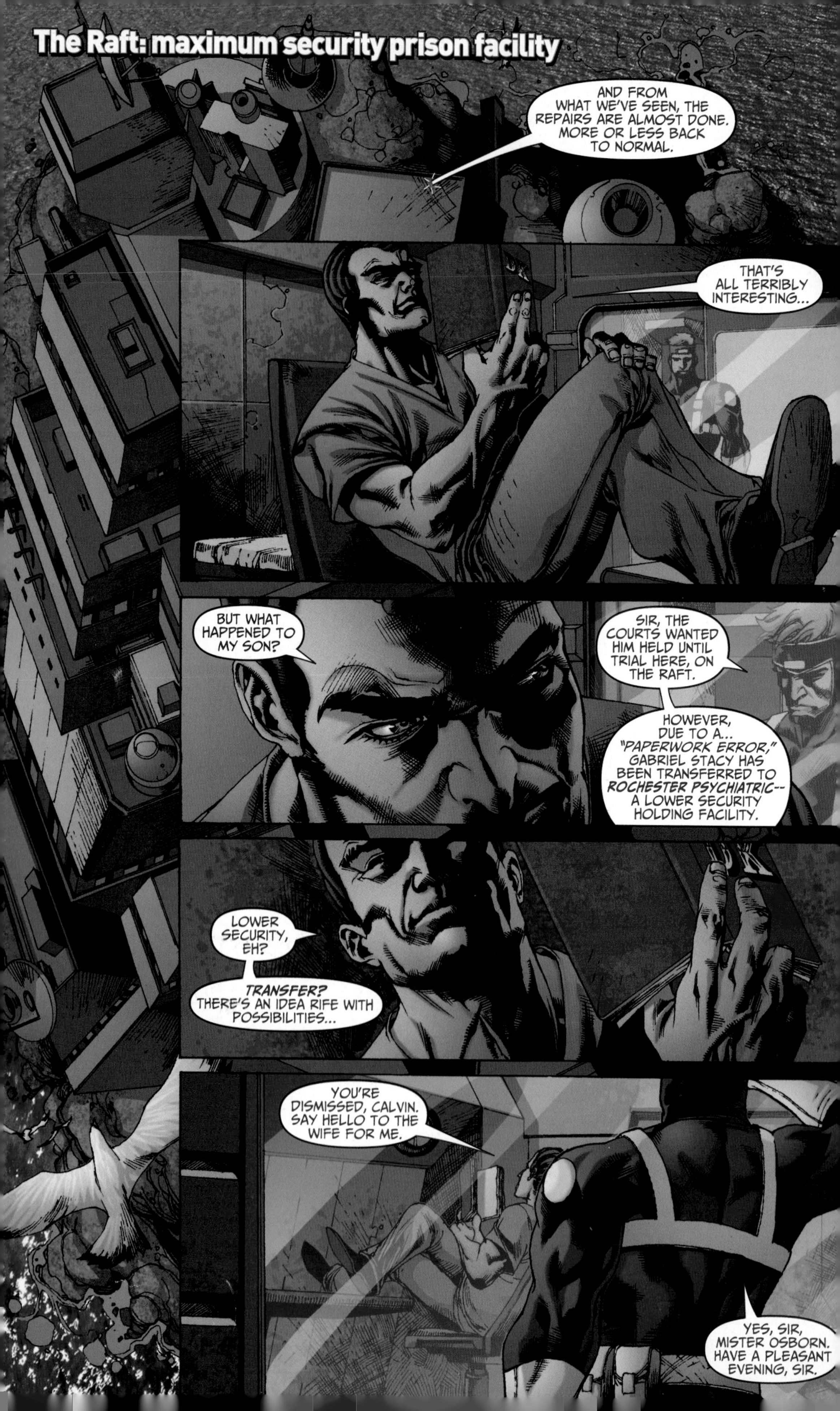
The Raft: maximum security prison facility
AND FROM WHAT WE'VE SEEN, THE REPAIRS ARE ALMOST DONE. MORE OR LESS BACK TO NORMAL.
THAT'S ALL TERRIBLY INTERESTING...
BUT WHAT HAPPENED TO MY SON?
SIR, THE COURTS WANTED HIM HELD UNTIL TRIAL HERE, ON THE RAFT.
HOWEVER, DUE TO A... "PAPERWORK ERROR," GABRIEL STACY HAS BEEN TRANSFERRED TO ROCHESTER PSYCHIATRIC-- A LOWER SECURITY HOLDING FACILITY.
LOWER SECURITY, EH?
TRANSFER? THERE'S AN IDEA RIFE WITH POSSIBILITIES...
YOU'RE DISMISSED, CALVIN. SAY HELLO TO THE WIFE FOR ME.
YES, SIR, MISTER OSBORN. HAVE A PLEASANT EVENING, SIR.

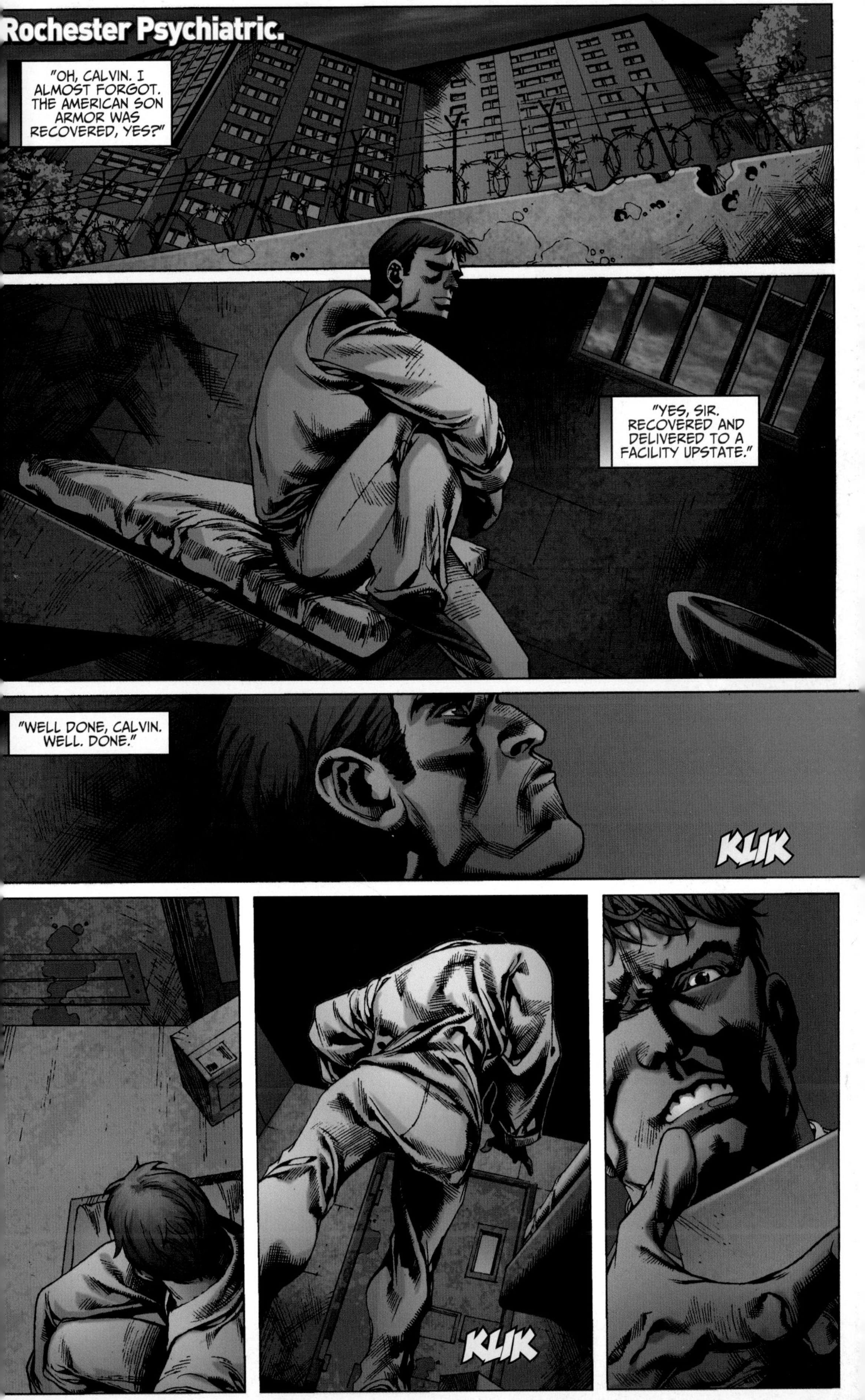
Rochester Psychiatric.
"OH, CALVIN. I ALMOST FORGOT. THE AMERICAN SON ARMOR WAS RECOVERED, YES?"
"YES, SIR. RECOVERED AND DELIVERED TO A FACILITY UPSTATE."
"WELL DONE, CALVIN. WELL. DONE."
KLIK
KLIK

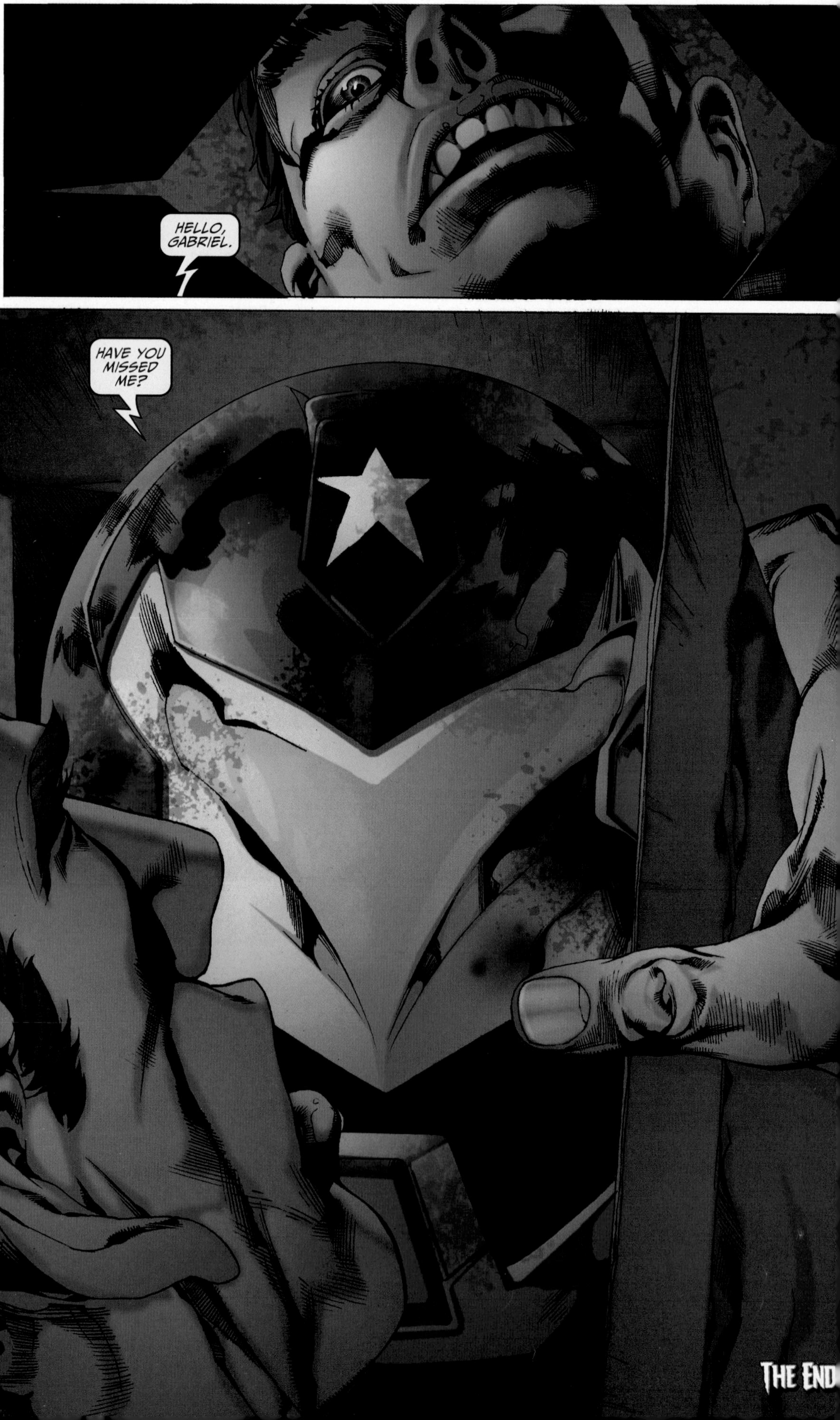
HELLO, GABRIEL.
HAVE YOU MISSED ME?
THE END

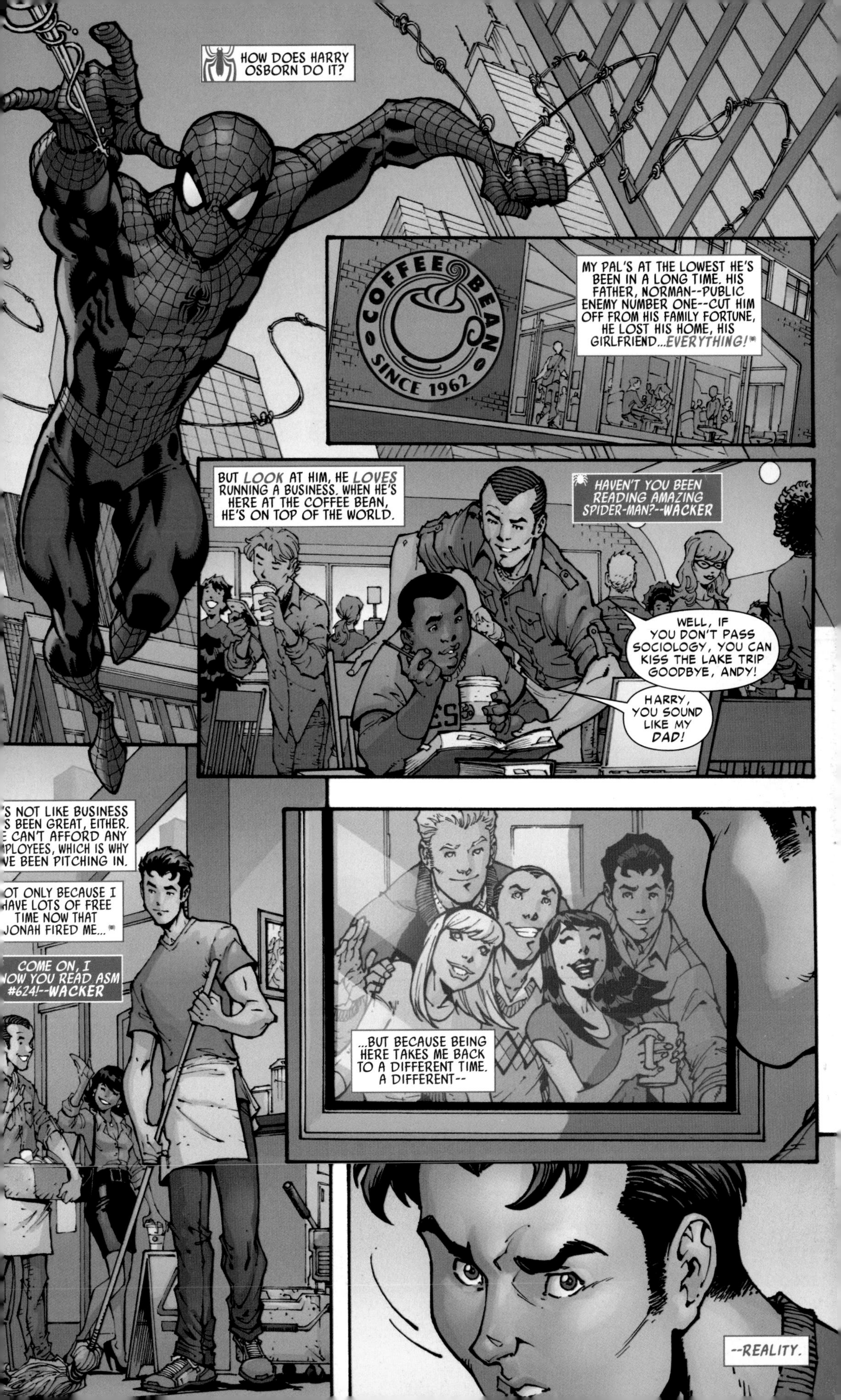
HOW DOES HARRY OSBORN DO IT?
COFFEE BEAN SINCE 1962
MY PAL'S AT THE LOWEST HE'S BEEN IN A LONG TIME. HIS FATHER, NORMAN--PUBLIC ENEMY NUMBER ONE--CUT HIM OFF FROM HIS FAMILY FORTUNE, HE LOST HIS HOME, HIS GIRLFRIEND...EVERYTHING!*
BUT LOOK AT HIM, HE LOVES RUNNING A BUSINESS. WHEN HE'S HERE AT THE COFFEE BEAN, HE'S ON TOP OF THE WORLD.
*HAVEN'T YOU BEEN READING AMAZING SPIDER-MAN?--WACKER
WELL, IF YOU DON'T PASS SOCIOLOGY, YOU CAN KISS THE LAKE TRIP GOODBYE, ANDY!
HARRY, YOU SOUND LIKE MY DAD!
'S NOT LIKE BUSINESS S BEEN GREAT, EITHER. CAN'T AFFORD ANY PLOYEES, WHICH IS WHY VE BEEN PITCHING IN.
OT ONLY BECAUSE I HAVE LOTS OF FREE TIME NOW THAT JONAH FIRED ME...*
*COME ON, I NOW YOU READ ASM #624!--WACKER
...BUT BECAUSE BEING HERE TAKES ME BACK TO A DIFFERENT TIME. A DIFFERENT--
--REALITY.

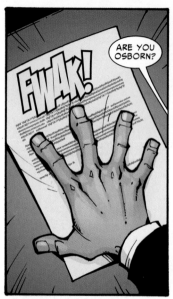

ARE YOU OSBORN?

FWAK!

ME? UH...*NO*, UMM...HE HAD TO STEP OUT.

CAN I HELP YOU?

I'M FROM THE BLACK GOLD COFFEE COMPANY. HE HASN'T PAID HIS BILL IN THREE MONTHS.

TERRIBLE MOTORCYCLE ACCIDENT. NOT SURE IF HE'LL *EVER* COME BACK...

WELL, WHEN YOU SEE "*HIM*," TELL HIM HIS FREE RIDE IS *OVER*...

...WE'RE CUTTING OFF HIS CREDIT.

WHOA, WHOA, WHOA, HANG ON! PROBABLY JUST AN OVERSIGHT, THAT'S ALL.

IF MR. OSBORN *WERE* HERE--AND HE'S *NOT*--HE'D SAY WE CAN'T RUN A COFFEE SHOP WITHOUT *COFFEE*.

SO, PLEASE, TAKE WHAT'S HERE AND I'LL--I MEAN *HE'LL*--

--GET YOU THE REST AS SOON AS HE CAN, ALL RIGHT?

WHATEVER. I'LL BE BACK.

TELL "*OSBORN*" HE CAN'T HIDE FOREVER. EVEN IF THE NEW PLACE ACROSS THE STREET PUTS YOU OUT OF BUSINESS, I'LL FIND YOU...

...AND I *WILL* GET THE REST OF MY MONEY!

"*NEW PLACE?*"

OH.

BARGAIN DONUTS

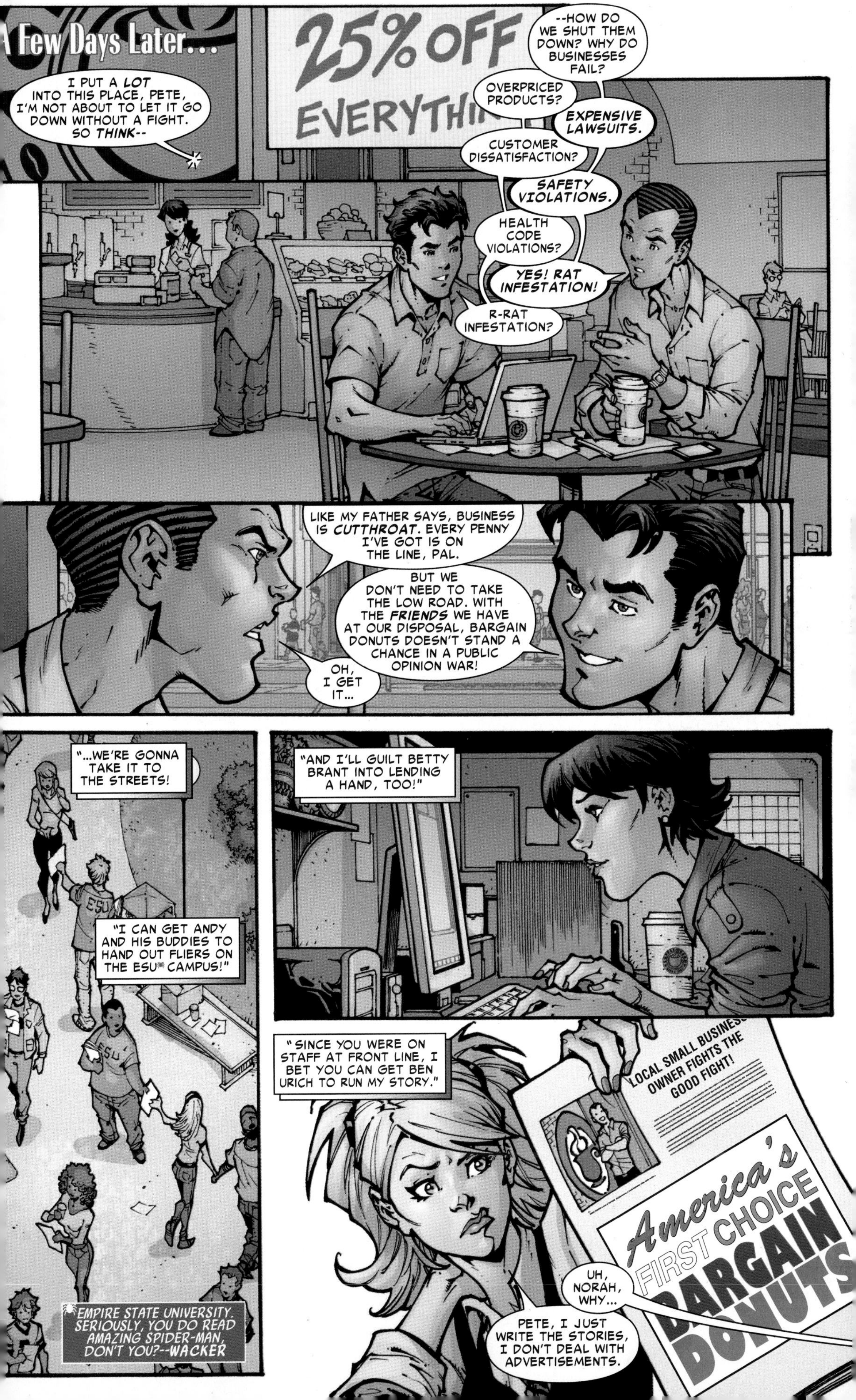
A Few Days Later...
I PUT A LOT INTO THIS PLACE, PETE, I'M NOT ABOUT TO LET IT GO DOWN WITHOUT A FIGHT. SO THINK--
25% OFF EVERYTHI
--HOW DO WE SHUT THEM DOWN? WHY DO BUSINESSES FAIL?
OVERPRICED PRODUCTS?
EXPENSIVE LAWSUITS.
CUSTOMER DISSATISFACTION?
SAFETY VIOLATIONS.
HEALTH CODE VIOLATIONS?
YES! RAT INFESTATION!
R-RAT INFESTATION?
LIKE MY FATHER SAYS, BUSINESS IS CUTTHROAT. EVERY PENNY I'VE GOT IS ON THE LINE, PAL.
BUT WE DON'T NEED TO TAKE THE LOW ROAD. WITH THE FRIENDS WE HAVE AT OUR DISPOSAL, BARGAIN DONUTS DOESN'T STAND A CHANCE IN A PUBLIC OPINION WAR!
OH, I GET IT...
"...WE'RE GONNA TAKE IT TO THE STREETS!
"I CAN GET ANDY AND HIS BUDDIES TO HAND OUT FLIERS ON THE ESU* CAMPUS!"
ESU
*EMPIRE STATE UNIVERSITY. SERIOUSLY, YOU DO READ AMAZING SPIDER-MAN, DON'T YOU?--WACKER
"AND I'LL GUILT BETTY BRANT INTO LENDING A HAND, TOO!"
"SINCE YOU WERE ON STAFF AT FRONT LINE, I BET YOU CAN GET BEN URICH TO RUN MY STORY."
LOCAL SMALL BUSINESS OWNER FIGHTS THE GOOD FIGHT!
America's FIRST CHOICE BARGAIN DONUTS
UH, NORAH, WHY...
PETE, I JUST WRITE THE STORIES, I DON'T DEAL WITH ADVERTISEMENTS.

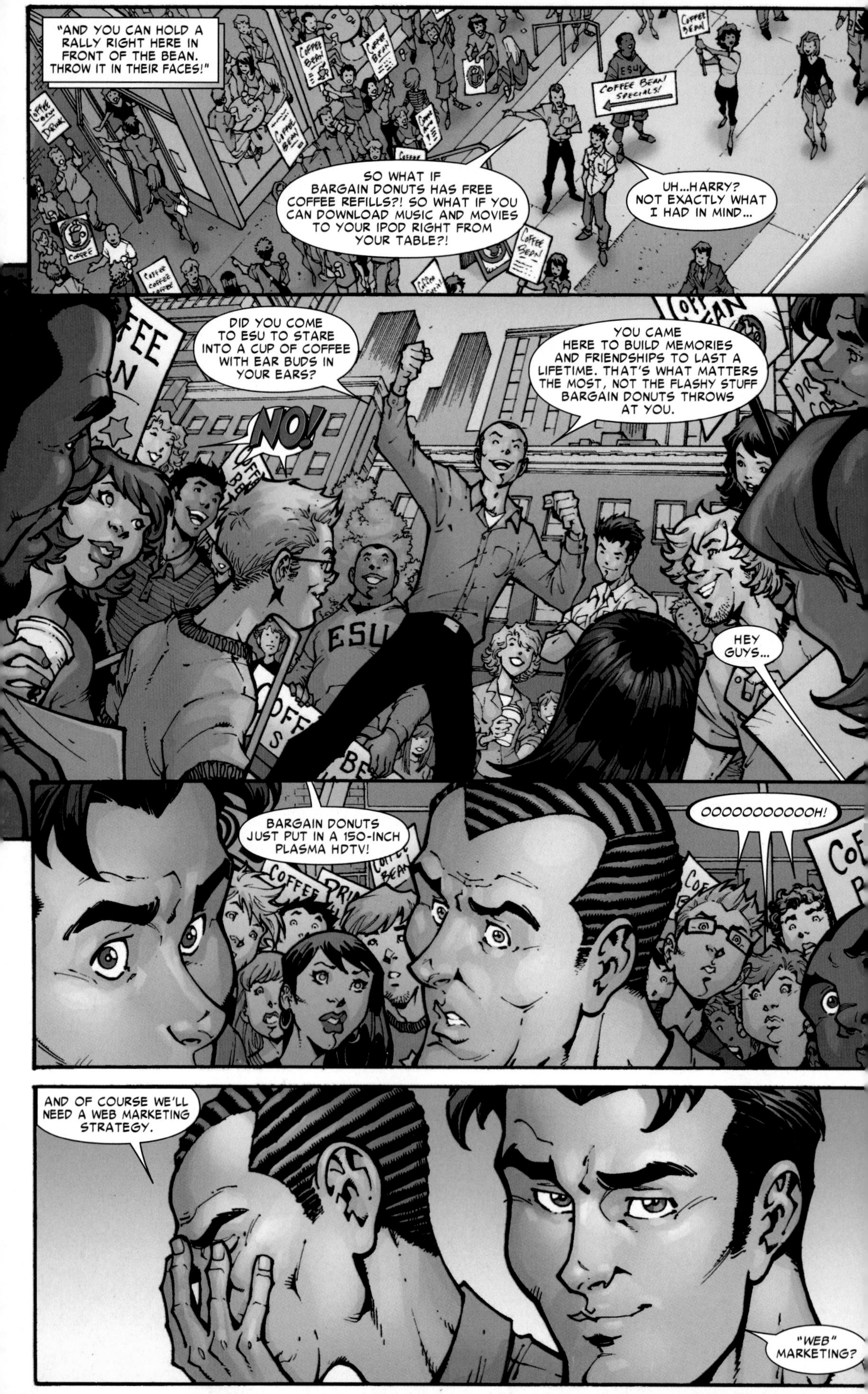
"AND YOU CAN HOLD A RALLY RIGHT HERE IN FRONT OF THE BEAN. THROW IT IN THEIR FACES!"
SO WHAT IF BARGAIN DONUTS HAS FREE COFFEE REFILLS?! SO WHAT IF YOU CAN DOWNLOAD MUSIC AND MOVIES TO YOUR IPOD RIGHT FROM YOUR TABLE?!
UH...HARRY? NOT EXACTLY WHAT I HAD IN MIND...
DID YOU COME TO ESU TO STARE INTO A CUP OF COFFEE WITH EAR BUDS IN YOUR EARS?
NO!
YOU CAME HERE TO BUILD MEMORIES AND FRIENDSHIPS TO LAST A LIFETIME. THAT'S WHAT MATTERS THE MOST, NOT THE FLASHY STUFF BARGAIN DONUTS THROWS AT YOU.
HEY GUYS...
BARGAIN DONUTS JUST PUT IN A 150-INCH PLASMA HDTV!
OOOOOOOOOOOH!
AND OF COURSE WE'LL NEED A WEB MARKETING STRATEGY.
"WEB" MARKETING?

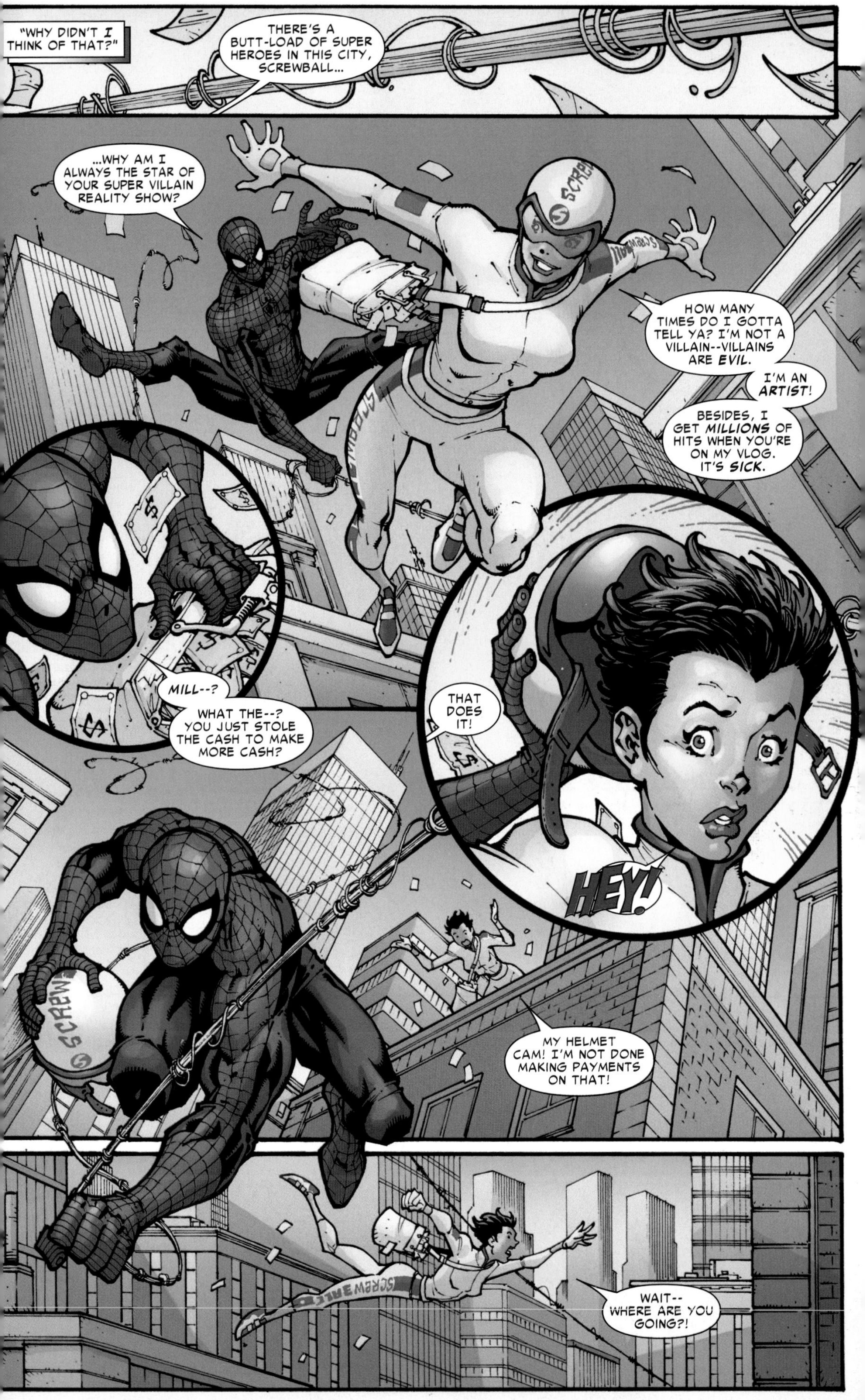
"WHY DIDN'T I THINK OF THAT?"
THERE'S A BUTT-LOAD OF SUPER HEROES IN THIS CITY, SCREWBALL...
...WHY AM I ALWAYS THE STAR OF YOUR SUPER VILLAIN REALITY SHOW?
HOW MANY TIMES DO I GOTTA TELL YA? I'M NOT A VILLAIN--VILLAINS ARE EVIL.
I'M AN ARTIST!
BESIDES, I GET MILLIONS OF HITS WHEN YOU'RE ON MY VLOG. IT'S SICK.
MILL--?
WHAT THE--? YOU JUST STOLE THE CASH TO MAKE MORE CASH?
THAT DOES IT!
HEY!
MY HELMET CAM! I'M NOT DONE MAKING PAYMENTS ON THAT!
WAIT-- WHERE ARE YOU GOING?!

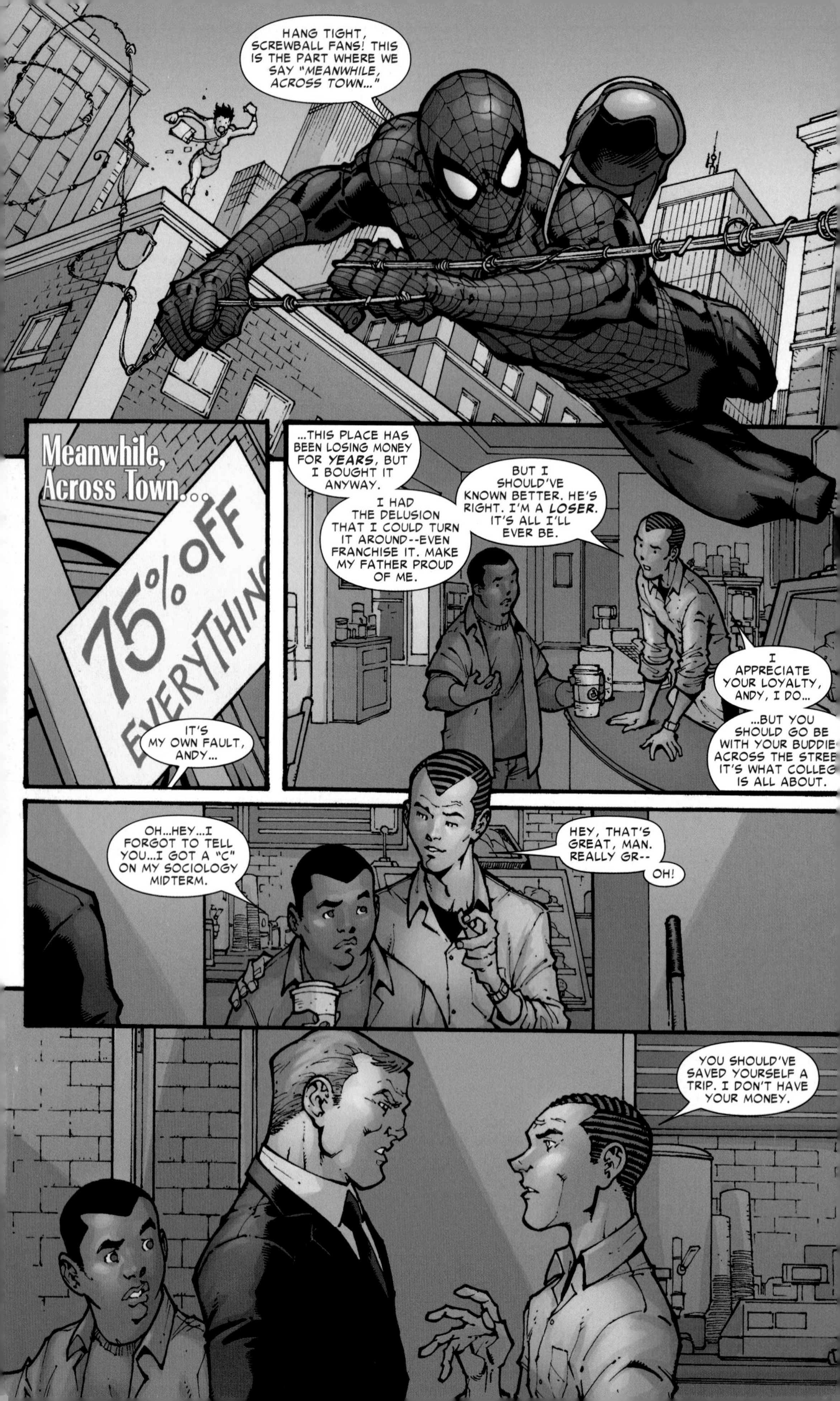

HANG TIGHT, SCREWBALL FANS! THIS IS THE PART WHERE WE SAY "MEANWHILE, ACROSS TOWN..."
Meanwhile, Across Town...
75% OFF EVERYTHING
IT'S MY OWN FAULT, ANDY...
...THIS PLACE HAS BEEN LOSING MONEY FOR YEARS, BUT I BOUGHT IT ANYWAY.
I HAD THE DELUSION THAT I COULD TURN IT AROUND--EVEN FRANCHISE IT. MAKE MY FATHER PROUD OF ME.
BUT I SHOULD'VE KNOWN BETTER. HE'S RIGHT. I'M A LOSER. IT'S ALL I'LL EVER BE.
I APPRECIATE YOUR LOYALTY, ANDY, I DO...
...BUT YOU SHOULD GO BE WITH YOUR BUDDIE ACROSS THE STREE IT'S WHAT COLLEG IS ALL ABOUT.
OH...HEY...I FORGOT TO TELL YOU...I GOT A "C" ON MY SOCIOLOGY MIDTERM.
HEY, THAT'S GREAT, MAN. REALLY GR--
OH!
YOU SHOULD'VE SAVED YOURSELF A TRIP. I DON'T HAVE YOUR MONEY.

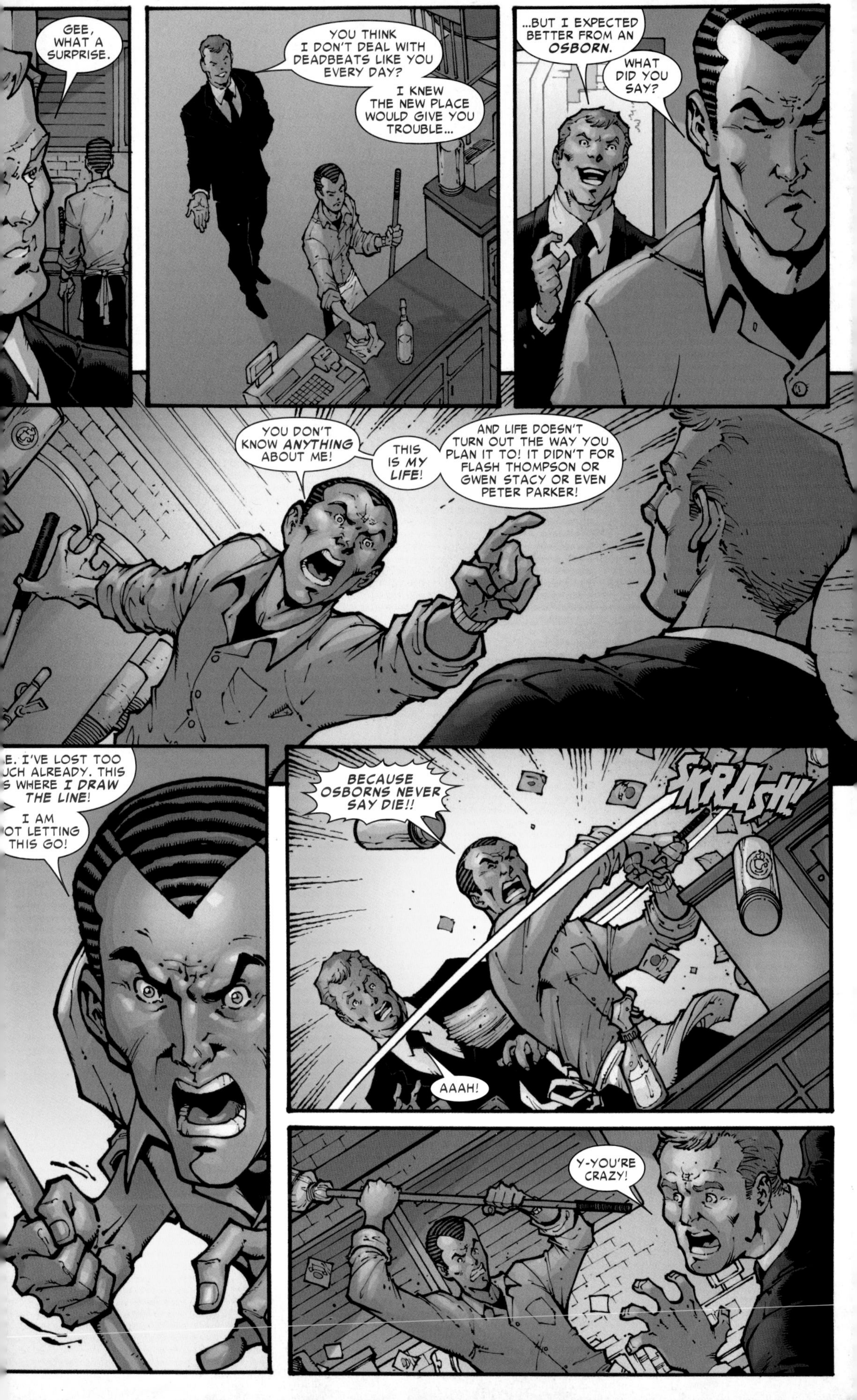
GEE, WHAT A SURPRISE.
YOU THINK I DON'T DEAL WITH DEADBEATS LIKE YOU EVERY DAY?
I KNEW THE NEW PLACE WOULD GIVE YOU TROUBLE...
...BUT I EXPECTED BETTER FROM AN OSBORN.
WHAT DID YOU SAY?
YOU DON'T KNOW ANYTHING ABOUT ME!
THIS IS MY LIFE!
AND LIFE DOESN'T TURN OUT THE WAY YOU PLAN IT TO! IT DIDN'T FOR FLASH THOMPSON OR GWEN STACY OR EVEN PETER PARKER!
E. I'VE LOST TOO UCH ALREADY. THIS S WHERE I DRAW THE LINE!
I AM OT LETTING THIS GO!
BECAUSE OSBORNS NEVER SAY DIE!!
SKRASH!
AAAH!
Y-YOU'RE CRAZY!

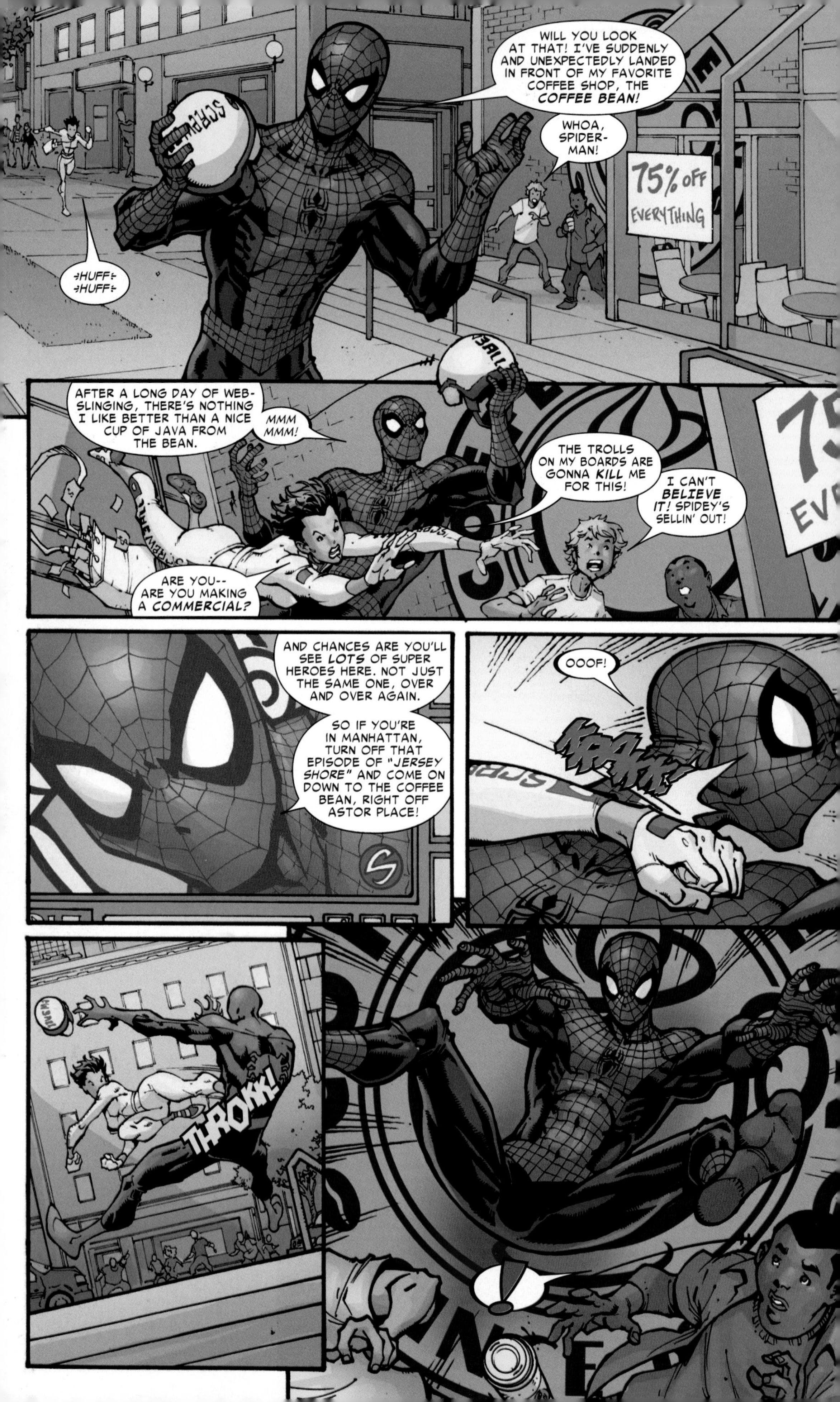

WILL YOU LOOK AT THAT! I'VE SUDDENLY AND UNEXPECTEDLY LANDED IN FRONT OF MY FAVORITE COFFEE SHOP, THE COFFEE BEAN!
WHOA, SPIDER-MAN!
75% OFF EVERYTHING
HUFF HUFF
AFTER A LONG DAY OF WEB-SLINGING, THERE'S NOTHING I LIKE BETTER THAN A NICE CUP OF JAVA FROM THE BEAN.
MMM MMM!
THE TROLLS ON MY BOARDS ARE GONNA KILL ME FOR THIS!
I CAN'T BELIEVE IT! SPIDEY'S SELLIN' OUT!
ARE YOU-- ARE YOU MAKING A COMMERCIAL?
AND CHANCES ARE YOU'LL SEE LOTS OF SUPER HEROES HERE. NOT JUST THE SAME ONE, OVER AND OVER AGAIN.
SO IF YOU'RE IN MANHATTAN, TURN OFF THAT EPISODE OF "JERSEY SHORE" AND COME ON DOWN TO THE COFFEE BEAN, RIGHT OFF ASTOR PLACE!
OOOF!
KRAKK!
THROKK!

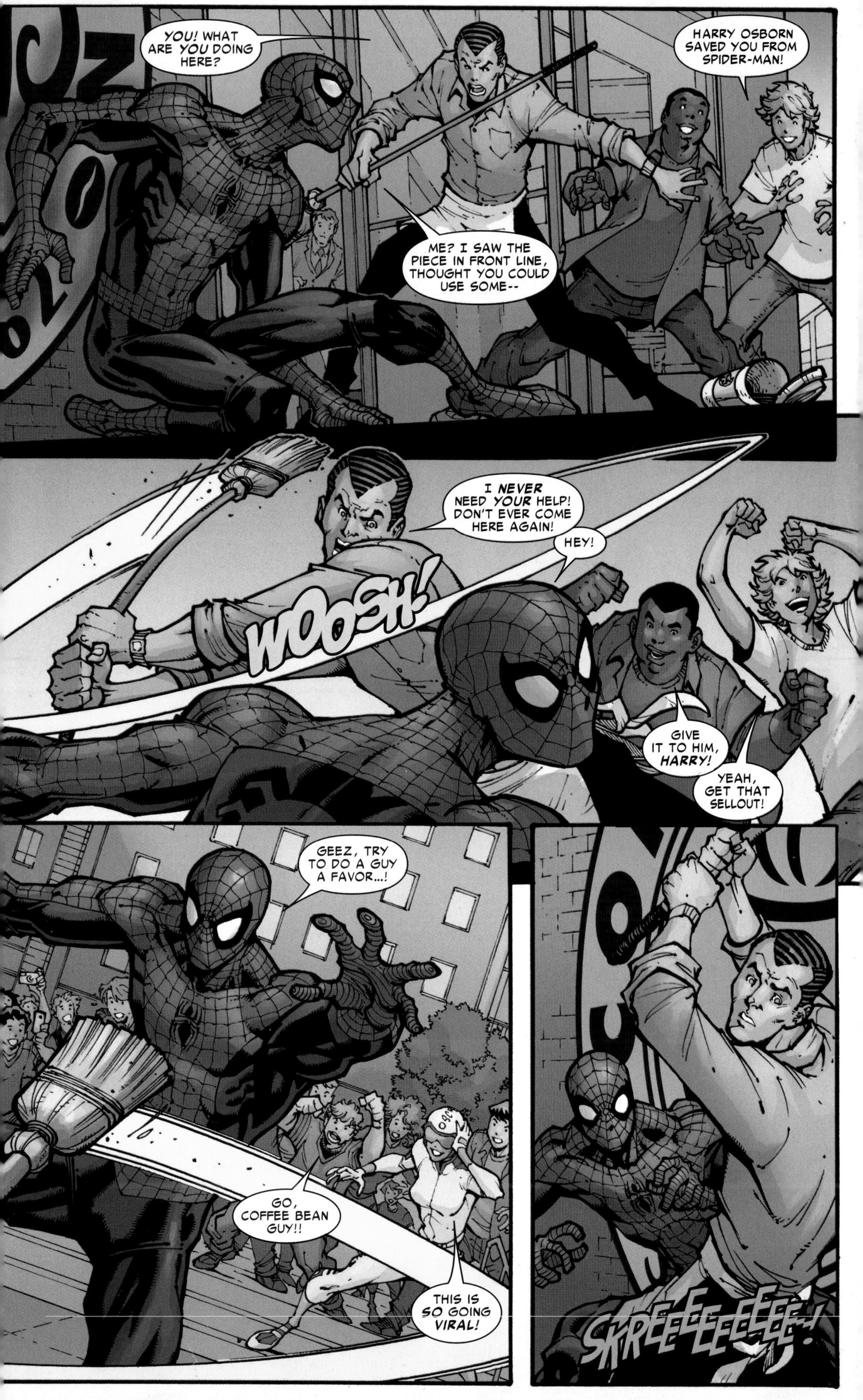

YOU! WHAT ARE YOU DOING HERE?
ME? I SAW THE PIECE IN FRONT LINE, THOUGHT YOU COULD USE SOME--
HARRY OSBORN SAVED YOU FROM SPIDER-MAN!
I NEVER NEED YOUR HELP! DON'T EVER COME HERE AGAIN!
HEY!
WOOSH!
GIVE IT TO HIM, HARRY!
YEAH, GET THAT SELLOUT!
GEEZ, TRY TO DO A GUY A FAVOR...!
GO, COFFEE BEAN GUY!!
THIS IS SO GOING VIRAL!
SKREEEEEEEEEE!

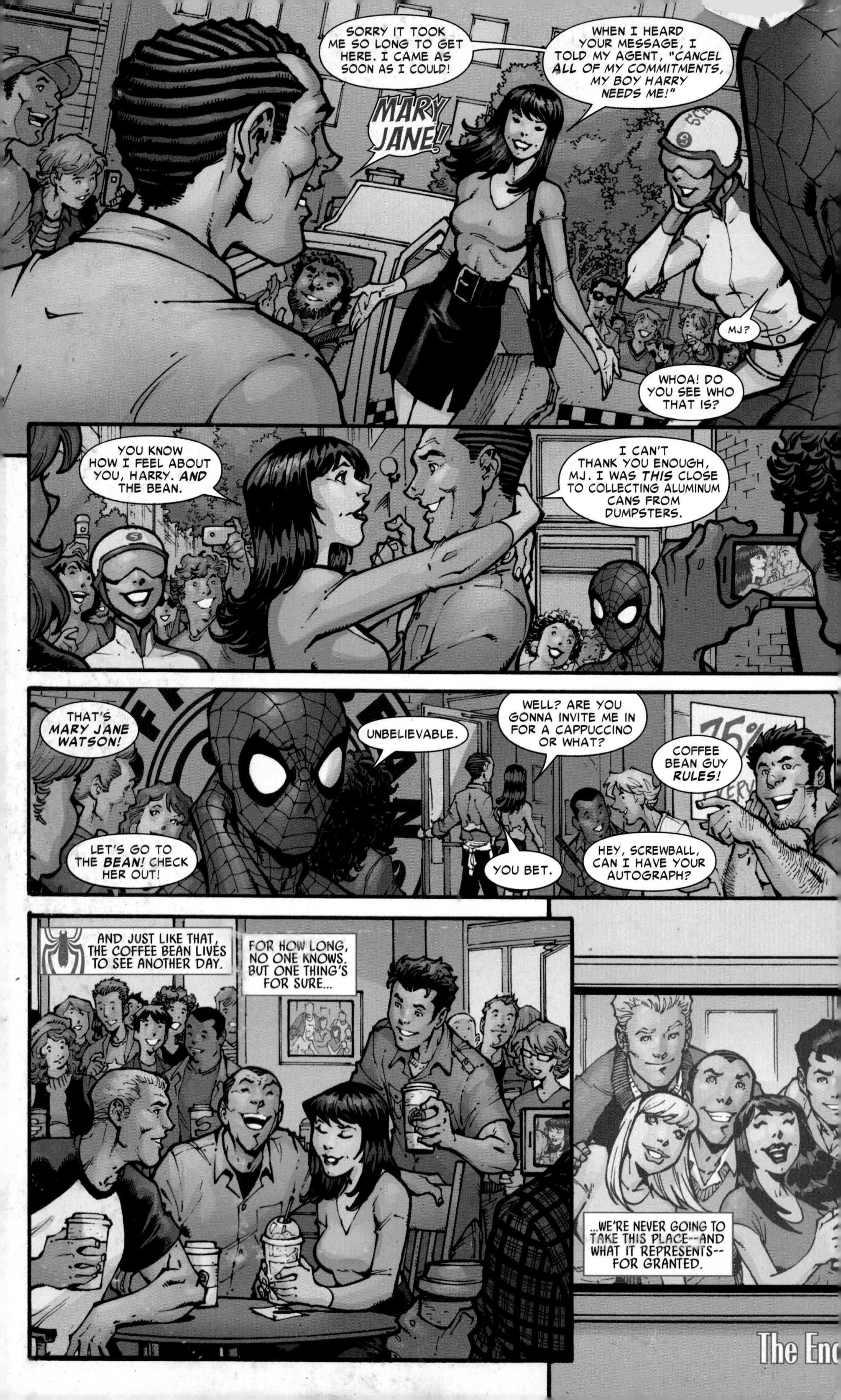

SORRY IT TOOK ME SO LONG TO GET HERE. I CAME AS SOON AS I COULD!
WHEN I HEARD YOUR MESSAGE, I TOLD MY AGENT, "CANCEL ALL OF MY COMMITMENTS, MY BOY HARRY NEEDS ME!"
MARY JANE!!
MJ?
WHOA! DO YOU SEE WHO THAT IS?
YOU KNOW HOW I FEEL ABOUT YOU, HARRY. AND THE BEAN.
I CAN'T THANK YOU ENOUGH, MJ. I WAS THIS CLOSE TO COLLECTING ALUMINUM CANS FROM DUMPSTERS.
THAT'S MARY JANE WATSON!
UNBELIEVABLE.
WELL? ARE YOU GONNA INVITE ME IN FOR A CAPPUCCINO OR WHAT?
COFFEE BEAN GUY RULES!
LET'S GO TO THE BEAN! CHECK HER OUT!
YOU BET.
HEY, SCREWBALL, CAN I HAVE YOUR AUTOGRAPH?
AND JUST LIKE THAT, THE COFFEE BEAN LIVES TO SEE ANOTHER DAY.
FOR HOW LONG, NO ONE KNOWS. BUT ONE THING'S FOR SURE...
...WE'RE NEVER GOING TO TAKE THIS PLACE--AND WHAT IT REPRESENTS--FOR GRANTED.
The End